THE PLEASURES OF CHILDREN'S LITERATURE

THE PLEASURES OF CHILDREN'S LITERATURE

PERRY NODELMAN

The University of Winnipeg

Longman
New York & London

The Pleasures of Children's Literature

Longman, 10 Bank Street, White Plains, N.Y. 10606

Associated companies:
Longman Group Ltd., London
Longman Cheshire Pty., Melbourne
Longman Paul Pty., Auckland
Copp Clark Pitman, Toronto

Executive editor: Raymond T. O'Connell
Production editor: Kathryn Dix
Cover design: Renée Kilbride Edelman
Cover photo: Bill Binzen
Production supervisor: Richard C. Bretan

Library of Congress Cataloging-in-Publication Data
Nodelman, Perry.
The pleasures of children's literature / by Perry Nodelman.
p. cm.
Includes bibliographical references and index.
ISBN 0-8013-0219-6
1. Children—Books and reading. 2. Children's literature—History and criticism. I. Title.
Z1037.A1N63 1991
011.62—dc20 91-6595
CIP

2 3 4 5 6 7 8 9 10-MA-95949392

COPYRIGHT ACKNOWLEDGMENTS

Text excerpts from *Charlotte's Web* by E. B. White, illustrated by Garth Williams; copyright 1952 by E. B. White. Text copyright renewed © 1980 by E. B. White. Illustrations copyright renewed © 1980 by Garth Williams. All selections reprinted by permission of HarperCollins Publishers and Hamish Hamilton Ltd.

Text excerpts and an illustration from *The Tale of Peter Rabbit* by Beatrix Potter. Copyright © Frederick Warne & Co., 1902, 1987. Reproduced by permission of Frederick Warne & Co.

Text excerpts from *The Tale of Mr. Jeremy Fisher* by Beatrix Potter. Copyright © Frederick Warne & Co., 1906, 1987. Reprinted by permission of Frederick Warne & Co.

''The Frog'' and excerpts from ''Sara Byng'' and ''The Tiger,'' from Hilaire Belloc's *Cautionary Verses,* published by Gerald Duckworth and Co. Copyright © The Estate of Hilaire Belloc 1940, 1964. Reprinted by permission of the Peters Fraser & Dunlop Group Ltd.

Text excerpt from *Dr. De Soto* by William Steig, published by Farrar, Straus and Giroux. Copyright © 1982 by William Steig. Used by permission of Farrar, Straus and Giroux.

Excerpt from *Anne of Green Gables* by Lucy Maud Montgomery. Copyright © 1908 by L. C. Page and Company, Inc. Copyright renewed 1935 by L. C. Page and Company, Inc. (Now Farrar, Straus and Giroux, Inc.) Used by permission of Farrar, Straus and Giroux.

''Small Song'' is reprinted from *The Selected Poems 1951–1977,* by A. R. Ammons, by permission of W.W. Norton and company, Inc. Copyright © 1977, 1975, 1974, 1972, 1971, 1970, 1966, 1965, 1964, 1955 by A. R. Ammons.

''Dreams'' from *The Dream Keeper and Other Poems* by Langston Hughes. Copyright © 1932 by Alfred A. Knopf Inc. and renewed by Langston Hughes. Reprinted by permission of the publisher and Harold Ober Associates.

''We Real Cool'' from *Blacks* by Gwendolyn Brooks, published by The David Company, Chicago USA 60619. Copyright © 1987 by Gwendolyn Brooks. Reprinted by permission of the author.

''The Muddy Puddle'' from *Garbage Delight* by Dennis Lee. Copyright © 1977. Reprinted by permission of Macmillan of Canada, a Division of Canada Publishing Corporation.

Excerpt from ''The Special Person'' from *Alligator Pie* by Dennis Lee. Copyright © 1974. Reprinted by permission of Macmillan of Canada, a Division of Canada Publishing Corporation.

''Balloon'' by Colleen Thibaudeau from *The New Wind Has Wings: Poems from Canada,* ed. Mary Alice Downie and Barbara Robertson, published by Oxford University Press Canada. Copyright © 1984. Used by permission of Colleen Thibaudeau.

''Listening to Grownups Quarrelling'' from *The Marriage Wig and Other Poems* by Ruth Whitman. Copyright © 1968 by Ruth Whitman, reprinted by permission of Harcourt Brace Jovanovich, Inc.

''The Dunce'' from *Collected Rhymes and Verses* by Walter de la Mare, published by Faber and Faber Limited. Copyright © 1970. Reprinted by permission of The Literary Trustees of Walter de la Mare and The Society of Authors as their representative.

''The Mutinous Jack-in-the-Box'' by John Cunliffe from *A Second Poetry Book,* published by Oxford University Press. Copyright © 1980 by John Cunliffe. Used by permission of David Higham Associates Limited.

"The Bird of Night" reprinted by permission of Macmillan Publishing Company from *The Bat Poet* by Randall Jarrell. Copyright © Macmillan Publishing Company 1963, 1964.

Reprinted by permission of Farrar, Straus and Giroux, Inc.: Illustration from *Bravo, Minski* by Arthur Yorinks, illustrated by Richard Egielski. Illustration copyright © 1988 by Richard Egielski. All rights reserved. Used with permission.

Reprinted by permission of Farrar, Straus and Giroux, Inc.: Illustration from *Jake and Honeybunch Go to Heaven* by Margot Zemach. Copyright © 1982 by Margot Zemach.

Illustration from *The Mysteries of Harris Burdick* by Chris Van Allsburg. Copyright © 1984 by Chris Van Allsburg. Reprinted by permission of Houghton Mifflin Co.

Excerpt from "The Highwayman" by Alfred Noyes. Copyright © by Alfred Noyes, 1913, renewed 1941. Used by permission of John Murray (Publishers) Ltd.

Illustration from *The Highwayman* by Alfred Noyes and Charles Keeping. Copyright © Charles Keeping 1981. Published by Oxford University Press.

Illustration from *The Happy-Ever-After Book* by Jack Kent. Copyright © 1976 by Jack Kent. Reprinted by permission of Random House, Inc.

Illustration and text excerpt from *The Visitors Who Came to Stay* by Annalena McAfee and Anthony Browne. Text copyright © Annalena McAfee 1984; illustrations copyright © Anthony Browne 1984. Reprinted by permission of Hamish Hamilton.

Illustration from *George Shrinks* by William Joyce. Copyright © 1985 by William Joyce. Reprinted by permission of HarperCollins Publishers.

Illustration and text excerpt from *Nijinsky* by Catherine Brighton. Copyright © 1989 by Catherine Brighton. Used by permission of Doubleday, a division of Doubleday Dell Publishing Group, Inc. and Methuen Children's Books.

Illustrations from *The Water of Life*. Copyright © 1986 by Trina Schart Hyman. Reprinted by permission of Holiday House.

Illustration and text excerpt from *Dance, Tanya,* text copyright © 1990 by Patricia Lee Gauch, illustrations copyright © 1990 by Satomi Ichikawa. Reprinted by permission of Philomel Books.

Excerpts from Grimms' *Tales for Young and Old,* translated by Ralph Manheim. Translation copyright © 1977. Used by permission of Doubleday, a division of Doubleday Dell Publishing Group, Inc.

Excerpt from *Folktales of China,* edited and translated by Wolfram Eberhard. Copyright © 1965. Used by permission of The University of Chicago Press.

Excerpt from *Mouse Woman and the Mischief Makers* by Christie Harris. Copyright © 1977. Used by permission of the author.

Excerpt from *People* by Peter Spier. Copyright © 1980. Used by permission of Doubleday, a division of Doubleday Dell Publishing Group, Inc.

Excerpt from *The Cat Ate My Gymsuit* by Paula Danziger. Copyright © 1974. Used by permission of Delacorte Press, a division of Doubleday Dell Publishing Group, Inc.

Excerpt from *The Shrinking of Treehorn* by Florence Parry Heide. Text copyright © 1971 by Florence Parry Heide. Reprinted from *The Shrinking of Treehorn* by permission of Holiday House.

Excerpts from *The Mystery Kiss* by Elaine Harper. Copyright © 1983 by Emily Hallin. All rights reserved. Reproduction with the permission of the publisher, Silhouette Books, 300 East 42nd Street, New York, NY 10017.

For Jill P. May, uncredited co-conspirator

Contents

Acknowledgments

The fact that this book is merely dedicated to Jill P. May is a little misleading: she might well have been listed as a co-author, for it's her book almost as much as it is mine.

Writing a book like this was Jill's idea in the first place. As a librarian with a strong interest in literature who teaches in a faculty of education, she was conscious of the many different fields of academic study that investigate children and their literature, and the surprising lack of communication between them. Cognitive, developmental, and perceptual psychologists, sociologists, folklorists, library and media specialists, reading specialists and other educational theorists, historians of childhood and family life, specialists in literature and literary theory and in art and art theory: all were arriving at intriguingly useful conclusions. But more often than not they seemed to be paying little attention to each other's work. Jill saw a strong need for an introduction to children's literature that would make use of recent research in as many of these different disciplines as possible, in order to place children's literature in the context of children's literary education.

Jill used her considerable energy and enthusiasm to persuade me to collaborate with her, in the flattering belief that our shared interest in children's literature and our different backgrounds—hers in library science and education, mine in literary studies—would make us the perfect team to produce the book she imagined. Together, she and I decided what the book should contain and mapped out a plan of how it would be presented, and together we set out on the intimidating task of trying to learn as much as two nonspecialists could about a variety of abstruse disciplines relating to the study of childhood.

If the book you have in your hands lacks the sort of balance Jill envisaged, it's only partially because of the inevitable limitations of our nonspecialist grasp of these many different disciplines. It's mainly because unavoidable scheduling conflicts prevented Jill from carrying on with her part in the project. While she and I continued to discuss the book extensively, and while she read the manuscript in various stages and provided me with valuable comments on it, I finally ended up doing all the writing myself. The good intentions, then, are all Jill's; I take all the blame myself for the flaws in my execution of them.

I also would like to thank a number of my friends and colleagues at the University of Winnipeg for their unfailingly constructive advice. Neil Besner, Murray Evans, Carol Matas, and Roland Huff read and offered perceptive comments on various sections of the manuscript. Kay Unruh-DesRoches gave me an honest and insightful response to the book as a whole, and made helpful comments about its structure. Mavis Reimer provided me with a thorough and useful commentary on the entire manuscript. I thank them all for making this a better book than it might have been.

The students I taught at the University of Winnipeg in 1989-1990, especially those in English 2131-5, Children's Fiction, were the first to try out parts of the book; their responses were honest, sometimes startling, and always provocative. I'm especially grateful to Guy Beauregard, Rebecca McCarton, Michael Melanson, and Arash Abizadeh for their straightforward and practical suggestions. Billie, Josh, Asa, and Alice Nodelman, who put up with me while I was writing the book, deserve medals for patience beyond the call of duty; so does the unflappable Patty Hawkins, my secretary at the University of Winnipeg, and Ray O'Connell, my fearless editor at Longman. And for showing me how to transform the chaos of my manuscript, my production editor, Kathryn Dix, and copyeditor, Susan Joseph, should have statues erected in their honor.

Finally, I would like to acknowledge my debt to the approach to literature outlined by Kathleen McCormick, Gary Waller, and Linda Flower in their *Reading Texts: Reading, Responding, Writing.* While I find much to quarrel with in this book—indeed, even more than what I don't quarrel with—my quarreling with it has greatly stimulated both my students and myself in our encounters with literature, and provoked us into a greater understanding of our own practices and assumptions about it. I have borrowed some of the terminology used in *Reading Texts,* even though I do not always use it as suggested there.

PART ONE

Introduction

This book has two main purposes. The first is to provide adults with contexts and strategies of comprehension that should help them understand and, above all, enjoy children's literature. The second is to suggest that children too can be taught—and would benefit from learning—these contexts and strategies.

We make sense of what we read in terms of expectations and strategies for determining meaning that we've developed earlier in response to our individual experiences. You read children's stories and poems differently from the way I might, or from the way a young child might. Parts One, Two, and Three of this book explore some specific expectations and strategies that might influence our response to children's literature. Such expectations and strategies influence our reading not only of literature but also of textbooks like this one. You'll inevitably approach this book differently from the way somebody with different expectations about textbooks would.

Unfortunately, not all the expectations that we bring to our reading are equally productive. For instance, people who read expecting to be bored are more likely to be bored than those who anticipate pleasure. In my own experience as a reader, I've found that my expectations hampered my response on two occasions in particular. When I was a student reading textbooks like this one, I sometimes found myself wanting to disagree with the conclusions the textbooks reached; but expectations based on previous classroom experiences convinced me that I had to pretend to accept these opinions in order to get through a course. Later, as a literary specialist in another field, I was assigned to teach a children's literature course, and I suddenly found myself trying to read and make some sense, as an adult, of books that were intended for children. I believed I should be thinking about how a child might read them, and couldn't imagine how.

I know that many other readers share the assumptions that caused me these problems. The two chapters in this introductory section explore the implications of these assumptions and recommend some reading strategies I believe to be particularly useful—first for getting the most from this book and second for reading texts of children's literature.

CHAPTER 1

How to Read and Respond to This Book

MATTERS OF OPINION AND BIAS

The fact that our opinions about a particular subject might not agree with those of others, even those of supposed experts, doesn't make them any less real or less important. Our individual opinions define who and what we believe ourselves to be. We all have both a responsibility to respect the opinions of others and a right to have our own.

Too often, however, we are expected to forget these different opinions of our own when they conflict with supposedly expert ones: to accept unquestioningly a teacher's interpretation of a poem or to assume that the conclusions presented in a textbook like this one are the only acceptable truth. I hope that you do not respond to this book with unquestioning acceptance. Instead, I hope you will acknowledge the ways in which what I say does not explain your own response or match your own views—the ways in which my opinions do not persuade you.

For this reason, I have expressed my opinions strongly enough to make it glaringly obvious that, despite my knowledge of children's literature, they *are* only my own personal opinions. I hope you will respond by saying something like, "Hey, wait a minute, that's just *his* opinion, based on *his* responses, emerging from *his* character. I'm not sure I can go along with it." Then, I hope, you will try to figure out *why* you might or might not accept something I have said: why it might or might not actually be true, how it connects with your own responses to literature and with knowledge and beliefs you already have, what it might suggest about your future reading or your dealings with children.

Reading in this way will protect you from being manipulated into accepting (or pretending to accept) ideas you don't really go along with. And that will have the wonderful advantage of making you conscious of what you yourself already know.

In other words, this book offers just one part of a conversation; I hope you will enter into a dialogue with it and provide the other part yourself.

If you do, the task of fitting the information and the opinions in this book into your existing context of knowledge and values will inevitably change your understanding both of my ideas and of your own. What you learn from my opinions will have some effect on your thinking, and you are bound to change my ideas in the process of coming to terms with them. What should emerge from this process is not your agreement with me but, instead, your own thoughtful opinions about children's literature, opinions that I hope will be as strongly felt as my own and as significant for you as mine are for me.

To facilitate your dialogue with my ideas and opinions, I have included short sections called ''Explorations'' throughout this book. They look like this:

EXPLORATION: Open this book at any page and begin reading. Read until you come to an idea that strikes you as being strange. Consider why it seems so, and what in your own experience of life or literature might cause you to accept or reject the idea.

Like this one, all the explorations relate to the sections of the book that immediately precede or follow them. They contain questions for you to explore, subjects for you to think about that will allow you to engage more actively with what follows, or suggestions of issues to think about that emerge from the passage immediately preceding them. You do not have to do any or all of the explorations: I've written the book so that it is possible simply to skip them. But if you decide to do what the explorations suggest, remember that they are meant to help you think actively about the issues and ideas that the book is investigating *as* you are reading. While there is no harm in reading a chapter first and then coming back to the explorations it contains, it will probably be more helpful for you to do what they suggest as you read.

Some of the explorations may sound like the questions that appeared in the literature textbooks in use when I was a child: ''Do you think Dick is doing the right thing? Why not?'' In other words, they may seem to imply that you should reach very specific conclusions about the questions they raise: the conclusions that I myself reach and tell you about. I have tried not to make them sound that way; if you think that I have not always succeeded, I urge you to defy me.

In addition to the explorations printed throughout the book, there is another—invisible—one that you might imagine appearing at the end of almost every sentence:

EXPLORATION: Is that true? Am I willing to accept it? Why or why not?

Reading the book with this question in mind should help make it a stimulating and productive experience.

WRITING ABOUT WHAT YOU READ

While you can simply do the thinking the explorations recommend, you may find it useful to write down what you think as you think it. In a book with the interesting name *Writing to Learn,* William Zinsser says, "Writing organizes and clarifies our thoughts. Writing is how we think our way into a subject and make it our own. Writing enables us to find out what we know—and what we don't know—about whatever we're trying to learn" (16). As we write, gaps and illogicalities in our thinking become apparent to us, and we can then think about ways of filling the gaps and clarifying the logic. You'll know you have done a useful piece of exploratory writing if you feel you know more about the subject or your thoughts about it when you are finished than you did when you started writing.

Writing down your ideas—not just your responses to explorations, but any thoughts that strike you as you read—has another benefit. It will provide you with a record that will help you develop insights into your patterns of reading and thinking. If you write down what you think as you think it, you'll be able to come back to it later, perhaps after reading further, and reconsider your ideas in the light of newer ones. You can explore the implications of any change, or lack of change, in your thinking. And if you are using this book in a course in which your instructor requires you to write essays, the job will be made easier by the fact that you have already written so much about the issues of the course.

The writing you do in response to the explorations or to other aspects of the book that interest you should be different from the writing you might submit as a finished essay. Essays represent the best way of presenting ideas you have already thought your way through and understand; the writing in them should be clear, correct, and controlled: organized to guide a reader through the ideas you want to present. But when you start to write an exploration, you don't yet know what your conclusions will be. You are writing your way toward a conclusion, not trying to find the best way to describe a conclusion you already have. In other words, your job is to describe the *process* of your thinking, not the product of finished thought.

What matters most is that you get your ideas down in as much detail as you can, before you forget what they are, and that you follow them wherever they take you. Do not be too concerned about contradicting yourself or about following a potentially useful thread of ideas that takes you far away from where you started, and don't worry about spelling or grammar or whether your writing is neat or your typing accurate. In order to make your explorations as useful as possible, try to describe your responses as completely as you can—not just general summaries, but detailed descriptions of what you thought in the order in which you thought it. Remember that your purpose here is *to know more when you've finished writing than you did when you began.* As you write, ask yourself questions about what you've written so far:

- What do I mean by that?
- Can I explain it more clearly, or in more detail?

- Why did I say it? Why does it seem to be important to me? Does it reveal something about my own assumptions concerning literature or my strategies for making sense of it?
- Why do I think it's true? What evidence do I have to support it? Can I test it out by a deeper consideration of or more detailed look at the text I'm discussing?
- What are its implications, either for the topic or for my own reading strategies?

Think about these questions, and write your answers to them—and then ask the same questions again about the answers you've given.

If you follow the process I recommend, you may find yourself concluding with questions rather than answers: you may at this point have no definite answers for the questions you have asked yourself. If that happens, avoid pretending that you do have an answer, and therefore leaving out information you know or ideas you have that seem to contradict a point you are trying to make; record everything, so you can think further about it later on. In the long run, the best thing to do about not having reached a conclusion is to not be concerned about it. There really aren't *any* definite answers about literature, only the answers we can reach based on our experience so far. Whether exploration or essay, a piece of writing that acknowledges contradictory possibilities and ends with an admission of inability to resolve them is more honest and more intellectually stimulating than one that deliberately distorts and leaves things out in order to arrive at a specific resolution.

Many of the explorations in this book could be done by children as well as by adults. As I suggest throughout and assert in some detail in Chapter 14, I firmly believe that everything in this book could be communicated to children, and that having a knowledge of these strategies for understanding children's literature can only deepen children's pleasure in it. As you read the book, then, I urge you to consider ways in which you might make use of its contents to enrich the literary experience of children.

WORK CITED

Zinsser, William. *Writing to Learn.* New York: Perennial Library–Harper & Row, 1989.

CHAPTER 2

How to Read Children's Literature

SEEING BEYOND THE ADULT PERSPECTIVE

Before you can understand children's literature, you have to read it. That's not necessarily as easy as it seems.

Something called "children's literature" exists only because people are convinced that children are different from adults—different enough to need their own special texts. Knowing that these texts are intended for people assumed to be unlike ourselves makes it difficult for us to respond to them. How can we develop the most useful understanding of them, in order to make judgments about them that will best serve children?

I once asked a group of adults beginning to study children's literature to consider whether or not a certain poem was good children's literature. The poem was Edward Lear's "The Owl and the Pussy-cat":

The Owl and the Pussy-cat went to sea
  In a beautiful pea-green boat,
They took some honey, and plenty of money
  Wrapped up in a five-pound note.
The Owl looked up to the stars above,
  And sang to a small guitar,
"O lovely Pussy! O Pussy, my love,
  What a beautiful Pussy you are,
    You are,
    You are!
  What a beautiful Pussy you are!"

Pussy said to the Owl, "You elegant fowl!
  How charmingly sweet you sing!
Oh let us be married! too long we have tarried:
  But what shall we do for a ring?"
They sailed away, for a year and a day,
  To the land where the Bong-tree grows,
And there in a wood a Piggy-wig stood,
  With a ring at the end of his nose,
    His nose,
    His nose,
  With a ring at the end of his nose.

"Dear Pig, are you willing to sell for one shilling
  Your ring?" Said the Piggy, "I will."
So they took it away and were married next day
  By the Turkey who lives on the hill.
They dined on mince, and slices of quince,
  Which they ate with a runcible spoon;
And hand in hand, on the edge of the sand,
  They danced by the light of the moon,
    The moon,
    The moon,
  They danced by the light of the moon.

EXPLORATION: After you have read "The Owl and the Pussy-cat" (and ideally, before you consider the discussion of it that follows), decide whether or not you think it's a good children's poem. Try to figure out the reasons that led you to your judgment of the poem.

My students decided that "The Owl and the Pussy-cat" is not a good poem for children. They told me that young children wouldn't be likely to know difficult words like "runcible" and "bong-tree" and that their frustration at not knowing these words would not only make them dislike the poem but possibly lead to a general dislike of poetry.

I asked these students if they enjoyed the poem themselves. They said they had. But when I asked them what "runcible" and "bong-tree" meant, it turned out that they didn't know, either. It was a sneaky question; in fact, they couldn't possibly have known. There's no such thing as a bong-tree, and "runcible" is in the dictionary only because somebody created a strange sort of fork shaped like a spoon and called it a runcible spoon *after* Lear made up the word and used it in this poem over a hundred years ago.

I had an ulterior motive for asking my sneaky question. I wanted my students to realize that while not knowing these words hadn't stopped them from enjoying the poem, they had ignored their own pleasure when they thought about it as literature for children. They had paid less attention to what the poem did for them than to what they imagined it might do for some hypothetical children.

Many adults base their judgments of children's literature upon guesses about how children might respond to it. Unfortunately, making accurate guesses of this sort is difficult, maybe even impossible, simply because it forces us to make generalizations about children—about how they read, how they think, and how they absorb information. Such generalizations cause more problems than they solve.

It's hard to talk about children's response to literature without making at least some generalizations, and it is true that most three-year-olds do respond differently from the way most twenty-year-olds do, if only because the former tend to have less experience of both literature and living. But as we'll see in Part Two, many adults tend to make generalizations about children based on too little information and with too little thought.

Worse, while we are trying to guess about how a typical child might respond, we are not paying attention to our own responses. If my students had thought more about their own pleasure in "The Owl and the Pussy-cat," they would have realized that their own lack of knowledge had not prevented them from enjoying it. If the pleasure this poem offered them didn't require absolute mastery of its vocabulary, then why might it not offer children a similar pleasure?

In fact, I know from experience that it does—that many children do enjoy "The Owl and the Pussy-cat." Even children too young to read the poem themselves will enjoy the experience of having it read to them, in spite of or perhaps even because of their unfamiliarity with its strange language.

But while texts of children's literature demand as honest a response as all other literature, they do tend to create their own special worlds, and to evoke moods and feelings unlike those provided by other forms of literature. Even though we should try to respond to a text of children's literature in the same way that we would respond to any other text, we should also be conscious of the ways in which it might differ from other texts. We should ask ourselves not only whether children's stories or poems are enjoyable, or interesting, or thought provoking, but also what is special about them *as* texts of children's literature.

Furthermore, it seems likely that the special qualities of these texts relate to the fact that they are written with an audience of children in mind. How can we both respond to children's literature honestly and take into consideration the fact that it was meant to be read by an audience unlike ourselves? I believe that the answer to this question lies in the concept of the implied reader.

THE IMPLIED READER

Appreciating the uniqueness of children's literature involves, first, thinking about who its audience might be. Who *are* the "children" in the phrase "children's literature"? As we have already discovered, we won't identify the audience by thinking about children or childhood, at least not if we are dissatisfied with inaccurate generalizations. Instead, we should look at the literature itself: what can *it* tell us about the children in its name?

As it happens, all texts imply in their subject and their style the sort of reader most likely to respond positively to them. Some texts dwell on sad characters and gloomy situations; they seem to imply a reader with a taste for sadness. Some texts are filled with complex descriptive paragraphs and strange symbols; they seem to imply a reader who takes pleasure in such writing and has the ability to integrate it into a meaningful whole. "The Owl and the Pussy-cat" implies a reader who enjoys unfamiliar words for their strangeness and doesn't worry too much about their meaning.

Actively responding to a text, then, means being able to become the audience that the text implies to us. We can use that as a strategy for understanding texts. Even though our individual perceptions of a text's implied reader will depend on our own skills and tastes, thinking about who the implied reader is will help us understand and enjoy it.

EXPLORATION: Choose (or have children choose) one text you liked and one you disliked. By exploring the kinds of characters and situations they dwell on, the kinds of mood and atmosphere they create, and the kinds of style and language they use, develop a description of the readers these texts imply to you. What are the tastes, interests, and skills of the readers you think would be best equipped to understand and enjoy these texts? To what degree do the implied readers you perceive in these texts match yourself? To what degree has the extent of the matching influenced your pleasure in these texts?

The implied readers of children's texts are, most obviously, children. Each text intended for children can be seen to imply a child reader with specific knowledge, skills of comprehension, and tastes. We can compare the implied readers of the children's texts we encounter both with ourselves as readers and with the actual children to whom we might recommend the texts. Doing so has a number of benefits:

- In order to make sense of literary texts, we need a *repertoire,* a body of knowledge of literature and life that texts assume and allude to, and as part of that repertoire, a set of *strategies,* ways of thinking about texts in order to see them as meaningful. In discovering how the repertoire and the strategies of the reader implied by a text intended for children vary from our own, we can learn what is distinctive about what that text offers.
- In thinking about the repertoire and the strategies that the implied readers of various children's texts share, we can learn something about the characteristics of children's literature.
- Many texts for children imply a supposedly typical reader, one whose characteristics are based on generalizations about children. Others imply a distinctive reader with particular skills and tastes. We can use our perceptions of these different readers as the basis for our evaluation of texts.
- By comparing our perception of a text's implied reader with children we know, we can determine what special strategies of comprehension might be required to understand and enjoy that particular text. We can decide whether the children we know are likely to be familiar with these strategies—and if they are not, how we might help them develop such strategies.

CHILDREN'S LITERATURE AND ADULT LITERATURE: DIFFERENCES AND SIMILARITIES

A consideration of implied readers makes it clear why children's texts are different from other texts and even, to some extent, *how* they are different, and how we must read them differently. There is obviously a great distance between the reader implied by a Mother Goose rhyme, who does not need to know much more than that words put into patterns can be fun to listen to, and the reader implied by T. S. Eliot's *The Waste Land,* who must be conscious of the history of the world and many of its mythologies.

But is the difference all that great? We cannot have a satisfying experience of either of these poems unless we are willing and able to make ourselves into the specific reader that each of them implies and is designed to make us become. And we cannot understand either of them unless we then stand back from the experience each has offered us and explore the character of the reader it has made us become. The two are equally literature, and offer similar pleasures.

The title of this book, *The Pleasures of Children's Literature,* suggests how centrally it focuses on the question of literary pleasure. While the book concentrates on the ways in which children's literature is distinct from other kinds, it does so in the belief that the differences are less significant than the similarities, that the pleasures of children's literature are essentially the pleasures of all literature.

Many of us assume that children read primarily in order to learn, and so our response to children's texts focuses on the messages those texts might teach. But anyone who likes to read knows that we do so primarily because we enjoy it, not because it is good for us. Even if we do sometimes read because it is good for us, we take pleasure in how and what our reading makes us think. If we are going to recommend works of literature for children and to children, we should base our recommendations on the aspects of reading that make committed readers want to and like to read.

THE PLEASURES OF LITERATURE

What *are* the pleasures of literature? The list presented here outlines a number of them.

EXPLORATION: Keep (or ask children to keep) an enjoyable literary text in mind while reading through the list below. Consider specific ways in which the text might be offering the pleasures described.

- The pleasure of words themselves—the patterns their sounds can make, the interesting ways in which they combine with each other, their ability to express revealing or frightening or beautiful pictures or ideas.
- The pleasure of making use of our repertoire of knowledge and our strategies of comprehension—of experiencing our mastery.

- The pleasure of recognizing gaps in our repertoire and learning the information or the strategy we need to fill them, and so developing further mastery.
- The pleasure of the pictures and ideas that the words of texts evoke—the ways in which they allow us to visualize people and places we have never actually seen or think about ideas we have not considered before.
- The pleasure of story—the organized patterns of emotional involvement and detachment, the delays of suspense, the climaxes and resolutions, the intricate patterns of chance and coincidence that make up a plot.
- The pleasure of formula—of repeating the comfortably familiar experience of kinds of stories we have enjoyed before.
- The pleasure of newness—of experiencing startlingly different kinds of stories and poems.
- The pleasure of story*telling*—our consciousness of how a writer's emphasis of particular elements or point of view shapes our response.
- The pleasure of structure—our consciousness of how words or pictures or events form cohesive and meaningful patterns.
- The pleasure of our awareness of the ways in which all the elements of a literary work seem to fit together to form a whole, or even of the ways in which texts sometimes undermine or even deny their own wholeness.
- The pleasure of finding mirrors for ourselves—of identifying with fictional characters.
- The pleasure of stepping outside of ourselves at least imaginatively and experiencing the lives and thoughts of different people.
- The pleasure of understanding—of seeing how literature not only mirrors life but comments on it, and makes us consider the meaning of our own existence.
- The pleasure of seeing through literature—of realizing how poems or stories attempt to manipulate our emotions and influence our understanding and our moral judgments in ways we are not prepared to accept.
- The pleasure of recognizing forms and genres, of seeing similarities between works of literature.
- The pleasure of getting insight into history and culture through literature.
- The pleasure of discussing with others their responses to texts we have read.
- The pleasure of developing a deeper understanding of our responses and of relating them to our responses to other texts and to our understanding of literature in general.

EXPLORATION: What are your *pleasures in literature? Consider (or have children consider) the kinds of pleasure you derive from your own reading. Think of specific examples of texts that gave you any of the pleasures listed above.*

These different pleasures all amount to one basic pleasure: the act of entering into communicative acts with others. They are like meetings and confrontations, bridges across the abysses that separate us one from another. Responding to a story or to a poem is a meeting with a text that conveys the flavor of a different personality or experience; talking about a text we have read with others is a meeting of different minds. We read literature to experience something we did not previously know or at the very least, an unfamiliar version of a familiar idea and experience. We talk about literature in order to enter into a dialogue with others about it, for good stories and poems have the ability always to be newly rewarding—whenever we hear new ideas about them, share new experiences of them, have newly read texts to compare them with. In other words, the pleasure of literature is the pleasure of conversation—of dialogues between readers and texts, and between readers and other readers about texts.

EXPLORATION: Some people believe that literary experience is essentially private and that analyzing our responses to literature or discussing them with others destroys them. Explore whether or not dialogue with others increases your understanding and enjoyment. Arrange with a friend or classmate to read the same story or poem and then have a discussion about it. Was the discussion enjoyable or destructive?

Understood as conversation, literature exists both in and out of the actual written texts or films or TV shows that contain stories and poems. In a sense, it is the entire body of writing, and of the thoughts people have had about writing, and also, all of the differing aspects of life that have ever been written about. One text reminds us of another text; our conversations with others about texts lead us to see connections with still other texts, with other conversations about texts, with aspects of our lives and our knowledge of the lives of others throughout history. In these ways, all literature and all experience of literature is tied together, a network of ideas and stories, images and emotions. Every time we read a text or discuss our response to a text with someone else, we become part of that network, learn more about it, and, in our own response and conversation, add something to it. All readers and all people who discuss their reading are in the process of making literature, of making it mean more to themselves and to others.

This process of making literature meaningful includes children: a child's response to a poem, based on limited experience of both life and literature, may in some ways seem to be less complicated than the response of an English professor; but it may also be more complicated in other ways. It is certainly no more and no less significant than the response of the English professor. In being different, it adds to the possibilities and thus enriches literature as a whole.

Nevertheless, exactly because literature is an interconnected network of texts and responses to them, both the child and the English professor can learn from, and gain pleasure from, each other's responses.

EXPLORATION: Share a story or a poem with some children, and discuss their response with them. Does it differ from your own? Can you see ways in which the discussion might enrich either their knowledge of literature or your own?

From the professor, or from other adults, the child can learn useful strategies. The ability to respond to literature with an understanding of its subtleties, and with a flexible attitude to the possibilities of meanings it might convey and emotions it might arouse—in other words, the ability to enjoy literature—is a learned skill. Those of us who enjoy reading may have developed our own skills for enjoying literature unconsciously, simply by reading a good deal. But many people who have read less can be encouraged by sensitive teachers to learn the skills of literary enjoyment. Children in particular can learn to become more perceptive readers of literature—and greatly increase their pleasure in the act of reading as a result of it.

In return for offering children something of our own sophisticated skills, we adults can gain something equally important from our discussions of literature with children. We can learn to share some of the more immediate, more sensuously direct, and less guilty pleasure that many children, too inexperienced to have learned otherwise, can still take from literature—specifically children's literature. We can learn to laugh at the jokes as hard as some children do, to become as involved as some children can. We can learn that exactly because it demands and encourages this sort of guileless intensity, children's literature can be a real pleasure for adults.

All engaged readers, adults or children, read intensely, without fear of strangeness or boredom with familiar pleasures—with commitment to the experience offered. And all engaged readers, adults or children, think intensely about what they read, without fear of what exploration of their responses will tell them about texts or, more significantly, about themselves. *The Pleasures of Children's Literature* expresses the faith that both adult students of children's literature and the children they teach or parent can become this sort of engaged reader, able to take pleasure both in the experience of literature and in the understanding of that experience.

EXPLORATION: Now that you have read this chapter, reconsider your previous exploration of whether "The Owl and the Pussy-cat" is a good poem. Does anything said in this chapter disagree with the opinions you expressed earlier? If so, has reading the chapter changed your opinions? How and why? If not, how would you counter the arguments presented here?

WORK CITED

Lear, Edward. "The Owl and the Pussy-cat." *The Complete Nonsense of Edward Lear.* Ed. Holbrook Jackson. New York: Dover, 1951.

PART TWO

Children's Literature in the Context of Childhood

As I suggested in Chapter 2, our previous experience of life, of language, and of literature provides us with a repertoire, a body of information and beliefs, including a set of strategies for comprehension that influence our response to a text. We all read the same texts differently, because we read them in the differing contexts of our individual repertoires and strategies. But our response to literary texts also depends upon our knowledge of another set of contexts that does not relate quite so immediately to our private experience—the contexts in which they were written. If we wish to deepen our understanding and enjoyment of literature, we need to learn something about a variety of other contexts, such as the following:

- We need to understand the vocabulary and the grammar of the language in which a text is written.
- We need to have some general ideas about what literary texts are—what their function is, what sorts of information or pleasure they can offer. If we do not understand the concept of "story," we are not likely to appreciate a particular story.
- We need knowledge of conventional strategies of comprehension—specific ways of making sense of literary texts that authors might expect us to use. For instance, we need to know how to think about a story in order to derive a moral from it and, also, what specific characteristics in a story make it appropriate for us to try to do so: not all stories have morals.
- We need knowledge of specific types of literature. For instance, fairy tales offer different pleasures and therefore require a different set of expectations from moral fables or realistic novels.
- In order to understand specific allusions and general assumptions about what constitutes normal human behavior, we need to know the social and historical

contexts in which a text was written. We might need to know about a particular event in history, or about popular attitudes toward women or children in the time the text was written.

As the name we give it implies, "children's literature" represents an intersection of two different sets of contexts: our ideas about children, and our ideas about literature. The three chapters in Part Two explore ideas about children, while Part Three explores ideas about literature.

In Chapter 2, we considered the ways in which texts imply readers. The next three chapters investigate the history and the characteristics of the implied readers in much of children's literature. They explore how the imaginary children who are the implied readers of children's literature came into existence over the centuries as our forebears developed a variety of ideas about childhood and about the nature of children; and they examine how those ideas of childhood have influenced our current assumptions about children. They also explore how those current assumptions relate to and are expressed by popular culture intended for children.

CHAPTER 3

Children and Children's Literature in History

CHILDREN BEFORE CHILDHOOD

If we accept Harvey Darton's definition of children's books as "works produced ostensibly to give children spontaneous pleasure, and not primarily to teach them" (1), then stories or poems that can readily be identified as children's literature didn't exist before the seventeenth century. It wasn't until 1744, when the publisher John Newbery had a great success with a collection of rhymes and descriptions of games called *A Little Pretty Pocket Book,* that the practice of producing such books became firmly established. Why did the invention of children's literature come so late in history?

The main reason is simply that, for much of the world's history, there was not much literature of any sort. Walter J. Ong points out that of the many thousands of languages that have existed, "only around 106 have ever been committed to writing to a degree sufficient to produce literature, and most have never been written at all" (7).

Nevertheless, stories and poems can exist outside of writing, in spoken forms. Like all the nonliterate cultures around the world that we sometimes condescendingly identify as "primitive," the European, African, Asian, and North American precursors of contemporary culture all had poems and stories that they communicated orally: myths and legends about supernatural beings like the Greek Hercules or the Ojibwa Nanabozho. But as we'll see in Chapter 11, when we consider myths and legends as children's literature, we cannot assume that these stories had the same function for their original audiences that our own literature has for us. Many of them were simultaneously sacred texts, like the Bible or the Koran, and humorous or adventurous tales meant to give pleasure. If Ong is right in suggesting that the ability to read and write has profound effects on the way human beings think, then the fact that we see important distinctions between stories conveying sacred truth and ones meant for entertainment seems to be an aspect of our literacy.

Our distinction between children and adults as audiences for stories also reflects our literacy, for in oral cultures children would most often simply have been considered an indistinguishable part of the overall audience listening to stories. Philippe Ariès says that in medieval Europe, which was primarily an oral society, "as soon as the child could live without the constant solicitude of his mother, his nanny or his cradle-rocker, he belonged to adult society" (128).

Ariès goes on to say, "That adult society now strikes us as rather puerile: no doubt this is largely a matter of its mental age, but it is also due to its physical age, because it was partly made up of children and youths" (128). "Puerile" has unfortunate negative connotations of a foolish immaturity; Ariès takes for granted that our current culture is superior to an earlier one, and we might just as easily see that earlier society as superior. It seems to have been more successful than we are in finding a balance between the opposing values we now identify with youth and age. But Ariès does explain why so many of the stories of oral cultures—fairy tales, myths, legends, tall tales—have come to be part of children's literature: they speak to the tastes and interests of an audience we would now identify as childlike.

Ariès has also provided an answer to our original question—although an answer that has caused considerable controversy: there was no children's literature until a few hundred years ago because, in an important sense, there was no childhood. There were children, of course: but if Ariès and a number of other historians of childhood are right, adults didn't think of these children in a way that made them distinct enough from other human beings to need their own separate literature.

EXPLORATION: The idea that children are not significantly different from adults is at odds with attitudes toward childhood that are common today. The following paragraphs describe still other attitudes toward children commonly held in different periods of history. As you read about these varying attitudes, record and consider the implications of your response to them. To what degree do you think children in all cultures and periods of history have been basically alike? To what degree have the nature of childhood and the characters of children been influenced by the values and assumptions of particular times and cultures?

Childhood from Ancient Times through the Middle Ages

Some ancient cultures had attitudes toward children substantially different from the ones we now take for granted. Both the Greeks and the Chinese exposed unwanted or deformed babies to the elements and left them to die, and the Carthaginians and others practiced child sacrifice. While many of the children who survived were cared for and educated, the ways in which they were distinctly childlike were not considered to be particularly important. Barbara Kaye Greenleaf says that the ancients "had no interest in the mysterious inner workings of childhood, because maturity was everything to them . . . . the ancients gave little thought to the child *as a child*'' (24). In this context, Jesus' idea that adults should become like children because it is children who are wise was a startling innovation, meant to shock his contemporaries. It led to the beginnings of attitudes a little more like our own.

After the fall of Rome these newer attitudes became mingled with the more traditional ones of the Germanic tribes. Ariès presents a variety of evidence to make the case that in the Middle Ages in Europe there was no concept of childhood as we now understand it—a stage of life with characteristics distinct enough to be noticed and seriously examined. Before the thirteenth century, European medieval art contained few depictions of children, and the children portrayed have the proportions of adults. While we might assume this phenomenon represents a lack of technical expertise, we might ask why that expertise didn't develop—why artists did not feel the need to depict the distinctive appearance of children. Furthermore, children were dressed like adults of their class as soon as they stopped being babies.

Ariès believes that behavior of this sort might suggest a lack of interest in children—that parents did not invest much love in their children for fear they might lose them: ''The general feeling was, and for a long time remained, that one had several children in order to keep just a few. . . . People could not attach themselves to something that was regarded as a probable loss'' (38). In fact, there were low survival rates for children: some scholars believe that in the fourteenth century as many as three-fourths of children died before the age of five.

Even so, many scholars doubt that parents loved their children any less for fear of losing them; Linda Pollack describes personal diaries written as early as the sixteenth century in which parents recorded deep concern about their children, and C. H. Talbot points to the fact that many biographical narratives of medieval times record stories of mothers dying from grief at the loss of a child.

Those children who survived early death seem to have simply taken their part in a communal life along with their elders, as soon as they stopped being infants and needing special care. Even in the seventeenth century, paintings show men, women, and children all playing games together. They also shared the same sermons, saints' lives, miracle tales, folk tales, and the cycle plays of Corpus Christi, the street theater depicting episodes of biblical history.

For historians of childhood like Ariès, differences between medieval society and our own signal significant differences in the way adults thought about and behaved toward their children. As I have suggested, some scholars doubt these conclusions. Pollack asserts: ''I believe there is no reason to assume that parental care must vary according to developments and changes in society as a whole. The history of childhood is an area dominated by myths'' (viii). Pollack claims that views of childhood like Ariès's depend too much on secondary sources, such as religious tracts and books offering advice to parents. Her investigations of diaries written as early as the sixteenth century show that parents acted on such advice no more often than parents nowadays heed the advice of experts—which is, according to some studies, not very often—and that parental instincts led them to an apparently modern awareness of different developmental stages and of children's need for care, protection, and guidance.

Similarly, Talbot shows that at least some medieval people were conscious of the psychological differences between children and adults. Talbot quotes a description of the distinguishing characteristics of boys written in the thirteenth century: "Their minds are docile, without a care or an anxiety in the world, and because they lead a sheltered life, the only things they appreciate are those that make them laugh" (18).

Nevertheless, there seems to be some truth in Hiner and Hawes's statement that, while "Ariès has been justly criticized for his selective and sometimes uncritical use of evidence, no one has successfully challenged his essential point that childhood is *not* an immutable stage of life, free from the influence of historical change" (xvi). Medieval scholars make it clear that medieval children did indeed live different lives from modern children. Even Pollack has to admit that the earliest diarists she considers do not discuss their feelings about raising children or being parents, as modern parents surely would. She also speaks of "the rise of the training aspect of parental care—that of moulding a child into shape. It would seem to be non-existent in the 16th century, rising to a peak in the 18th" (113). While most parents throughout history have loved their children, their ways of expressing that love have not always been our own.

The ways parents have expressed their love for their children have sometimes been so unlike our own that they might strike us as implying negligence or even malicious cruelty. Judged in terms of our own ideas, the indiscriminate mixing of children with adults in medieval society seems neglectful. But Talbot asserts that medieval people actually had an understanding of children superior to our own, because they didn't try "to enforce an artificial childhood on girls and youths who had reached the stage of puberty" (32). Perhaps it is *we* who harm children in our determined efforts to protect and mold them.

EXPLORATION: Do you agree that it is possible for parental love and concern to manifest themselves in ways that might strike people in different times or places as neglectful or abusive? To what degree can we generalize about what constitutes abusive or neglectful behavior? To what degree might modern attitudes to childhood be considered more harmful to children than medieval ones?

THE INVENTION OF CHILDHOOD

We have seen that because people in the past thought about childhood differently, they probably treated children differently—and they certainly did not produce a special kind of literature for them. What happened to change these attitudes? How did an idea of childhood develop that would lead to the invention of children's literature?

The focus on childhood as a distinct stage of life worthy of careful thought and attention that began to develop in the Middle Ages relates to the transition from a primarily oral culture to a literate one. With the introduction of printing in the fifteenth century, books and the ability to read became more widespread. If Ong's theories are correct, people automatically became more self-conscious—more aware of their separateness from others and more concerned with who they were as individuals. Whereas oral communication demands involvement with other people, writing demands isolation: as we read we separate ourselves from the people we are with, a process that may lead to introspection and self-analysis. As introspection develops, childhood becomes a subject of interest, for our knowledge of ourselves depends on our thoughts about our past experience. The contemporary idea that childhood is significant as the time in which we form the personalities we will have as adults dates from the development of literate society.

Another major component of our idea of childhood did not come into existence until after the Middle Ages: the idea that all children need a formal education. While the ancient Greeks and Romans educated at least some upper-class children, in the Middle Ages few children outside the church had a formal education. Most learned what they needed to know by imitating adults. Even in school, children were mixed with adults: it took many centuries for educators to decide that children should begin school at a certain age, that they should be separated from adults and placed in classes based on their age, and that they should begin their studies with simpler materials and move on to harder ones.

In fact, the development of the idea of childhood as a distinct period of life is connected with the development of distinctions between simple and hard subjects and between the capabilities of young children and older ones. Ariès suggests that these distinctions "were the manifestations of a general tendency toward distinguishing and separating: a tendency which was not unconnected with the Cartesian revolution of clear ideas" (314). The new respect for clear thinking can itself be explained by the influence of books and reading, for, as Ong says, "abstractly sequential, classificatory, explanatory examination of phenomena or of stated truths is impossible without writing and reading" (8–9).

Not surprisingly, those who did the classifying saw themselves as the superior class. Childhood became distinct not so much because children were singled out as different, but rather because wealthy adult males saw *themselves* as different enough from (and superior enough to) servants, children, and women to separate themselves from the rest of the community. When male children began to dress differently than their fathers in the seventeenth century, they did so not because a new style was invented for them but because they continued to wear the old styles while their fathers adopted new ones; and while the dress of middle-class boys became different from that of middle-class men, it tended to be the same as that worn by servants.

Other aspects of culture developed similarly to clothing. The poor and the children of the rich continued to enjoy games, like blindman's buff, that everybody had played before middle-class adults decided in the seventeenth century that such games were beneath them. More significantly, the poor and the children of the rich continued to hear the oral stories that are the basis for fairy tales after wealthy literate adults came, during the seventeenth century, to consider themselves superior to these stories. As Ariès says, "Childhood was becoming the repository of customs abandoned by the adults" (71). We might conclude that our current conceptions of the nature of childhood accurately sum up the characteristics of people in general in the Middle Ages—that it was not so much a concept of childhood that developed but, as Neil Postman says, "a new definition of adulthood" (20).

As conceptions of adulthood evolved, there developed some specific assumptions about childhood. The basic one was that children were, like adults of the lower classes, weak and vulnerable enough to need protection, both from adults and from themselves. It became a matter of significance for adults that children were *innocent*—that is, either ignorant of the restraints of adult maturity and therefore savagely primitive and weakly prone to evil, or else, unsullied by the laxity of adult corruption and therefore delightfully pure and in need of being sheltered.

Both attitudes led to the need to isolate children, either from the corrupting immodesty of adult sexuality or from the corrupting limitations of adult rationality. The essence of childhood as we now understand it is that children need to be kept separate from adult society and culture—kept off the streets, sent to schools with other children of their own age, and provided with a literature primarily defined by what aspects of adult thought and feeling it leaves out. A special children's literature began at the end of the sixteenth century, when adults perceived a need for expurgated editions of classics for children. Even today, the questions most adults ask about children's books relate to what they should leave out rather than to what they should contain.

CHILDREN'S LITERATURE IN HISTORY

The history of children's literature parallels the history of childhood: the stories and poems that children have experienced throughout history express the vast differences in the ideas of childhood of different cultures and times.

Misconceptions about Early Children's Literature

Gillian Adams suggests that about four thousand years ago in what is now Iraq, the Sumerian culture produced the earliest literature that can be identified as being intended for children—clay tablets containing texts designed to train scribes. One of these is a story about a schoolboy, and Adams says, "If it can be assumed that the Sumerians believed a story about a young schoolboy was appropriate for use by students of the same age, much as primers today have first- and second-graders as major characters, then it seems likely that this story was written for the use of elementary students and that those students were young. The student's misadventures would be amusing to young children" (19).

But there is no clear evidence that the student scribes were actually children at all, or even that, as Adams's modern developmental assumptions lead her to take for granted, easier texts like this one would have been studied before more complicated ones, and therefore, by younger students. If we are not willing to assume that the Sumerians made the same distinctions and educational assumptions that we make, there's no reason to believe that this particular story was intended for a young audience. It seems just as likely that, in a society less prone to making distinctions between children and adults than our own, both children and adults would have read such materials and enjoyed them for the same reasons. The claim that this text must have been primarily literature for children because it had some of the characteristics of modern children's literature might well be a distortion of history.

Similar claims have been made for much early literature. For instance, scholars have tried to identify the aspects of medieval literature that might have appealed to children. Thomas Hanks suggests that the medieval miracle plays "attracted children by portraying children on-stage, by presenting villains of highly entertaining frightfulness, and even by incorporating children's games into the plays" (21). But as Meradith Tilbury McMunn and William Robert McMunn say, "it seems almost a certainty that the 'children's literature' of the Middle Ages was simply the literature of the entire culture. . . . Perhaps it would be an anachronistic modern inference to suppose that medieval children would have preferred the beast fables to the courtly romances" (24)—or that, because we believe that modern children like frightening villains, we can assume that medieval children would have too.

Early Texts for Children

There were, of course, texts intended primarily for children in earlier times, but they had educational purposes and were purely didactic. For instance, *The Babees Book,* from the late fifteenth century, tells its readers "O Babees ynge,/My Book only is made for youre lernynge"—"Young babies, my Book is for you only" (Demers and Moyles 11). We shouldn't forget, though, that it was common in the Middle Ages to call all beginners—even grownups—"babees": the book gave such beginners, apprentice courtiers acting as servants, advice about table manners. Similarly, one of the books Caxton produced in the fifteenth century was a collection of Aesop's *Fables.* While these animal stories with morals were often used in the education of children over the next three or four hundred years, Caxton explicitly asserted that his version was meant not just for children but "to shew al maner of folk what maner of thyng they ought to ensue and folowe" (Darton 9). In the following pages, we will examine how a literature developed in England that was more exclusively intended for child readers.

The Puritans. The didactic tradition intensified with the Puritans of the seventeenth century, who were, according to Ruth MacDonald, "the first child-centered group in history" (153). Since their faith focused on the need for each individual to find his or her own salvation, the Puritans developed the conviction that children were as prone to sin and in need of salvation as were adults, and they produced books specifically aimed at directing young children to the right path. For instance, James Janeway's *Token for Children: Being an Exact Account of the Conversion, Holy and Exemplary Lives, and Joyful Deaths of Several Young Children,* first published in 1672, contains the story of Sarah Howley, who gave herself to Christ after hearing a sermon when she was eight, and who then became seriously ill at the age of fourteen:

"She was full of Divine Sentences, and almost all her discourse from the first to last in the time of her sickness, was about her Soul, Christs sweetness, and the Souls of others, in a word, like a continued sermon" (Demers and Moyles 48). She died in the blissful knowledge of her eternal salvation.

Books like this may strike us as being both excessively preachy and unnecessarily depressing—"a continued sermon" isn't what we expect of children's literature. But as Darton says, "It is true that they do not provide 'amusement,' except unintentionally. But that is exactly why, at that time, they *were* 'children's books.' They *were* meant to give pleasure: the highest pleasure, that of studying and enjoying the Will of God" (53). Despite our own vastly different ideas about what children like, there surely can be no doubt that children immersed in the values of the adults who loved them took great pleasure in these books.

EXPLORATION: Or can *there be doubt about that? Consider your own response to this somewhat presumptuous assertion.*

Chapbooks and Street Literature. Meanwhile, other children were enjoying materials that would strike most modern readers as more obviously entertaining. The invention of printing meant that versions of old tales of heroes and adventures from the oral tradition became available. While sophisticated readers viewed these tales as crude and old-fashioned, they continued to be widely read by a developing audience of less-sophisticated readers. From the sixteenth through the eighteenth centuries, stories of giants and heroes like Tom Hickathrift and Robin Hood appeared in numerous cheaply printed chapbooks, often in lurid versions that eliminated the poetry of the medieval originals and concentrated on the excitement of the action. These chapbooks were the first popular literature. As with contemporary comic books or romance novels, educated people considered them to be trash, but they were widely read and enjoyed by a mixed audience of adults, primarily of the lower classes, and by children of all classes.

Locke and Newbery. In 1690, in *An Essay Concerning Human Understanding,* John Locke had argued that people are neither innately good nor bad, that at birth the human mind is a blank page and that all our ideas depend on experience. In *Some Thoughts Concerning Education,* first published in 1693 and reprinted in edition after edition throughout the next century, Locke spelled out the educational implications of his theory. Adults influenced by it began to think seriously about what they should try to write on those blank pages in the minds of children and, also, to worry about what they ought to prevent from being written—such as the excitement and violence of the old tales of heroes. Locke himself had recommended that children read Aesop's fables, "which being stories apt to delight and entertain a child, may yet afford useful reflections to a grown man" (Darton 17). John Newbery's genius was to see that there might be a market for literature that offered the pleasure of the chapbook tales, but that also encouraged children to develop the right values and attitudes; in an advertisement, he proclaimed that *A Little Pretty Pocket Book* was "intended for the Instruction and Amusement of little Master Tommy and pretty Miss Polly." In following Locke's suggestion and combining instruction and amusement in this way, Newbery invented what we now recognize as children's literature.

After Newbery: The Pleasures of Rationalism. The children's literature that developed after Newbery had little in common with our own, however. Locke had encouraged adults to believe that their primary obligation to children was to encourage the development of rational thought and moral judgment; and while the equally influential Jean-Jacques Rousseau didn't accept Locke's idea that children began with empty minds, he wanted to preserve what he saw as their natural wisdom by creating educational situations that allowed them to reach their own conclusions rather than enforcing their acceptance of adult authority. Influenced by both Locke and Rousseau, many writers produced children's books designed to lead children to reach the right conclusions by considering both good and bad examples. The central characters of these books tend to be wise adult teachers who guide children to the truth by encouraging them to consider the moral and intellectual implications of their experiences. In Maria Edgeworth's "The Purple Jar" (1801), for example, young Rosamund's mother allows her to spend her money on an attractive purple jar instead of a needed pair of shoes, and to suffer and learn from the consequences when the purple disappears as she pours out the jar's contents and she has stay home for want of proper footwear.

If we consider such stories from the viewpoint of our own assumptions, it's not easy to admire them. Darton says of "The Purple Jar": "You hate the mother. . . . You know she is right, and you loathe rectitude accordingly" (141). Demers and Moyles say that Mrs. Mason, the wise teacher of Mary Wollstonecraft's *Original Stories from Real Life* (1788), is "icily rational" (138). Geoffrey Summerfield finds the children's literature of this period so offensive that he calls *A Little Pretty Pocket Book* "a sneaky piece of work" that "serves only to show how calamitous the didactic book for children could be" (86). He also says that Wollstonecraft's *Original Stories* "has a strong claim to be the most sinister, ugly, overbearing book for children ever published" and calls Mrs. Mason "a veritable monster" (229).

In "Wise Child, Wise Peasant, Wise Guy," Mitzi Myers asserts that the attitude implied by comments like Summerfield's is "a presentist one that orders the past to validate today's needs" (108): in her view, Summerfield attacks these writers for not sharing his own twentieth-century convictions that fantasy is healthy and that appeals to reason are oppressive, and forgets that for writers and even for children of earlier times, there might well be genuine pleasure to be found in stories about people who learn to be more rational.

In "Impeccable Governesses, Rational Dames, and Moral Mothers," Myers herself presents an alternate interpretation to these "presentist" ones, focusing on the fact that writers like Darton and Summerfield direct most of their ire at characters, like Mrs. Mason, who are powerful (and therefore, apparently, threatening) *women.* She suggests that writers like Edgeworth and Wollstonecraft represent an "under-valued and almost unrecognized female literary tradition" (33) and "show how girls should be educated in a new mode of female heroism—in rationality, self-command, and moral autonomy" (34). Myers sees Mrs. Mason not as a monster but as a model of "the heroic potential available in ordinary female life, in everyday female roles" (50); she represents not icy repression but emancipating empowerment.

EXPLORATION: Read a text such as Wollstonecraft's Original Stories *or Edgeworth's "The Purple Jar" in the light of the arguments described here. Which position do you find most persuasive?*

A Delight in Childishness. Before contemporary literature could come into existence, a new idea of childhood had to develop—the idea that the way in which children are different from adults is not so much a limitation as a blessing—that, as the poet Wordsworth says in his "Ode: Intimations of Immortality in Early Childhood" (1807), a child is a "Mighty Prophet! Seer blest!" (l. 114), and that it is actually so-called maturity that is limited, a "prison-house" (l. 67) of false perception. Only after it had become possible to believe that the innocence of childhood might represent greater wisdom than does adult reason, could writers find charm in poems pretending to be spoken in the voices of children, as did Jane Taylor in her well-known "Twinkle, Twinkle, Little Star" (1806). Other writers could then invest the voices and attitudes of children with great power and use them to attack the supposed rationality and wisdom of adults, as did the poet William Blake in *Songs of Innocence and Experience,* in which a child's limited understanding contrasts with the hypocrisy and corruption of an adult's supposedly wiser view of the same subjects.

A similar attack on adult reason is implied even in the title of Edward Lear's *Book of Nonsense* (1846) and in the anarchic events of what was probably the first children's novel with no clear moral, Lewis Carroll's *Alice in Wonderland* (1865). Lear's absurd limericks about people who have incredibly long noses or who eat nothing but buns, and Carroll's description of a young girl's encounters with arrogant caterpillars and disappearing cats, represent a radical celebration of childishness that undermines the claims of adult reason and maturity. That these writers could be as popular as they were suggests how much adults had come to accept the positive power of childishness.

The Balancing of Entertainment and Instruction. The books by Lear and Carroll were oddities. Like Catherine Sinclair's novel *Holiday House* (1839) and John Ruskin's fairy tale "King of the Golden River" (1851), most of the children's books produced throughout the nineteenth century combined a delight in childish innocence with a need for instruction in adult values. "Torn between the opposing demands of innocence and experience," Uli Knoepflmacher says of Victorian fantasists, "the author who resorts to the wishful, magical thinking of the child nonetheless feels compelled, in varying degrees, to hold onto the grown-up's circumscribed notions about reality" (499).

That's still true: most children's books balance their praise of childishness with a consciousness of the values of maturity, and as we'll see later, Knoepflmacher's assertion about Victorian children's books applies to today's children's books: "In the better works of fantasy of the period, this dramatic tension between the outlooks of adult and childhood selves becomes rich and elastic: conflict and harmony, friction and reconciliation, realism and wonder, are allowed to interpenetrate and co-exist" (499). In other words, by the middle of the nineteenth century, attitudes toward childhood were much like our own, and children's literature had become much like what it is today.

EXPLORATION: Test the conclusions of this section by reading some children's literature from a specific period in history—the Puritan books of the seventeenth century, the rational novels of the early nineteenth century. Examine the extent to which they imply child readers and ideas of childhood unlike your own.

THE LESSONS OF HISTORY

In trying to find out why children's literature has existed for such a short time, we have uncovered opinions and ideas that might influence our understanding not only of history but also of children and of children's literature itself. To summarize briefly:

- In order to make sense of the fact that people in the past expressed their concern for children by treating them in ways that we now consider objectionable, but that, as far as we know, worked as well as our own approaches to children, we might develop some humility toward the past. We should consider if our own behavior is only different from, not necessarily better than, that of people in earlier times.

EXPLORATION: Consider whether you believe that our current ideas and attitudes represent an evolutionary improvement over past values or just a different state of affairs.

- In learning about the values of the past, we might find ourselves becoming more conscious of the specific nature of our own values. The fact that people once thought differently forces us to realize that what we take for granted is not necessarily the complete or the only truth. Our knowledge of the past might stop us from being too confident in our own generalizations about children—a topic we'll explore further in the next chapter.

WORKS CITED

Adams, Gillian. "The First Children's Literature? The Case for Sumer." *Children's Literature* 14 (1986): 1–30.

Ariès, Philippe. *Centuries of Childhood: A Social History of Family Life.* Trans. Robert Baldick. New York: Vintage–Random House, 1962.

Darton, F. J. Harvey. *Children's Books in England: Five Centuries of Social Life.* 1932. 3rd ed. Rev. Brian Alderson. Cambridge: Cambridge UP, 1982.

Demers, Patricia, and Gordon Moyles. *From Instruction to Delight: An Anthology of Children's Literature to 1850.* Toronto: Oxford UP, 1982.

Greenleaf, Barbara Kaye. *Children Through the Ages: A History of Childhood.* New York: McGraw-Hill, 1978.

Hanks, D. Thomas, Jr. "Not for Adults Only: The English Corpus Christi Plays." *Children's Literature Association Quarterly* 10.1 (Spring 1985): 21–22.

Hiner, N. Ray, and Joseph M. Hawes, eds. *Growing Up in America: Children in Historical Perspective.* Urbana: U of Illinois P, 1985.

Knoepflmacher, U. C. "The Balancing of Child and Adult: An Approach to Victorian Fantasies for Children." *Nineteenth Century Fiction* 37.4 (1983): 497–530.

MacDonald, Ruth. *Literature for Children in England and America from 1646 to 1774.* Troy: Whitston, 1982.

McMunn, Meradith Tilbury, and William Robert McMunn. "Children's Literature in the Middle Ages." *Children's Literature* 1 (1972): 21–30.

Myers, Mitzi. "Impeccable Governesses, Rational Dames, and Moral Mothers: Mary Wollstonecroft and the Female Tradition in Georgian Children's Books." *Children's Literature* 14 (1986): 31–59.

———. "Wise Child, Wise Peasant, Wise Guy: Geoffrey Summerfield's Case Against the Eighteenth Century." *Children's Literature Association Quarterly* 12.2 (Summer 1987): 107–110.

Ong, Walter J. *Orality and Literacy: The Technologizing of the Word.* London: Methuen, 1982.

Pollack, Linda A. *Forgotten Children: Parent-Child Relations from 1500 to 1900.* Cambridge: Cambridge UP, 1983.

Postman, Neil. *The Disappearance of Childhood.* New York: Dell Laurel, 1984.

Summerfield, Geoffrey. *Fantasy and Reason: Children's Literature in the Eighteenth Century.* Athens: U of Georgia P, 1984.

Talbot, C. H. "Children in the Middle Ages." *Children's Literature* 6 (1977): 17–33.

Wordsworth, William. *Poetical Works.* Ed. Thomas Hutchinson, rev. Ernest de Selincourt. London: Oxford UP, 1936.

CHAPTER 4

Contemporary Attitudes toward Children

CHILDHOOD AS DIFFERENT

"When we deal with the distant and relatively alien society of seventeenth-century France," says David Hunt, "it is not hard to accept the notion that the plight of children was related to the character of the social and political order in which they lived. We lack the corresponding understanding of parenthood and society today" (196). Despite, and even to some degree because of our unconscious acceptance of it, our own social and political order strongly influences our attitudes toward children and children's literature.

If anything, contemporary ideas about childhood have a more profound effect on the lives of children than did the ideas of previous eras. In the twentieth century, we have invented entire academic disciplines devoted to the study of childhood: Freudian, developmental, and educational psychology, the sociology of childhood, the history of childhood, even the criticism of children's literature. These disciplines claim to be scientific, and we tend to accept their conclusions as fact. We often approach children with the misleading conviction that our general knowledge of childhood allows us to understand the significance of their lives.

Our ideas about childhood boil down to one key assumption. We believe that children are significantly different from adults, that they think differently, feel differently, and need different treatment from their elders.

COMMON GENERALIZATIONS ABOUT CHILDREN

EXPLORATION: As you read the following list of generalizations about children, consider (or have children consider) their implications. Which of them do you believe to be true? What experiences have you had that might confirm or contradict them? Are there any you've assumed without being conscious of doing so? Were you right to make such assumptions?

Children Are Innocent

We believe children are blissfully happy—presumably because they have not yet learned what adults know about the miserable world they have been born into. In terms of children's literature, this assumption usually takes the form of censorship: children shouldn't be told stories about subjects that adults find painful, because "they'll know about that soon enough." Meanwhile, we assume that children will respond positively to "childlike" books—bright, colorful ones describing pleasant experiences—and will be bored by ones with pictures too somber and events too painful to represent their own blissful vision of reality. According to Charlotte Huck, "Cynicism and despair are not childlike emotions. Some books . . . are destructive of values before children have had time to develop them" (5). On the other hand, children may respond all too deeply to such books, as the next generalization suggests.

Children Are Vulnerable

We believe that children are highly emotional and need to be protected from experiences that might give them nightmares or scar them permanently. As a consequence, we may engage in a vigilant effort to keep children away from potentially traumatic books or films. When the movie *Batman* came out, a news report quoted a psychiatrist as saying that "the film's dark eerie atmosphere, coupled with gratuitous violence, could cause nightmares in children and make them afraid of the dark" (Toronto *Globe and Mail,* July 14, 1989).

Children Are Influenceable

Because children are deeply impressionable, we believe, they are easily influenced—prone to corruption because they're not yet shielded from their animal instincts or primitive desires by the repressions of maturity. They need protection not only from potentially traumatic experiences but also from those that might encourage them in immoral or antisocial behavior.

The result of such an assumption is an effort to censor potentially damaging books. Many adults are far more interested in determining what children should *not* experience than what they should. Huck reports that, when Maurice Sendak's *In the Night Kitchen* first came out, librarians in Caldwell Parish, Louisiana, sought to protect young children from an apparently harmful knowledge of human anatomy by painting diapers on the book's naked hero. Similarly, many people prevent children from reading books containing what they consider to be sexist portrayals of characters. Speaking of E. B. White's *Charlotte's Web,* Masha Kabakow Rudman says, "Fern, the human female protagonist, changes from a girl interested in animals to a girl interested in boys—one of the only flaws in this beautiful book" (354).

Children Are Limited

Because children are usually less experienced and less knowledgeable than adults, we assume that they have short attention spans and can understand only simplified information. Assumptions like these can lead to a concern that books not overtax children by being too long or too complex. We tend to praise books for having the straightforward predictability that we condemn in adult books.

Children Are Cute

Children's limitations often endear them to us. When children try to act like adults and fail—when babies look charmingly chubby in imitation tuxedos or when older children mispronounce or misuse words—we call them adorable. While we claim to be appreciative of their childishness, we may actually be confirming our idea that children are so incapable of handling the adult world that they need supervision and protection. This assumption leads to praise for "cute" books, like those in which small, cuddly animals are rewarded for their smallness or their ignorance.

Children Are Creative

On the other hand, there are some ways in which children are *less* limited than adults. Because they haven't yet been totally fixed in the repressions of maturity, they are, we believe, freer and more spontaneous than adults, and highly imaginative. Some adults who stress children's creativity are likely to allow children access to stimulating and rewarding literary experiences. But such assumptions influence other adults to do just the opposite—for instance, to deprive children of picture book versions of fairy tales because somebody else's visualization might hamper their own creativity.

Children Are Conservative

Despite their presumed creativity, we also believe that children tend to find it hard to respond to new or different ideas—that they like only what they already know, and that they will be bored or discouraged by new and unfamiliar experiences. Such assumptions lead many adults to recommend books for children on the basis of their supposed current likes or interests, or because there is evidence that these books are already popular among children.

All Children Develop in Clearly Defined Stages

According to the Swiss psychologist Jean Piaget, children pass through a number of stages as they develop and mature. These stages always occur in the same order, and each child tends to enter them at approximately the same point in his or her life. As popularly understood, the stages are as follows:

- In the *sensorimotor* period, from birth to approximately two years of age, children form simple, nonverbal ideas by manipulating objects.

- From age two to six or seven, children are in the *preoperational* stage. They begin to use symbols, but lack the ability to think about what they're doing; furthermore, they are egocentric, that is, unable to understand any point of view but their own.
- From age six through twelve, children are in the *concrete operational* stage. They begin to understand some of the basic concepts that underlie our ability to think about the world, but only in terms of concrete examples.
- It is not until the *formal operational* period, between ages twelve and fifteen, that children can begin to think abstractly, to reason about ideas that don't relate to their direct experiences.

Piaget's theory has led to the idea that children are conservative by suggesting that development occurs in this series of separate stages. Many people assume that, therefore, it is impossible for a child at one stage to learn tasks that require the kind of thinking characteristic of a more advanced stage. Furthermore, Piaget's idea of discrete stages has influenced many other theories of development, including Erik Erikson's theory of psychological development and Lawrence Kohlberg's theory of moral development. As usually understood, these theories reinforce the conception of the inflexibility of childhood by confirming the inability of children to act in ways uncharacteristic of their current stage.

In terms of children's literature, this focus on stages has produced the labeling of books as being appropriate for children of certain ages or readable only by children of certain ages, and has led to the assumption that each book is appropriate for only one specific level of development. For instance, Nicholas Tucker bases his discussion of how to choose books for children on such a focus: "Following Piaget, I shall chiefly describe the more typical ways in which children seem to approach and make sense of their stories at various ages, leaving particular details—of how individuals or whole cultures can then sometimes react to such stories quite differently—to one side" (5–6). It is this sort of determined avoidance of "details" like individuality or culture that leads adults to ask bookstore salespeople questions like "What do you recommend for a five-year-old?"

Judgments of books based on Piagetian stages more often relate to what children cannot understand than to what they can. According to Alan Purves and Dianne Monson, for instance, "the reader must possess a certain lack of egocentricity in order to be able to relate to the characteristics, problems, etc., of a story character living, let us say, in the Middle Ages. According to Jean Piaget's work on children's development, that egocentricity does dissipate during the period of formal operations, reached by most children at about age eleven. . . . Therefore, it may be that children in the intermediate grades and junior high are better suited for understanding and relating to historical fiction than are younger children" (77).

Piaget also insisted that learning is active, that each of us must make our own sense of the world in the process of interacting with it. His experiments persuaded him that each child must in effect re-create the world and that therefore children cannot learn through being given information or instructions by others. Ideas like this have led many people to assume that children are, in effect, uneducable. Since children must move from one stage to the next on their own, many adults believe that it is pointless for adults to offer them information or attempt to teach them more complex tasks.

Indeed, some people believe that adult interference is dangerous, for attempting to teach children more than their current stage makes them capable of absorbing will merely frustrate and confuse them. For adherents of this view, the main goal in choosing books for children is to ensure that the books are not likely to challenge them too much and so "turn them off" literature.

Children Are Always (or Should Always Be) Learning

The reason for our concern about whether books will frustrate children or give them nightmares or bad ideas is our conviction that childhood is malleable, a period of constant development, and that therefore it is and should be a state of constant learning. We assume that everything in children's lives ought to be educational. We decorate their rooms with an eye to their learning of colors, and we provide them with educational toys, educational television programs, even educational clothing and dinnerware. As Nancy Weiss says in her discussion of Dr. Spock, "The language in which child rearing is discussed is often that of modern marketing. Children are a product to be turned out by the home. The mother, not only literally the original producer, is more importantly its refiner and packager. The lure is held out before her that with attentiveness, emotional vigilance, and her uninterrupted presence she can provide an environment from which a superior individual will emerge" (302).

The conviction that children should always be learning moves the significance of childhood from the immediate experience of living to the future consequences of that experience. Rather than spontaneously engaging with children, parents and teachers are constantly alert to the future results of their current behavior toward children. An attitude of this sort leads to an evaluation of books in which the main consideration is what they might teach and how they might affect a young reader's future. Instead of praising a funny book because it is funny, we may say that it is good because it will help children develop a sense of humor.

EXPLORATION: Are these generalizations really all that common? Test them (or have children test them) by looking for evidence of them in newspapers or magazines, in conversations or classroom discussions, or on TV programs. If they are not common, what generalizations about children do *you find evidence of, and what effect might they have on our decisions about children's literature?*

EXPLORING THE GENERALIZATIONS

The most obvious flaw in these assumptions is the fact that they are generalizations, and that generalizations rarely apply in all cases. In a less interesting world, it might be safe to say something like, "This is a book that six-year-olds will enjoy." In the real and more interesting world, some six-year-olds like a particular book, and many others hate it. In the real world, children have as few generally true group characteristics as do, say, all lawyers, or all university students. In this world, each child is his or her own person, an individual being whose values and capabilities are influenced both by heredity and environment. When we make assumptions about the similarity of all six-year-olds, we lose sight of the immense significance of individual differences in the process of literary response.

Are Children Innocent?

Some of the differences in children's responses have nothing to do with differences in character or potential. When we speak of the innocence of childhood, we forget about the 40 million children in the world who live on the streets, without homes or parents or enough food. Most of our generalizations about the kind of literature children can "relate" to imply the degree to which we assume that all children live the comfortable, protected lives of white, middle-class North Americans.

We also forget—or, perhaps, try to hide from ourselves—the extent to which the innocent bliss of even fairly well-off children is a fiction. Weiss suggests that Spock's *Baby and Child Care,* still the most popular guide for parents, is such a fiction: "This world of rearing the young . . . is free of dissonance or conflict, or the recognition of poverty or cultural difference. Such a world has invented a motherhood that excludes the experience of many mothers" (303). It also excludes the experience of the many children who are sexually or physically abused, and of the even more numerous ones who go through the ordinary but nevertheless painful traumas of growth and of adjustment to human existence. The psychoanalyst Sigmund Freud developed a complex theory about the ways in which children inevitably experience and come to repress feelings of sexual desire, particularly for their own parents. Even those who refuse to accept Freud's theory must acknowledge that children's desires and feelings about themselves and their parents are intense, difficult, and often sexual.

EXPLORATION: Is that statement true? To what extent are children sexual beings? Find out something about Freud's theories of child sexuality, and consider the degree to which the theories might be valid.

If we are willing to acknowledge that the lives of all children contain some degree of pain and difficulty, then perhaps we will begin to see why attempts to censor children's literature may be misguided. Because of assumptions about what sort of language is childlike, few children's texts contain as much vulgarity as can be heard in most schoolyards and playgrounds. Because of assumptions about what sorts of attitudes and experiences are childlike, few children's texts describe the kinds of disturbing thoughts about sex or antisocial behavior that many children do have, or the cruelty or violence many children do experience. To deprive children of the opportunity to read about such things will either make literature irrelevant to them or else leave them feeling they are alone in their thoughts or experiences.

Those who believe in censorship think that providing children with an ideal vision of the way things ought to be—with literature that describes a world without pain or poverty or sexism—will prevent them from ever learning how to do wrong. My own conclusion is that those who are deprived of knowledge of certain attitudes or forms of behavior, and therefore, prevented from thinking about why they might be harmful, are the ones most likely to take such attitudes or commit such acts.

EXPLORATIONS: (1) To what degree do you believe that it is important to expose children, through literature, to many kinds of experiences, however unpleasant. Should children's reading or the contents of children's books be censored in any way? Why or why not?

(2) Read (or ideally, have children read) a children's or young adult book that is often the subject of censorship, such as Maurice Sendak's In the Night Kitchen, *Toshi Maruki's* Hiroshima No Pika, *John Neufeld's* Freddy's Book, *Judy Blume's* Are You There God? It's Me, Margaret *or* Forever, *or Robert Cormier's* Chocolate War. *Should children be given access to the book you have chosen? In what way might it harm them or help them?*

Are Children Limited?

As well as forgetting about the actual experiences of many children, the generalizations we have considered focus on limitations rather than on strengths. We assume that children are different from adults in being more limited, less capable, more susceptible, less flexible. I believe that our doing so misrepresents the real capability and potential of many children. Our assumption that sexist or racist books will pervert children implies a distressing lack of faith in their good sense. The chance that a child brought up to abhor stereotypes could be perverted by one sexist portrayal in a book must be slight.

Furthermore, while some children may have short attention spans or a predisposition to nightmares after hearing scary stories, not all do. Our assumption that they will is a case of supposing that extreme cases represent typical examples, with the unfortunate effect of keeping worthwhile and pleasurable books out of the hands of many children who would not be harmed by them. The reaction of a young moviegoer to the psychiatrist's fears about the effect of *Batman* on children reveals the folly of such generalizations: " 'Old people are real stupid,' said 8-year-old Daniel LaJeunesse. 'Everybody knows Batman is a comic' " (Toronto *Globe and Mail,* July 14, 1989). We can only hope that Daniel's generalization about all old people is no more valid than is the psychiatrist's about all children.

Unlike Daniel's, furthermore, the psychiatrist's generalization has the potential to become a self-fulfilling prophecy. The more we believe that children are limited in various ways, the more we deprive them of experiences that might make them less limited. If we believe that children have short attention spans, we won't expose them to long books; if we believe they cannot understand complicated language, we will give them only books with limited vocabularies; if we believe they are susceptible, we will keep them away from interesting books that may contain potentially dangerous ideas or attitudes; and if we believe they like only certain kinds of books, we will not give them access to other kinds. Deprived of the experience of anything more than the little we believe them capable of, children often do learn to be inflexible, intolerant of the complex and the unconventional.

Was Piaget Right?

We base our faith in the limitations of children on stage theories of development like those of Erikson, Kohlberg, and above all, Piaget. But some assumptions about children's learning that claim to be based on Piaget do not necessarily represent Piaget accurately. Moreover, serious criticisms of Piaget's work have been raised.

Piaget's description of the mechanisms through which learning occurs suggests a serious misunderstanding on the part of those who believe stage theory means that children cannot deal with unfamiliar ideas or experiences. In fact, Piaget makes it clear that children *need* such ideas and experiences in order to move to a new stage. He speaks of *assimilation,* the process by which we integrate new information into our previously established systems of meaning, and of *accommodation,* the reverse process by which we adapt our systems of meaning-making in the light of new information. Both processes require new information in order to take place.

Furthermore, Piaget himself did not claim that the relationships between developmental stages and the chronological ages of children are as rigid as many of his followers suggest. Given the degree to which his theory of learning depends upon experience, he knew that children reach different stages in their development at different ages from each other and spend differing amounts of time in each stage.

On the other hand, Piaget himself did assert that it is impossible for children to learn concepts that he defined as being above their current stage of development. He did believe that they could only teach themselves, and that teaching by giving instruction merely communicated verbal pseudo-ideas that lacked meaning for children. These and many other aspects of his work have been seriously questioned in the past few decades. Indeed, as Charles Brainerd says, "Until the mid-1970s, Piaget's ideas dominated the landscape the way Freudian thinking once ruled abnormal psychology. Since then, however, the picture has changed dramatically. Empirical and conceptual objections to the theory have become so numerous that it can no longer be regarded as a positive force in mainstream cognitive-developmental research, though its influence remains profound in cognate fields such as education and sociology" (*Recent Advances* vii). Because of the continuing faith in Piagetian ideas that underlies so many of our attitudes to children's literature, we should consider these objections carefully.

The most basic objections to Piaget stem from reconsideration of the experiments on which he based his conclusions. Slightly different versions of the experiments have shown that children can accomplish theoretically impossible kinds of thinking at surprisingly early stages. What was thought to be theoretically impossible has proven to be possible in the right circumstances—when we make the task relevant, and couch it in language or in circumstances that children can understand.

Not only can children do tasks theoretically beyond their capability, but those not yet at a particular stage can be *taught* tasks that Piaget associated with that stage. According to Brainerd, "Children who uniformly fail pretests for Piagetian concepts have not proved to be untrainable—far from it" ("Learning Research" 98). Training is both possible and desirable; experiments show that those with training seem to learn more than those left to teach themselves through self-discovery.

Research also challenges the assumption that development is a series of periodic changes from one distinct state to another. In fact, the perception of separate stages may simply result from the preconceptions that developmental psychologists bring to their experiments. Recent studies suggest that learning occurs gradually in a continuous series of small steps, as long as there are new experiences for children (and adults) to learn from. While distinct stages do seem to exist, studies suggest they may be culturally imposed, and relate to matters such as typical school entrance ages and our expectations of the sorts of experiences children can process. "Thus, what appears to be maturationally 'normal' in cognition and performance reflects, upon closer examination, a culturally imposed system of 'prods and brakes' " (Zimmerman 14).

In addition to questioning the validity of Piaget's experiments, contemporary psychologists question the logic and value of the theoretical conclusions Piaget derived from them. For instance, one of Piaget's justifications for his theory that children are egocentric was an experiment requiring them to imagine how a display might look from another point of view. In assuming that the inability to imagine something from a different physical point of view indicated an emotional inability to empathize, he made an illogical connection between the physical and the emotional. Not surprisingly, experiments asking children questions about how others might feel establish that they can understand and empathize with the point of view of others as early as one-and-a-half years of age (Borke 35, 38). This would suggest that we underestimate children when we assume, as Purves and Monson do, that their egocentricity will prevent them from enjoying books about people different from themselves.

Piaget often seriously underestimated children in this way. Many commentators have suggested he did so because he always assumed that their actual performance accurately represented the extent of their potential. According to Susan Sugarman, "Piaget invariably claims that when children *are not* doing something . . . they *cannot* do it" (112). This confusion of performance with potential is common in discussions of children's books based on Piagetian ideas. We assume that because children don't like a certain kind of book they cannot like it until they reach a new stage, or, as Arthur Applebee suggests in his analysis of how children discuss stories, that because the descriptions of six-year-olds "seem to take the simplest possible form" (105), it is impossible for them to achieve more complex responses: they are preoperational, and so their descriptions will inevitably and immutably display characteristics like egocentricity—at least until they reach the next stage. Opinions like this neglect the fact Robert Protherough points out: "Less fluent children may seem to react inadequately, not because of a limited response but because of inability to express it" (37).

Some of the most powerful criticisms of Piaget go far beyond attacks on the design of his experiments or the logic of his conclusions. They condemn the basic assumptions upon which his theory is based—in particular, his conviction that someone like himself represents the height of human accomplishment, and that moral views and intellectual operations like his own are the final result of an evolutionary process.

As Carol Gilligan suggests, this bias "leads Piaget to equate male development with child development" (10). Gilligan suggests that the assumption that male behavior is in fact the norm leads Piagetian psychologists, themselves mostly male, to see as a deviation from the norm behavior that is in our society characteristically female. In the process, furthermore, they usually assume that the characteristically female behavior is inferior to the characteristically male behavior, rather than merely different from it.

Women are not the only human beings misrepresented in Piaget's theories. Piaget's cultural bias led him to assume that the ability to handle certain concepts represents intellectual accomplishment. But, as Brainerd reports, "There is now reason to believe that familiar concrete-operational concepts such as conservation are not culturally universal. It seems that mother nature has been shamefully neglecting the spontaneous development of primitive peoples" ("Learning Research" 83). Mother Nature also seems to have been shamefully neglecting the moral development of people of other cultures; the theories of moral development postulated by Piaget and followers like Kohlberg define stages that advance to the ultimate goal of belief in something like the Christian golden rule of acting toward others as you would have them act toward you. Many non-Christian cultures do not accept adherence to that sort of rule as the most sophisticated form of moral behavior.

Piaget's bias is intellectual as well as cultural; he assumes that the ability to think scientifically represents the pinnacle of mental achievement. "Looking at Piaget's protocols that report actual experiments," says Jean-Claude Brief, "one is struck by his selection of logical factors at the expense of those that are affective, sensorial, sociocultural, and linguistic. As a result, many possible interpretations are eliminated from the start" (185).

This scientific bias leads Piaget to make the assumption that thought develops in an evolutionary process in which what comes later is considered to be superior to what comes earlier. As a result, he sees the stages through which childhood thinking passes as imperfect approximations of an ideal adult standard of mental functioning, and assumes that the worlds children invent at earlier stages of development are false and deficient versions of an objective truth only available to mature adults. The danger in this sort of thinking is obvious. As Brief says, "The child is in charge of a particular reality which is appropriate to his body and to his thinking. Hence, to privilege the adult's reality under the pretext that it represents the true world does seem presumptuous . . . " (31). The philosopher Gareth Matthews, who calls Piaget's descriptions of children's thinking "dismissive, even contemptuous" (*Philosophy* 31), suggests what such dismissiveness may prevent us from understanding as he wonders why adults fail to recognize the degree to which children are capable of philosophical reflection: "Perhaps it is because so much emphasis has been placed on the development of children's abilities, especially their cognitive abilities, that we automatically assume their thinking is primitive and in need of development toward an adult norm. What we take to be primitive, however, may actually be more openly reflective than the adult norm we set as the goal of education" (*Dialogues* 53). It may also be more open to the pleasure of literary response and analysis, which require a focus on specifics rather than abstractions, and on individual differences rather than on generalized observations—in other words, the sort of thinking we usually define as childlike.

The fact that we set the so-called adult norm as the goal of education merely confirms the degree to which Piagetian assumptions control our educational ideas. As Joseph T. Lawton and Frank H. Hooper say, "Piaget's views have been rather glibly accepted as demonstrating prima facie validity and relevance for educational application" (170). Fortunately, anyone who refuses to accept these views so glibly quickly discovers that children have more potential than Piagetian theories of development might seem to suggest. For instance, Matthews's descriptions of his discussions of philosophy with children reveal that the sort of imaginative suppositions that Piaget dismisses as primitive actually represent accurate versions of philosophical positions taken by sophisticated adults. Robert Coles, reporting his experiences with children involved in traumatic situations of poverty and racial strife, points out the degree to which the intensity and maturity of their moral attitudes "contrasts, alas, with the categorical assurances of some theorists who have moral development all figured out, as if life were a matter of neatly arranged academic hurdles, with grades given along the way" (28).

EXPLORATION: It might be argued that teachers don't always have the time or the knowledge to pay detailed attention to the individual tastes and abilities of individual children, and that Piagetian and other developmental stage theories provide useful guidelines in book selection and other dealings with children. Is that a relevant consideration, or a dangerous one?

Freed from such categorical assurances, I believe, we can worry less about what children cannot do at a certain age and, instead, consider what they might be taught to do. We can worry less about what literature children should not read and start thinking about what literature they might be taught to enjoy.

Is Literature Mainly Educational?

As we seek to stimulate children's interest in literature, we must never forget why we read literature ourselves and what we would like children to know about it. I believe and would like children to know that experiencing literature, and thinking and talking about the experience of it, are pleasures requiring no justification other than the fact that they exist. For that reason, I believe the assumption that childhood is a time in which all things must be educational is dangerous. It suggests that children read only in order to learn, that their books provide entertainment only as a way of getting them to pay attention to facts or values. And if we provide children with books that entertain *only* in order to teach, we will deprive them of much of the real pleasure of literature. Furthermore, if we try to persuade children that the pleasure in literature is just the spoonful of sugar that lets the medicine of education go down, they may well end up thinking that it is, basically, just medicine—and no fun at all.

ARE CHILDREN THE OPPOSITE OF ADULTS?

The various generalizations we have considered all confirm the basic idea that children are not only different from adults but opposite to them. As Bronwyn Davies says, "Children are defined as *other* to adults in much the same way that women are other to men" (4).

The literary theorist Jacques Derrida points out the possible significance of this when he says, "Man *calls himself* man only by drawing limits excluding his other . . . : the purity of nature, of animality, primitivism, childhood, madness, divinity" (244). In other words, our idea that we are different from something which came before us and which we have evolved away from is what allows us to understand who we are; we are that which is not natural, not bestial, not mad, not divine—and most important, not childish.

At first glance, all these other qualities are different from humanity in being superior to it: nature is more natural, divinity more spiritual. Derrida suggests that this privileging of the prior and more primitive is a dangerous act of self-abuse on the part of those who see themselves as coming after and, thus, degenerated from, a state of innocence. We often view childhood as this sort of self-abusing "other." Our clichés about the ways in which children are closer to nature or to God, about how their ignorance is really a saving innocence, disguise a profound distrust of the realities of life as we must view it as adults—and, perhaps more significant, a nostalgia for that which in fact never was.

A surprising proportion of adult commentaries on children's literature view it in terms of this kind of celebration of child-like otherness, and focus on the appeal of "childlike" qualities like joy and wonder. Jacqueline Rose suggests that children's literature as a whole, just by existing, also represents this sort of nostalgia. She believes that the actual nature of childhood—particularly childhood sexuality—frightens adults. Because we have come to accept one form of thinking and being as normal, we see all others as chaotic and threatening, particularly those of a childhood we once shared and believe ourselves to have grown beyond. We protect ourselves from knowledge of this chaos by constructing images of childhood that leave out everything threatening; and we present such images to children in their literature in order to persuade them that their lives actually are as we want to imagine them to be. "If children's fiction builds an image of the child inside the book, it does so in order to secure the child who is outside the book, the one who does not come so easily within its grasp" (2).

In fact, says Rose, children's literature represents a massive effort by adults to *colonize* children: to make them believe that they ideally ought to be the way adults would like them to be, and to make them feel guilty about or downplay the significance of all the aspects of their selves that inevitably don't fit the adult models.

EXPLORATION: Do you think Rose's view is correct? Consider (or have children consider) the degree to which children's literature works to encourage children to believe in an untrue representation of childhood, by exploring the implications of a group of children's texts.

To some degree the colonization of children is unavoidable. As Raymond Williams says, "Any process of socialization of course includes things that all human beings have to learn, but any specific process ties this necessary learning to a selected range of meanings, values, and practices. . . . Education transmits necessary knowledge and skills, but always by a particular selection from the whole available range, and with intrinsic attitudes, both to learning and social relations, which are in practice virtually inextricable" (117–18). Children's literature partakes in this sort of selective education simply because authors always take for granted, and thus work to persuade young readers, that one particular view of childhood represents normality.

But while misrepresentation is inevitable, I believe there is particular danger in any view of childhood that insists on its otherness. If children as a group are different from adults, I'm convinced it is merely because they are less experienced. I therefore conclude that our obligation is not to deprive children of knowledge because we believe that their ignorance represents a wonderful otherness. Our obligation is, instead, to allow them to know as much as possible about the world they share with us, to enrich their experience in ways that will allow them to develop deeper consciousness of who they are. And because literature and techniques of responding to it are not only a part of that world but windows opening onto the rest of it, I believe that children particularly need and can be taught to share our own strategies for making sense of literature.

WORKS CITED

Applebee, Arthur N. *The Child's Concept of Story: Age Two to Seventeen.* Chicago: U of Chicago P, 1978.

Borke, Helen. "Piaget's View of Social Interaction and the Theoretical Construct of Empathy." Siegel and Brainerd 29–42.

Brainerd, Charles J. "Learning Research and Piagetian Theory." Siegel and Brainerd 69–109.

———. "Preface." Brainerd, *Recent Advances.*

———, ed. *Recent Advances in Cognitive Developmental Research.* New York: Springer-Verlag, 1983.

Brief, Jean-Claude. *Beyond Piaget: A Philosophical Psychology.* New York: Teachers College, 1983.

Coles, Robert. *The Moral Life of Children.* Boston: Houghton Mifflin, 1986.
Davies, Bronwyn. *Frogs and Snails and Feminist Tales: Preschool Children and Gender.* Sydney: Allen and Unwin, 1989.
Derrida, Jacques. *Of Grammatology.* Ed. Gayatri Chakravorty Spivak. Baltimore: Johns Hopkins UP, 1976.
Gilligan, Carol. *In a Different Voice: Psychological Theories and Women's Development.* Cambridge: Harvard UP, 1982.
Huck, Charlotte S. *Children's Literature in the Elementary School.* 3rd ed., updated. New York: Holt, Rinehart and Winston, 1979.
Hunt, David. *Parents and Children in History: The Psychology of Family Life in Early Modern France.* New York: Basic, 1970.
Lawton, Joseph T., and Frank H. Hooper. "Piagetian Theory and Early Childhood Education: A Critical Analysis." Siegel and Brainerd 169–199.
Matthews, Gareth. *Dialogues with Children.* Cambridge: Harvard UP, 1984.
———. *Philosophy and the Young Child.* Cambridge: Harvard UP, 1980.
Protherough, Robert. *Developing Response to Fiction.* Milton Keynes, England: Open UP, 1983.
Purves, Alan C., and Dianne L. Monson. *Experiencing Children's Literature.* Glenview: Scott, Foresman, 1984.
Rose, Jacqueline. *The Case of Peter Pan: or The Impossibility of Children's Fiction.* London: Macmillan, 1984.
Rudman, Masha Kabakow. *Children's Literature: An Issues Approach.* Lexington: Heath, 1976.
Siegel, Linda S. "The Relationship of Language and Thought in the Preoperational Child: A Reconsideration of Nonverbal Alternatives to Piagetian Tasks." Siegel and Brainerd 43–67.
Siegel, Linda S., and Charles J. Brainerd, eds. *Alternatives to Piaget: Critical Essays on the Theory.* New York: Academic, 1978.
Sugarman, Susan. *Piaget's Construction of the Child's Reality.* Cambridge: Cambridge UP, 1987.
Tucker, Nicholas. *The Child and the Book: A Psychological and Literary Exploration.* Cambridge: Cambridge UP, 1981.
Weiss, Nancy Pottishman. "Mother, the Invention of Necessity: Dr. Benjamin Spock's *Baby and Child Care.*" *Growing Up in America: Children in Historical Perspective.* Eds. N. Ray Hiner and Joseph M. Hawes. Urbana: U of Illinois P, 1985. 283–303.
Williams, Raymond. *Marxism and Literature.* Oxford: Oxford UP, 1977.
Zimmerman, Barry J. "Social Learning Theory: A Contextualist Account of Cognitive Functioning." Brainerd, *Recent Advances* 1–50.

CHAPTER 5

Children's Literature in the Context of Popular Culture

THE CULTURE OF CHILDHOOD

The context in which children look at picture books and read novels includes not only their dealings with parents, teachers, and other adults who might make some of the assumptions outlined in Chapter 4; it also includes their encounters with video games, Barbie dolls, and Saturday morning cartoons. Toys, TV shows, and movies intended for children are the most immediate background of many children's response to literature—the models of imaginative play and storytelling they are most likely to be familiar with. Because these products of popular culture have a powerful influence on children's expectations and attitudes—not only about literature but about life in general—they deserve particular attention. This chapter considers implications of the context that popular culture creates for children's understanding and enjoyment of literature.

EXPLORATION: The cultural theorists whose ideas form the basis of this chapter tend to work from positions that are often highly critical of values and assumptions that many North Americans take for granted. Does this divergence from the norm give these theorists the advantage of objectivity, or does it make them too biased to be considered seriously?

Ideology and Hegemony

Like all productions of the human mind, toys and TV shows inevitably express the values and assumptions of their creators. As a result, they provide children with messages about human behavior—messages that at least some adults consciously or unconsciously believe to be appropriate for children. For instance, many of the toys available for young children confirm (and therefore teach) traditional ways of distinguishing gender: the colors of dolls' clothes for girls tend to be delicate pastel pinks and mauves, those for boys strident reds and blacks.

Values assumed and expressed in this way are called *ideologies,* and as Raymond Williams says, our ideologies are "in effect a saturation of the whole process of living—not only of political and economic activity, nor only of manifest social activity, but of the whole substance of lived identity and relationships" (*Marxism* 110). While we may realize that the values of others are merely matters of opinion, we tend to take it for granted that our own ideology is nothing more than an accurate description of reality. As a result, the ideology dominant in our culture—the *hegemony*—"constitutes a sense of reality . . . beyond which it is very difficult for most members of the society to move, in most areas of their lives" (110).

Toys and TV shows are as much a part of this hegemony as are social institutions and political practices. They too support and sustain our culture's most powerful assumptions, perhaps even to the extent that, as Simon Frith says, "Popular culture produces 'the people,' not vice versa" (56).

EXPLORATION: Frith, in fact, claims that we are so saturated with the values of the hegemony that "the public/private distinction common in cultural sociology is hard to maintain. People do not have 'private' knowledge, particularly not private emotional knowledge, knowledge independent of public cultural meanings and experiences" (56–57). Do you believe this assertion to be true? Explore your own values, and decide whether any of them represent something different from the values current in your culture's hegemony.

The Ideal as Ordinary

Cultural theorists believe that the products of a hegemony tend to express the assumptions of the dominant group within it in a way that confuses the ideal with the ordinary. For instance, toys like Barbie represent a white middle-class ideal of feminine beauty as if it were the usual appearance of ordinary teenage girls, and TV situation comedies like *The Cosby Show* present an upper-middle-class life-style of huge houses and constant changes of clothing as if it were the norm. While there is nothing inherently wrong with the way Barbie looks or the kind of house the Huxtable family occupies, our unconsidered acceptance of these as a norm encourages our complacency about the way things are. We tend to ignore our knowledge of less ideal ways of looking and living. It also encourages our anxiety about the ways in which we ourselves differ from these supposed norms, and our desire to make ourselves more like them, most often by purchasing the right equipment, clothing, or furniture. It is clearly in the interest of those whom the current state of affairs benefits that we see these limited depictions as the norm.

Yet despite the fact that they are not often represented in toys or on TV, we all really do know that there are other images of femininity than the one implied by Barbie, other ways of being human than the ones presented on television situation comedies. Once we lose faith in the absolute truthfulness of the versions of reality these objects and activities express, we can develop more inclusive versions. We can free ourselves from the insecurity caused by our perception that we differ from supposed norms and from the complacency and intolerance that often accompany a total commitment to a one-sided view. The ability to do so is particularly significant for children, whose limited experience tends to make them prone to an unconsidered acceptance of the propaganda of a hegemony.

The Hidden Curriculum

Furthermore, knowing the degree to which toys and popular TV programs transmit messages supporting the hegemony, we can see how they provide children with ideas about themselves and the world they live in. Such an awareness has broad educational implications. The values of the hegemony are the *hidden curriculum* in all aspects of experience. Parents and teachers are likely to be most effective in their dealings with children when they remember that what happens in school or in a child's relationship with parents can only reinforce (or perhaps sometimes attempt to contradict) what is already happening in a far more powerful way in the rest of the child's life. In particular, those interested in helping children develop a deeper experience of stories and poems should consider how the messages conveyed by popular toys and entertainment might influence the ways in which children respond to literature.

TOYS AND GAMES: THEIR EFFECT ON CHILDREN'S ENJOYMENT OF LITERATURE

EXPLORATION: Because of the constant changes in the toy industry, the examples discussed in the section that follows may have gone out of fashion by the time you read this book. Visit a toy store, and consider the values and assumptions implied by the toys you see there.

In the film *E.T.*, the extraterrestrial alien can hide from adults while staying in full view in a child's closet simply because the closet is already filled with various dolls and stuffed toys that look no less strange than E.T. does. When alien creatures like Transformers and Teenage Mutant Ninja Turtles populate toy stores, they permeate the imaginations of contemporary children and affect their response to literature. Those who worried, when Maurice Sendak's *Where the Wild Things Are* first came out, that the book might give young children nightmares were wise to be concerned, for in the context of the toys, games, and other books of the time, these creatures would have seemed unsettlingly strange. But many of today's young readers, their closets and their heads full of Inhumanoids, Dino-riders, and even the by-now-commonplace Grovers and Cookie Monsters, find Sendak's Wild Things reassuringly familiar.

The closet in *E.T.* isn't unusual; toys fill the lives of North American children. Wendy Saul reports that in 1980, "$144 million was spent on infant toys and $412 million on 'pre-school' items. These figures do *not* include another $113 million on pre-school playsets, $333 million on stuffed animals, $46 million on 'non-pedal-driven riding vehicles,' $88 million on musical toys and $47 million on stuffed dolls" (2).

TV advertising generates these sales by persuading children that their lives will be incomplete without a certain toy. The result is that their lives *are* incomplete without it: they must deal with the stress of friends taunting them for not having what everyone else has. Manufacturers encourage this focus on ownership by producing toys in collectible sets, so that much of the pleasure of My Little Ponies or Transformers is in the sheer possession of them, in the satisfaction of completing the set. Since the main significance of these toys is the mere ownership of them, it is not surprising that they often end up in closets and are not much played with. Manufacturers encourage this built-in boredom by dropping advertisements for one set of toys just about when many children will have completed their sets, and focusing their attention on a new one.

These commercials, and cartoon tie-in shows, teach children how each of these sets implies its own fantasy world—its own geography and social structure. And each of these worlds can be seen to be supporting the central values of our culture's hegemony in a specific way. For instance, Barbie and Ken dolls immerse children in our society's understanding of gender distinctions and relationships between men and women. In her appearance and in her behavior, as we noted earlier, Barbie represents the supposedly ideal North American woman: young and theoretically innocent but highly conscious of her sexiness. She is less interested in boys than in the business of attracting boys, and so she is obsessed with clothing and is highly responsive to new fashions. As a post-puberty teenager with a boyfriend, Barbie allows young girls to try out in their fantasy play the life-style that their society encourages them to hope for in their future.

While the fantasies implied by other toys are less directly expressive of our culture, they have significant connections with it. Transformers, each of which can be converted from a carlike machine to a humanlike one, reinforce the pleasures of flexibility and imply the value of being able to adapt to new circumstances. At first that adaptability seems to represent a defiance of convention that ought to undermine the dominance of the established hegemony. But a glance at the advice about jobs and relationships given in any popular magazine shows how often our culture feels the need to reinforce the idea that change is growth, so that the ability to "transform" whenever one feels like it and a commitment to transience in values and relationships is a sign of maturity. A firmly embedded faith in the positive value of change reinforces the consumption of fads and fashions in a way that supports the conservatism and inflexibility of the hegemony rather than leads to real changes in it.

It is clear, then, that these toys can have a profound effect on the way children respond to literature. Barbie supports interests and values that prepare young girls to enjoy reading teen romances and to consider much other children's literature childish or beside the point. The fascination with change implied by Barbie's ever-renewing wardrobe and the bodies of Transformers prepares children to enjoy the randomized plots of Choose-Your-Own Adventures and to accept the growth-oriented morality of many contemporary junior novels.

EXPLORATION: Test the possible truth of that conclusion by considering (or by having children consider) the implications of one particular toy or set of toys. Are there messages suggested by its appearance and by the fantasy evoked by the copy on its packaging? If so, might those messages relate to or influence children's reading of literature? How?

Video Games as Narrative

A powerful example of the influence of toys on literature is the way in which the video games that fascinate so many children use narrative conventions. The stories implied by many of these games have clear relationships with traditional folktales: a hero, in this case the player, embarks on a quest and struggles with villains for a prize. But unlike other narratives, what happens in these games has no relation to moral choices. Because the games are often programmed to engender actions randomly, and because victory or defeat depends purely upon manual dexterity, the games indiscriminately reward or punish both moral and immoral behavior. As a result, individual events don't build into a consistent or meaningful plot. Without a cohesive pattern, there is no suspense, and so the ending isn't climactic: it interrupts what has become the main pleasure, the continuing process of the game itself. According to Gillian Skirrow, "The fascination of video games is not related to resolution; rather it is to be looked for in the opportunities provided for repetition of a set of actions, performed with an almost neurotic compulsion" (129). While these games relate to traditional stories, then, children who play them will develop knowledge of a set of narrative conventions that might well hinder their understanding and appreciation of more conventional stories.

TV'S ROLE IN CHILDREN'S RESPONSE TO BOOKS

Many people interested in literature are snobs about TV and movies. We criticize film and TV versions of books for not being exactly like the originals. And while we often enjoy watching TV and movies, we feel guilty about doing so. We tend to believe that all books are somehow better than all TV, and would rather have children read mindless Choose-Your-Own-Adventures than watch serious TV. We assume that TV somehow limits children's imaginations or makes them lethargic, while books awaken them, and we conduct experiments to prove our assumption.

For instance, Jerome Singer and Dorothy Singer claim that studies they have conducted show that "television may produce difficulty for children in developing the more active aspects of memory, in developing social interchange with parents—

which also enhances language use—and in developing an attitude of playfulness and imaginativeness'' (130). These conclusions depend on a number of often unexplored assumptions that many people interested in literature share.

Because TV provides viewers with visual images, Singer and Singer believe, viewers do not need to work as hard to understand as readers do. While there may be some truth in this, I'll show in Chapter 10 that researchers have discovered that visual images require as much use of interpretive strategies as verbal ones do. The idea that TV requires less work leads Singer and Singer to propose that TV limits imagination, but Vivian Paley's vivid descriptions of the imaginative ways in which kindergarten children make use of movies and TV in their play reveals their richness as a basis for creative variation. In *Boys and Girls: Superheroes in the Doll Corner,* Paley shows how ''Star Wars, despite its commercial hokum, comes close to being a perfect vehicle for small boys' play'' (24).

Furthermore, while the experience of TV inevitably transforms the nature of social interchanges, it hardly prevents them, as Singer and Singer suggest. Many commentators point to the unifying effect of TV as a medium experienced in the context of family or communal life—a medium people can view together and discuss, whereas reading is an individual activity. Roger Silverstone claims that TV is "an oral rather than a literate medium . . . generative of a folk culture" (35)—that it serves the same unifying function for our world as myth did for earlier societies. John Fiske and John Hartley say that "television functions as a social ritual, overriding individual distinctions in which our culture engages, in order to communicate with its collective self" (85). If, as I speculated in my earlier consideration of history (Chapter 3), the development of literacy led to the isolation of individuals, TV may bring them back together into a community—encourage rather than prevent social interchange.

Finally, Singer and Singer complain that TV does not encourage the development of memory. Their point is not surprising, for memory isn't especially necessary for enjoying TV—and not particularly important in a world of recordings and calculators and computers. But the fact that memory has not been developed doesn't mean that it can't be, or that children confronted with a need for facility in retention would not quickly acquire it.

TV does make those who spend a good deal of time watching it different from their predecessors. But the difference may not be a deficiency. The moral and social attitudes, even the art and literature, produced by those who grow up with TV are different from those of earlier generations, but not necessarily inferior.

TV and Literary Pleasure

While the absorption of children in TV does complicate the process of their responding to literature, it might also actively help them develop literary enjoyment. Children who watch a lot of TV may respond more perceptively to the stories in books simply because they already have familiarity with stories. The average young TV viewer experiences far more stories, in the form of cartoons and adventures and situation comedies, than children in any previous generation even had access to. Furthermore, the main feature of these TV and movie stories is their adherence to formula. Saturday morning cartoons often involve lovable small creatures who fight with and defeat less lovable larger creatures. Situation comedies often involve inflexible characters who learn each week to be less rigid and then start out next week's program just as stubborn as they always were.

EXPLORATION: Test the adherence of TV programming to formula by watching (or having children watch) a number of shows of the same type: superhero cartoons, police adventures, or situation comedies. Is a formula apparent? If so, what is it, and how might this particular story pattern relate to children's stories in written form?

By telling similar stories again and again, TV equips children with a repertoire of basic *story patterns* that allows them to recognize and make sense of the new stories they experience not just on TV but also in books, for the story patterns of popular movies and TV shows are also those of many children's books. Consider how much the following stories have in common:

- The ordinary clothing of a mild-mannered reporter hides a fancy costume. When the costume is exposed, he uses his secret powers to defeat powerful opponents.
- The wretched clothing of a powerless young girl hides her great beauty. Once her beauty is exposed through the secret powers of a magical assistant, she triumphs over powerful opponents.
- A casually dressed, mild-mannered young man has the ability to put ordinary objects to ingenious use. He uses that almost magical ability to triumph over powerful opponents.
- The ordinary clothing of a boy hides a rabbit's fur. When the clothes come off, he is able to escape a powerful enemy.
- A small, apparently powerless child dons a fancy costume and uses his secret power of staring to defeat powerful opponents.
- A small, apparently insignificant spider uses her secret power of web spinning to defeat powerful opponents.
- An apparently plain young girl with red hair uses the secret power of her charm to win over powerful opponents.

These are, in order, the basic plots of the comic books and Saturday morning cartoons about Superman, the fairy tale "Cinderella," the action series *McGyver,* the picture books *The Tale of Peter Rabbit* and *Where the Wild Things Are,* the novel *Charlotte's Web,* and the novel *Anne of Green Gables.* Whether TV cartoons or treasured classics, these stories all follow one basic pattern, and it is the experience of many different versions of that pattern that allows children to develop a sense of the pattern itself. We will consider in the next chapter how essential this sort of consciousness of patterns is to our ability to make any sense of literature at all.

Jon Stott suggests that the similarity in the narrative patterns of comic books and serious literature can have educational value: "Not that the teacher should teach comic books, but, knowing students' familiarity with the comics, he can show how certain elements reappear in great literature, how they are used to give symbolic significance to that literature, and how, unlike the comic books, the great works help to provide pattern and meaning to human lives" (11). It might well be argued that comic books—and TV shows and movies—do provide pattern and meaning, and that teachers *should* teach them, in order to bring children to a consciousness of the repetitive nature of formulas that will allow them a richer perception and enjoyment of less formulaic texts.

EXPLORATION: Nevertheless, many people believe that comic books and TV cartoons are vulgar and simplistic, and that there is no point in encouraging children's indulgence in them. Look at (or have children look at) some currently available comic books or cartoons. Are they good or bad for readers and viewers? Why? Should they be part of what children study in literature? Why or why not?

TV AS DISTINCT FROM LIFE AND LITERATURE

Despite the repetitiveness of its narrative content, storytelling on TV is different from storytelling in books. In examining TV's particular approach to storytelling, we will consider, first, its relationship to myth, and second, how the process of watching TV differs from the process of reading.

TV as Bard

Because it would lose its audience if it did not express mainstream tastes and interests, TV must confirm a society's hegemony. For that reason, Fiske and Hartley see the function of TV as "bardic." Like the bards who recited stories of epic heroes in the oral culture of the past, TV works to "*articulate* the main lines of the established cultural consensus about the nature of reality" (88) in a way that causes viewers to feel they are part of that consensus. It does so by constantly showing us images that represent our culture's norms or ideals of appearance and behavior—for instance, what female beauty is, or what acceptable feminine behavior is—as if they were the whole and only truth, and consequently the only truth about ourselves.

Fiske and Hartley also believe that TV works to explain away the threatening quality of individuals and events apparently alien to the culture's central values, by a process they call *claw back:* "for example, nature programmes will often stress the 'like-us-ness' of the animals filmed, finding in their behaviour metaphoric equivalences with our own culture's way of organizing its affairs" (87). Similarly, many TV shows work to prove that people with handicaps or of different races are really "just like us" despite their apparent differences. This apparently positive idea may cause us to lose consciousness of and tolerance for the validity of the "other-ness" of these other ways of being human.

EXPLORATION: Can you find evidence of the articulation of "cultural consensus" or of "claw back" in TV programming for children? Watch (or have children watch) cartoons or programs like Sesame Street *and think about the ways in which they might be confirming a specific view of reality and/or dissipating the threat of apparently alien ideas or behavior.*

Because its central focus is the expression of hegemonic values, TV storytelling tends to be symbolic rather than natural—to provide something more like myths than like realistic fiction. For instance, Fiske and Hartley claim that the significance of violence in television fiction is that "it externalizes people's motives and status, makes visible their unstated relationships" (34). In other words, the violent encounters of specific individuals on TV actually represent something less specific. TV "personalizes impersonal social conflicts between, for example, dominant and subordinate groups, law and anarchy, youth and age. It is never a mere imitation of real behavior" (34–35).

In a survey of prime-time TV shows in the late 1970s, Ben Stein discovered that almost all the murderers were upper-middle-class whites, and that educated people were always criminals: "On television . . . only villains have a library" (127). Such patterns seriously distort reality, for statistics reveal that, for obvious economic reasons, much real violence is committed by uneducated members of deprived minority groups. Nevertheless, the distortions of TV do accurately express a mythic version of the world that our society finds preferable to reality, a mythic world in which the powerful are always corrupt and always vulnerable and the weak are always pure and always able to triumph. By repeating these inaccurate representations of violence and its perpetrators, TV works to deflect our consciousness of the part played by racial and economic inequality in societal conflict and the difficulty individuals have in managing to change the way things are.

While many observers agree that TV performs these culture-sustaining functions, they take different attitudes toward it. Silverstone is positive. Saying that "television, above all, is a machine for the reduction of the ambiguous and uncertain" (180), he concludes that "television translates history, political and social change, into manageable terms" (182). But others worry about the deception that accompanies that manageability. Laura Kipnis is concerned that what we see on TV "disguises what it really is—relationships among people and classes—into an appearance of the objective and the natural. . . . it subjugates people to its monopoly of appearance, and proclaims: 'That which appears is good, that which is good appears' " (20–21).

EXPLORATION: Which of these opposing views, Silverstone's or Kipnis's, do you share? Why?

Watching TV as a Context for Reading

Whether we consider TV's influence to be positive or negative, there is little doubt that TV plays a large part in our ideas about our world and ourselves. When children who watch TV approach literary texts they are already equipped with a system of values, a set of attitudes toward rich and poor, young and old, male and female. They are also equipped with the unconscious knowledge that TV relates to life by providing myths that make it comprehensible. Such an understanding of the purpose of stories will influence how they understand written fiction.

But children's viewing of TV has an even more immediate impact, for TV communicates differently from the way books do. Unlike books, TV simultaneously uses a variety of media, and those accustomed to receiving information from music and pictures as well as from words might have problems in decoding books.

Furthermore, books end. TV continues, each program being succeeded by another in an endless flow of pictures, words, stories—a flow that is made to seem even more amorphous because the stories themselves are interrupted and fragmented. Most programs are series in which any single episode is merely part of an ongoing longer story, a story filled with events but with a decidedly shapeless plot. While individual programs often have recognizable narrative plots, they are constantly interrupted with commercials. In contemporary TV style, furthermore, few shots or sequences last for long, and within one thirty-second commercial we may see more than twenty images, moving quickly from a face to a glass to a beach scene and back to a face again. In their constant movement from one short sequence to another, distinctly different one, *Sesame Street* and many Saturday morning shows duplicate this pattern.

EXPLORATION: Test out the prevalence of this pattern by recording (or having children record) the shots and sequences of a particular television program. How might the awareness of these patterns affect your response to the program?

Describing his difficulties with interpreting one specific experience of this sort of flow, in which one film was interspersed with commercials and promotions for other films, Raymond Williams says, "I can still not be sure what I took from that whole flow. I believe I registered some incidents as happening in the wrong film, and some characters in the commercials as involved in the film episodes, in what came to seem—for all the occasional disparities—a single irresponsible flow of images and feelings" (*Television* 92). Such a reaction is clearly different from the connected meanings we can derive from our experiences of individual written stories.

One significant result of fragmentation and flow is that TV tends to discourage attentiveness. Given an endless flow of fragmented stories, we have no choice but to pay close attention only to that which specifically interests us. Rick Altman observes that "there is a growing body of data suggesting that intermittent attention is in fact the dominant mode of television" (42). But while intermittent viewing is an acceptable approach to TV, children used to it may well have trouble giving most written fiction the kind of attention it demands. If we want children to enjoy reading fiction, we cannot assume that the strategy of paying the necessary attention to it comes naturally; we might well have the responsibility of teaching it to them. If we do, we will have helped them enjoy two different but equally pleasurable means of telling stories.

EXPLORATION: Devise a means of showing children the difference between the cohesiveness of written stories and the fragmentation and endless flow of TV. Explore the effect of their awareness of these differences on their response to both forms of storytelling.

WRITTEN LITERATURE IN OTHER FORMS

Despite their differences from written texts, TV and movies often offer direct substitutes for specific books. Many children see film versions of fairy tales and classic novels in addition to or even instead of reading the originals.

Educators and literary commentators often accuse versions of children's books in other media of not being authentic—that is, they don't duplicate the plot and the tone of the original texts. But because film and TV use other means to tell stories—visual images, music, action rather than description—the stories they tell are inevitably different from the written versions.

If we wish to evaluate versions of children's literature in other media, we need to take these unavoidable differences into account. Since these works claim to represent the original texts, we have a right to demand some faithfulness, at least to the overall tone or feeling of the original. But as Jill May says in her introduction to a *Children's Literature Association Quarterly* special section on the audiovisual arts, "Film literature is not the same as book literature, and film should not be required to reproduce a book in its entirety" (3). Instead, we should try to judge adaptations in terms of the success with which they use the techniques of the medium they have been translated into. In order to do that, we need to find out about the differing natures of the various media. We need to find out how films or television productions use images and sound as well as words to tell stories in a distinctive way—how camera angles and choices of music contribute to our understanding.

EXPLORATION: Do some research and reading about the specific nature of film communication; some useful books are listed in Chapter 15. Then use the information you gather to explore (or have children explore) the distinctive ways in which a particular film tells a story.

Disney Films: An Appraisal

An important example of the difference between books and movies is the work of Walt Disney studios, which has produced an astonishing number of movie and TV versions of children's stories since its first success, a filmed version of "Snow White" in 1937. These versions are the subject of intense controversy. The children's librarian Frances Clarke Sayers once asserted that in Disney productions, "I find genuine feeling ignored, the imagination of children bludgeoned with mediocrity, and much of it overcast by vulgarity. . . . He does strange things. He sweetens a folk tale. Everything becomes very lovable" (117, 118).

Sayers's reaction suggests two problems: first, that Disney's values are inadequate, and second, that the Disney versions are not authentic. Many commentators have continued the attack on both these grounds. In terms of Disney's values, for instance, Jill May complains that ''He used black voices for monkeys and apes (*The Jungle Book*)'' and ''depicted Italians as aggressive, mindless people who spoke in broken English and were strongly influenced by their emotions (*The Lady and the Tramp* and *Pinocchio*)'' (''Walt Disney's Interpretation,'' 464). In regard to authenticity, Douglas Street says that *Pinocchio* and *Snow White* ''epitomize the 'Disney touch': they were technical masterworks but travesties of their literary sources'' (14).

In a defense of Disney, Lucy Rollin says that comments like those of Sayers ''represent the classic elitist position: a distrust of anything mass marketed for children and a confidence that one's educated personal judgment can decide what is best for others'' (91). Rollin insists that ''Disney was no more and no less than a product of this time [the mid-twentieth century], and if therein lies the weakness of his work, there must be its strengths as well'' (92). In other words, Disney's genius was merely that he was able to capture the values of his culture's hegemony; if we wish to condemn Disney, then we must also condemn the society that admires his films.

EXPLORATION: Is that statement true? Watch a Disney film such as Snow White *or* Cinderella. *Is it vulgar? Do its values merely represent those of its audience, or are they manipulative?*

As for the authenticity of Disney films, once we have accepted the idea that filmed versions inevitably differ from written originals, the real question is not whether the film duplicates the written text, but whether it finds appropriate equivalents for the original in the particular techniques of a different medium. My own opinion is that the Disney version of *Alice in Wonderland* does not constitute a successful adaptation. It overdoes the slapstick and cuteness in a way that dissipates the unsettlingly threatening tone of the original. But I would argue that the Disney version of *Treasure Island* is successful. Much of its plot revolves around a pistol that the pirate Long John Silver gives the boy Jim—a pistol that doesn't appear in the novel. Silver first wins Jim over by giving him the gun; Jim sees it as a symbol of manhood, but his boyish excitement about it reveals his actual lack of maturity. The gun is a visual symbol that communicates some of the central meanings of the original novel—meanings that the book itself expresses in terms of an extended and subtle verbal narrative that the film could not easily or entertainingly duplicate.

Disney's versions of fairy tales are often substantially different from written ones. For instance, much of the Disney *Cinderella* shows the adventures of a pair of mice who try to help Cinderella and eventually do save the day. These mice don't appear in the Perrault version of the story that the film claims to be based on. But as we will see later, in Chapter 11, fairy tales are by definition stories that can be told in different ways. If that is true, then Disney's versions are no more and no less authentic than any other telling.

Furthermore, the fact that Disney's *Cinderella* centers on the antics of these mice and their friends provides action and visual interest—characteristics that are necessary to films but that are not much present in the Perrault version. The film succeeds because its variation from the written text gives it the qualities that audiences find entertaining in most movie or TV cartoons: chases and slapstick jokes involving humanized animals.

Meanwhile, the focus on these small animals allows the film to achieve its own unity. They represent what becomes a central theme in their ability as weak creatures to triumph over strong ones by trying to accomplish what they dream of: trying (although unsuccessfully) to provide Cinderella with a dress that will allow her to go to the ball and later, despite their tiny size, successfully freeing her from a locked room. The film focuses on this theme in a number of other ways as well. At one point or another, it shows each of its major characters dreaming, and the characters we admire all achieve their dreams by believing in them enough to work at them. Furthermore, a song heard often in the film insists that wishes come true if you believe in them hard enough. While Disney's version is different from Perrault's, then, it is both entertaining and internally consistent.

TV, MOVIES, AND THE LITERARY EDUCATION OF CHILDREN

Our explorations of the entertainment for children provided by TV and other media have suggested at least four important considerations in helping children enjoy literature.

1. Since the formulaic nature of much children's TV inculcates basic story patterns, we can use children's knowledge of TV to deepen their appreciation of books. By encouraging them to compare TV cartoons with books based on the same formula, we can help them both to develop a consciousness of story patterns and to use that consciousness to focus on the interesting differences of TV shows and books from each other.
2. Assuming that the fragmentation and flow of TV storytelling encourages attitudes toward narrative that might hinder appreciation of written stories, we can understand what particular skills children immersed in TV might need to learn in order to appreciate literary texts.
3. Understanding the extent to which TV and filmed versions of novels differ from literary texts, we can help children develop an awareness of these differences, and thus deepen their appreciation of the pleasures of TV, movies, and books. We can help them develop strategies to deal with the effects of TV flow or movie visualization.
4. Our efforts to achieve the tasks in items 1, 2, and 3 will also provide us with ways of helping children break the limiting hold that hegemony-supporting toys, movies, and, particularly, TV might have over their imaginations and their conceptions of reality.

WORKS CITED

Altman, Rick. "Television Sound." *Studies in Entertainment: Critical Approaches to Mass Culture.* Ed. Tania Modleski. Bloomington: Indiana UP, 1986. 39–54.

Fiske, John, and John Hartley. *Reading Television.* London: Methuen, 1978.

Frith, Simon. "Hearing Secret Harmonies." MacCabe 53–70.

Kipnis, Laura. " 'Refunctioning' Reconsidered: Towards a Left Popular Culture." MacCabe 11–36.

MacCabe, Colin, ed. *High Theory/ Low Culture: Analysing Popular Television and Film.* New York: St. Martin's Press, 1986.

May, Jill P. Introduction. "The Audio-Visual Arts and Children's Literature." Spec. section. Jill P. May. *Children's Literature Association Quarterly* (Fall 1982): 2–5.

———. "Walt Disney's Interpretation of Children's Literature." *Jump Over the Moon: Selected Professional Readings.* Ed. Pamela Petrick Barron and Jennifer Q. Burley. New York: Holt, Rinehart and Winston, 1984. 461–472.

Paley, Vivian Gussin. *Boys and Girls: Superheroes in the Doll Corner.* Chicago: U of Chicago P, 1984.

Rollin, Lucy. "Fear of Faerie: Disney and the Elitist Critics." *Children's Literature Association Quarterly* 12.2 (Summer 1987): 90–93.

Saul, E. Wendy. " 'All New Materials': Reflections on the American Toy Scene." *Children's Literature Association Quarterly* 7.1 (Spring 1982): 2–5.

Sayers, Frances Clarke. "Walt Disney Accused." *Children and Literature: Views and Reviews.* Ed. Virginia Haviland. Glenview: Scott, Foresman, 1973. 116–125.

Silverstone, Roger. *The Message of Television: Myth and Narrative in Contemporary Culture.* London: Heinemann, 1981.

Singer, Jerome L., and Dorothy G. "Television and Reading in the Development of Imagination." *Children's Literature* 9 (1981): 126–136.

Skirrow, Gillian. "Hellivision: An Analysis of Video Games." MacCabe 115–142.

Stein, Ben. *The View from Sunset Boulevard: America as Brought to You by the People Who Make Television.* New York: Basic, 1979.

Stott, Jon C. "Pseudo-sublimity and Inarticulate Mumblings in Violent Juxtaposition: The World of Comic Books." *Children's Literature Association Quarterly* 7.1 (Spring 1982): 10–12.

Street, Douglas. "An Overview of Commercial Filmic Adaptation of Children's Fiction." *Children's Literature Association Quarterly* 7.3 (Fall, 1982): 13–17.

Williams, Raymond. *Marxism and Literature.* Oxford: Oxford UP, 1977.

———. *Television: Technology and Cultural Form.* New York: Schocken, 1974.

PART THREE

Children's Literature in the Context of Literary Experience

According to the cognitive psychologist Ulric Neisser, ''Not only reading, but also listening, feeling, and looking are skillful activities that occur over time. All of them depend upon pre-existing structures . . . called *schemata,* which direct perceptual activity and are modified as it occurs'' (14). In Chapter 5, we considered how a number of stories found on TV and in children's books followed one same basic pattern, and I suggested that consciousness of such patterns is essential to an understanding of literature. These story patterns are examples of *schemata* (*schemata* is plural; one such pattern is a *schema*).

By developing schemata and then applying them to our new experiences, we perceive by means of what we have taught ourselves to expect. As Neisser says, ''Because schemata are anticipations, they are the medium by which the past affects the future; information already acquired determines what will be picked up next'' (22). For instance, the contexts of assumptions about children that we have already explored operate as schemata in our response to children's literature, and TV shows are schemata for children's reading of literature.

But these are not the only schemata we can apply to literary texts. In this section, we will explore how our previous experience of literature provides schemata that determine our response to the new texts we encounter.

Since our understanding of any given text depends on the schemata we apply to it, reading is an interactive process. Like the instructions in a recipe, the words of a text are incomplete until somebody makes them into an experience by applying the schemata of information and skills learned earlier. A story or a poem does not exist until a reader makes it exist.

For knowledgeable readers, however, a text implies some of the particular skills and information needed to complete it. For such readers, for instance, the visual pattern ''blue'' evokes the idea of one particular color. So texts are not as incomplete as they might seem. Just as proficient cooks know which tools and operations are implied by the words "beat egg whites into stiff peaks" in a soufflé recipe, proficient readers "produce" similar stories or poems from the limited information present in a printed text.

But never the same stories or poems. What are stiff peaks for some cooks are not quite stiff enough for others. Because we all have different previous experiences of language and of life, different schemata, we all have different ideas about what the words we share mean. That is why each of us finds a different story in the same text, and why each of us responds uniquely to the same reading.

While the existence of many versions of the same text is inevitable, however, not all of them are equally plausible—no more plausible than the soufflé of a cook who did not in fact know what "stiff peaks" were, and so hardly beat the eggs at all. While the resultant gooey dish might be interesting, it would not be a soufflé. Knowing how to derive meanings from a text with some confidence in their plausibility is a learned skill.

Children's literature seems so simple from an adult point of view that we forget how many schemata are required to understand it. A baby given a book for the first time does not know whether to taste it or tear it or toss it in the air. Only after experiencing a number of books and developing some schemata can the baby approach a new book in the anticipation that the experience it offers can be understood best by looking rather than by tasting.

And not just any kind of looking—a very specific kind, as we can discover if we try to forget our own assumptions and consider the aspects of books and reading that our complex contexts of schemata cause us to take for granted. We could not enjoy books before we learned to read them from front to back and to read the words on each page from left to right and from top to bottom.

As their experience of books and of life widens, children develop more subtle schemata, wider contexts that allow them to make greater sense of and get deeper pleasure from texts. But that does not necessarily mean that they understand and enjoy either as much as is there to enjoy or as much as they might be capable of enjoying. Many children have a repertoire of knowledge and of literary strategies that do not match the ones demanded by the books they read.

That's a pity, because even simple children's texts may communicate rich experiences—but only to those equipped with the skills to understand them. There is nothing inherently wrong with applying oversimple meaning-making strategies to the books we read, with getting simple meanings out of rich texts. But such an approach has less potential to enlighten or to satisfy us than if we can respond with more complex strategies.

In Chapter 14 we will explore how children can be taught such strategies—helped to develop schemata to make their reading as rewarding as possible. But first we will survey schemata that might influence our own reading, specifically of children's literature.

WORK CITED

Neisser, Ulric. *Cognition and Reality: Principles and Implications of Cognitive Psychology.* San Francisco: Freeman, 1976.

CHAPTER 6

Strategies for Reading a Literary Text

GAPS IN TEXTS

As is true of recipes, most of what a written text is capable of communicating is not actually on the page. What *is* there is the minimum amount of information needed to evoke a reader's knowledge of the ways it might be made meaningful. We make sense of the minimal information on the page by understanding that it is minimal, that it leaves *gaps,* but that our knowledge of a context—our reading strategies and our repertoire of information—can tell us how to fill those gaps. If we possess expertise in filling the gaps, we can turn a small amount of information into a surprisingly rich experience. The pages that follow explore how, by considering one highly popular children's novel, E. B. White's *Charlotte's Web,* as an example.

Charlotte's Web begins this way:

> ''Where's Papa going with that ax?'' said Fern to her mother as they were setting the table for breakfast.

Even if we can understand the basic meaning of the words, we need a repertoire of knowledge of conventional behavior to fill in the many gaps here. We specifically need to know the following:

- That Fern is called ''her,'' and so must be female. (Note that we do not yet know if she is human—our repertoire for children's literature includes the possibility that she might be a talking animal.)
- That ''setting'' the table is the act of placing dishes and cutlery on it, and that ''breakfast'' is a meal eaten in the morning.
- That ''Papa'' is probably not a person's name, but a conventional designation for a father most often used by his children; so the word tells us that

Papa is most likely Fern's father. Furthermore, "Papa" is more old-fashioned than "Dad." Perhaps the story takes place some time ago.

- That the directness and tone of the question implies an easy, open relationship between Fern and her mother; there's no reticence or fear of being considered disobedient.
- That in earlier times when children were meant to be seen and not heard, a question like Fern's would usually be considered inappropriate; so her apparently casual asking of it implies either that this is an unusual family in the past or that the story takes place sometime in this century.
- That this family seems to take for granted that everyone sits down together and eats breakfast from a set table, and that setting the table is female work, done by a girl and her mother. These notions imply a fairly old-fashioned family life-style. While the story is contemporary, it probably is not set in the last twenty years or so.
- That, given the context of the rest of the sentence, the one surprising element is the ax—an implement we don't expect to appear during breakfast. Its presence makes us think about its customary uses, and its oddity evokes questions about what it might be used for here.

The few words of this sentence have implied much that they haven't actually said—for those who know how to fill in the gaps.

EXPLORATION: Consider (or have children consider) how another section of Charlotte's Web *or another children's text contains gaps that require a repertoire of contextual knowledge.*

As we continue reading past the opening, we can fill in more gaps. When Mother says that Papa is "out to the hoghouse," we understand that the events are probably taking place on a farm. And when Mother answers Fern's question about the ax with the statement that a runt was born, we fill in another sort of gap—an idea or even a picture of what Papa might do with the ax. The author does not need to provide a literal picture of Papa taking an ax to the runt; from the information White gives, we can imagine the scene.

In addition to filling in gaps that relate to the setting and the situation, astute readers will make use of other strategies. One is to assume that, because this is the beginning of a novel, what happens here will be of significance for what follows. Either Fern, or her father or mother, or the ax, will continue to be important, and we will look for further information to tell us which of them it might be. If we expect children's literature to concern children, then we may use the soon-provided information that Fern is eight not only to fill in a gap and specify that Fern is a child, but also, to guess that the story will revolve around her.

In making predictions as we read, we are using the basic strategy we apply to all stories—the idea that they are in some way complete, that everything in them relates in some way to their overall effect. In other words, we assume that they have *consistency* of direction and purpose, and we build our sense of what that consistency might be. So when we are suddenly told, later on the first page, "Fern pushed a chair out of the way and ran outdoors," we are not likely to assume that she has suddenly seen her best friend through the window. Instead, we assume that her action relates to what we have heard already—that she wants to stop her father from killing the runt. That turns out to be the case—not surprisingly, for the text has neither mentioned nor implied a friend in the yard, but it *has* made Papa's actions important.

But the next sentence, "The grass was wet and the earth smelled of springtime," seems to be unrelated to what has gone before. To make sense of this new information, we have to think about how the statement relates to what we know already: Why is it suddenly important that we hear about the grass and the earth? We might simply assume that the grass's moisture and the earth's fragrance are what Fern herself perceived at this moment, even though we're not in fact told so. In fact, if we are right that she is concerned about the runt pig, then she is not likely to notice the grass or the earth. We might guess that we are being told about the grass and the earth for other reasons: perhaps the author wants to confirm what those who know when pigs usually litter have guessed already, that the book is set in spring; or perhaps it is going to be important that it rained recently; or perhaps White simply wants to focus our attention on the way the world looks and smells for reasons that will become apparent later.

As it happens, we hear nothing further about rain, and so we have to dismiss the idea that rain will be a significant aspect of the events to follow. But the novel as a whole turns out to focus on sensuous impressions and express appreciation for what White eventually calls "the smell of manure, and the glory of everything" (183). One conjecture is right, the other wrong. As we read, we constantly imagine reasons for details we learn about that we either dismiss and forget or else remember and build on. We consciously or unconsciously process matters as apparently peripheral, such as information about the grass, in a way that builds consistency.

I've talked so much about the sentence about the grass because it surprised me. The previous conversation about breakfast and a runt had not prepared me for a description of outdoor sights and smells. The unexpectedness of this sentence suggests one of the basic strategies demanded by works of fiction: the way in which at any given point in our reading of text we build consistency out of what we know so far, and thus create a schemata, or set of expectations, for what follows—and then are surprised by something we had not expected and so must build a new consistency. Each new bit of information not only adds to but changes our understanding of all the former ones, so that, in the most interesting texts, we are continually forced to reconsider everything we knew before.

This basic pattern of expectation and surprise begins long before we get to a sentence like the one in *Charlotte's Web* about the grass. As soon as we see a book's cover, our context of previous knowledge leads us to develop expectations of what we'll find inside.

EXPLORATION: Choose any children's book you have not read before. Record (or have children record) the changing ideas and expectations you develop as you consider your general impression of its appearance, your response to its title and the name of its author, to the cover illustration, to the words on the back cover, and so on. Describe the expectations you have developed before you actually begin to read the text; then explore how the text itself either confirms or contradicts those expectations.

FILLING IN THE GAPS: STRATEGIES FOR BUILDING CONSISTENCY

There are five major ways in which competent readers conventionally build consistency from the information they gather as they work their way through a literary text: character, plot, theme, structure, and point of view. While these are sometimes identified as the elements of literary texts, they are actually elements of our repertoire of strategies for responding to texts: they are apparent only to those readers who have learned to look for them. Our knowledge of each of these strategies individually and all of them together allows us to find pleasing and meaningful patterns in the literary texts we read. We will examine each of the five strategies in detail.

Character

Character is what we discover in literature when we look for information about the personalities of the people the text describes. We assume that the consistency (and central significance) of a text depends on the ways in which it allows us to see the consistency in (and significance of) the motivations of those people—and of human nature in general. In considering the character of Fern or Wilbur or Charlotte, for instance, we can explore not just how *Charlotte's Web* holds together but also how and why people in general behave as they do, how the threat of death creates a love of life, how friendship makes existence meaningful.

We assume, too, that literature mirrors life, that it is "realistic." Consequently, the limited information that stories provide about their characters is, like the limited information we have about the people we meet, merely the tip of an iceberg of more detailed information about them. We can use our knowledge of the way people usually behave to guess further into their characters' motivations, their past, and even what they might do after the end of the story.

Using this strategy, we explain Fern's concern for the runt pig by suggesting that her grandmother may recently have died; or later, we might try to figure out whether her relationship with Henry Fussy will last after the book is over. Reading in this way implies that fiction is a kind of gossip: it assumes that authors tell us a little bit about the characters they describe so that we can have the fun of guessing about all the aspects of their character and experience they do not tell us about.

Guessing about literary characters allows us to see how their actions match what we assume to be true about human behavior. If we want the pleasure of perceiving something more than or something different from our everyday experience of human nature, however, then we must work with a different assumption: that authors carefully select what they choose to tell us, and that their choices—both what they tell and what they choose not to tell—define what they wish us to understand. For instance, White does not tell us that Fern's grandmother died or how long she will stay with Henry. If we assume that these matters are not important to his conception of Fern, we can build consistency out of what he *has* told us, and learn something about *his* conceptions of human behavior. And if we become conscious that he has not provided certain information that we expected, we can derive new understanding by thinking about *why* it isn't there.

EXPLORATION: In Charlotte's Web, *why might the author not have told us whether Fern's relationship with Henry will last?*

Plot

Plot is the sequence of events that make up a story. It is what we discover in literature when we look for information about how what happens forms a meaningful pattern. We do so on the assumption that the consistency (and central significance) of a literary text depends on the ways in which it allows us to see a consistent pattern of causes and effects underlying actions—and to understand the ways in which what happens in real life also has a history that gives it meaning.

If we assume that plot forms the basic pattern of *Charlotte's Web,* then, we can see how Fern's question about the ax leads her mother to provide her with the information that causes Fern to confront her father about the runt, how her concern saves the runt, and how that action eventually leads to her involvement with the animals in the barn. We see that events have consequences and how causes create effects.

In focusing on plot, our interest is continually on what happens next, on how each event develops from and sums up what went before. We are made to wonder where Papa *is* going with that ax, and when we find out, the answer makes us wonder how Fern will react to the information; and when we find that out, we wonder what she will do about it. Because each action is incomplete, we wonder about its result, and each action both completes the previous one and raises new questions about the future. This chain is what we call *suspense.*

In building suspense, a well-constructed plot captures and maintains our attention until the story comes to an end. It's hard to say exactly *why* such a patterning of events creates pleasure. We may enjoy it simply because it organizes experience into a recognizable or meaningful shape—provides the ordering of random human experience that we expect and enjoy in all works of art. Robert Scholes suggests a more specific reason for our enjoyment of plots when he considers the most basic plot pattern: a series of actions organized to encourage our gradually increasing involvement until the events reach a culminating point at which our interest is at its most intense—a *climax*—and then quickly come to an end. Scholes calls this "the orgastic pattern of fiction'' (26) and indicates that it gives us pleasure because it mirrors a basic human pleasure—the pattern of sexual excitement and fulfillment. Like the sexual pattern, plots provide a twofold pleasure—first, the pleasure of incompleteness, the tension of delaying and anticipating completion; and second, the pleasure of the completion.

In *Charlotte's Web,* for instance, we hope for a climactic moment at which Charlotte's scheme will work and Wilbur will be saved, and eventually we savor that moment. But our pleasure in the anticipation of the climax increases during the events that delay it: the efforts to get all the right animals to the fair, the discovery there of a pig much larger than Wilbur, and so on.

Some plots are pleasurably suspenseful because we can't figure out what will happen next. But some plots are pleasurable simply because we have read similar stories already and therefore *can* guess what will happen next. In the one case we are enjoying the excitement of that which is strange to us, in the other, the satisfaction of recognizing that with which we are familiar. In order to experience this satisfaction, we need a repertoire of plots. These are the basic *story patterns* I mentioned in Chapter 5; writers often expect us to bring such patterns into play as we try to make sense of their stories. As we'll see, children's fiction makes use of a number of story patterns—cumulative tales, fables, wish-fulfillment fantasies in which underdogs triumph, home/away/home stories.

Furthermore, even our pleasure in the unfamiliar depends on our knowledge of the familiar. For instance, we couldn't enjoy the specific humor of a story like Robert Munsch's *Paperbag Princess,* in which a princess rescues a prince from a dragon, unless we knew the conventional pattern it diverges from.

Plots form a spectrum between total familiarity and total strangeness. At one end of the spectrum are formula mysteries and teen romances that offer the pleasures of familiarity with very little surprise. Plots of this sort usually please readers only until they become familiar enough with the formula to be bored by it—that is, until they can use their knowledge of the formula to unlock the pleasures of less formulaic works. At the other end of the spectrum are totally innovative plots that seem to have no relationship to our repertoire of plot patterns. Ideally, readers should have the adaptability to enjoy stories all across the spectrum.

Theme

Teachers often ask elementary school students, ''What is the author's message or purpose?'' University students frequently try to determine the ''hidden meaning'' of a text. Both are building consistency in a literary text by understanding its central idea or *theme.*

Themes are meanings, and the search for meaning is a productive strategy to apply to literature. Indeed, it may be the *only* strategy: all the ways in which we think about texts are really only different ways of understanding their meanings and their relevance to ourselves. Furthermore, these meanings provide readers with insights into their own lives. Charlotte Huck asserts that ''the literary or artistic craft of a book is not as important as its message'' (705), and many politically conscious literary critics might agree with her: Marxist and feminist critics, for instance, focus on the validity of the messages literary texts imply. As we will see in Chapter 7, a consideration of the nature of these messages and of the subtlety with which they are conveyed can enrich our response to literature.

The Dangers in Message Hunting. Unfortunately, many readers approach texts with the idea that their themes or messages can be easily identified and stated in a few words. For instance, many readers suggest that the theme of *Charlotte's Web* is the joy of friendship. Reading in this way directs attention away from the more immediate pleasures of a text: away from language, away from the evocation of vivid pictures and the creation of pleasing patterns and structures—and therefore, away from other, deeper kinds of meaning the text might imply.

Readers may fall into this trap because trying to identify easily expressed general themes requires a strategy quite different from that used in thinking about other elements of a text. As we think about character or plot, for instance, we examine how authors evoke the people and events of the story; we are taking pleasure in the immediate experience of reading itself, in our awareness of how a text is unfolding and in our perception of the ways in which it forces us to fill its gaps. And our awareness of that process becomes part of our effort to obtain meaning from the text, so that our perceptions of meaning are richer. But when we look for a specific theme, we must defer our attempt to understand the message until we have finished reading the text. Instead of focusing on the process of perceiving and thinking that a text offers as we experience it, we must consider only the ideas the entire story has made us think of *after* we've experienced it. That limits both our enjoyment of and our perception of a text's subtleties.

In focusing exclusively on themes as messages for ourselves, we assume that all stories are *parables* or *fables*. These are stories that are not really about the characters in them, but about ourselves: their characters represent general human behavior in order to teach us specific truths that can govern our own future actions. When Jesus tells the parable of the Good Samaritan or Aesop tells the fable of the fox and the grapes, the storyteller does not expect us to be interested in what the characters are wearing or how they feel, but to think about how these events imply specific messages about ourselves.

Adults often assume that all children's stories are fables or should be read as fables. For instance, Charlotte Huck says that ''the theme of a book reveals the author's purpose in writing the story'' (8). Huck reveals the extent to which she believes themes are messages for readers by adding, ''The theme of a story should be worth imparting to young people and be based upon justice and integrity. Sound moral and ethical principles should prevail'' (8). Because it is so prevalent in discussions of children's literature, this particular strategy of consistency building needs detailed consideration.

If we view *Charlotte's Web* as a fable or a parable, we assume that it is not really about what happens to a pig and a spider; it is about how the experience of the pig and the spider can teach us how to act in our own lives. Reading it in that way will certainly deprive us of pleasurable insights into pigs and spiders.

Aesop's fables usually end with an explicit statement of a moral. But these stories have been retold by many different people, and Joanne Lynn points out that "those who retell the fables always manage to find 'morals' that mirror their own values" (6). For Caxton in the fifteenth century, the story of the fox and the grapes showed that the fox was *wise* not to want what he could not have. In more recent versions the fox's behavior is neither wise nor admirable but shallowly self-deceptive; the moral is something like, "It's easy to despise what we cannot have." It seems that, if we assume a story is a parable or a fable, the presence of a moral is so important that almost any one will do. Because we expect a moral or a message, we are sure to find one.

In doing so, we reveal the degree to which messages or themes are separate from the texts we relate them to. In reading for theme, we tend to confirm our own preconceived ideas and values: to take ideas from outside the text and assume that they are inside it. That prevents us from becoming conscious of ideas and values different from our own.

Nevertheless, because many adults assume that children's literature has the main purpose of educating its audience, many children's books *are* fables, and the most common meaning-making strategy that we teach children is to search for morals, messages, or themes. This strategy consists of two parts: first *identification,* and then *manipulation.*

Identification is the perception that a character in a work of literature is like oneself. Many of the characters of children's literature are young, small, concerned with testing their abilities or defying their elders—enough like many of their readers to make identification possible. Identification is so basic to the strategy of reading stories as fables that some adults encourage children to use the technique even when it is not required by a text. "Look," we say to a young child as we finish reading a story about the adventures of a bunny, "Now the bunny is tired and ready to fall asleep, *just like you.*"

After identification comes *manipulation.* If you have seen yourself as the bunny, then something in the story will happen to the bunny that will teach you a lesson about yourself. For instance, in Munro Leaf's *Noodle* children are obviously expected to identify with the dachshund who finds his shortness bothersome; it prevents him from digging holes easily. When a dog fairy agrees to grant Noodle's wish to be different, Noodle considers some other possibilities but finally decides to stay the way he is. Young readers are meant to see his decision as a message about themselves: the dog fairy explicitly asserts that his wish is a wise one. The logic here goes like this:

1. You are short, like the dog.
2. It is wise for the dog to accept its size.
3. Therefore, it is wise for you to accept your size.

But while a mature dachshund is stuck with its size and shape and had better learn to be content with it, children grow and change, and do not need to have such firmly entrenched attitudes of acceptance. Numerous other children's stories use the process of identification and manipulation to reach similarly illogical conclusions.

Even if it is sometimes misleading, the process of identification and manipulation can be an effective teaching device. But if assuming that all stories are fables and concentrating on finding the message in them is the *only* strategy we offer young readers for making sense of stories, then we will have seriously limited their ability to respond to literature. But if we provide them with a wider repertoire of consistency-building strategies and encourage them to be flexible in their use of them, they will be able to distinguish between texts that are fable and those that are not, and apply the appropriate consistency-building strategies to each.

EXPLORATION: Try (or have children try) to determine which ones of a random selection of children's stories and poems seem to be intended to be read as fables and which ones might not be so intended. How might or might not the strategy of looking for themes limit or distort a reader's perception of these texts?

Structure: Words, Images, Ideas

As we read, we may notice that certain words or descriptions or actions remind us of others we came across earlier in the text. In *Charlotte's Web,* for instance, we might notice how often White presents us with descriptions of places and that these descriptions consist of lists of objects. Early on, the description of Zuckerman's barn includes a list of the smells in it: "It smelled of hay and it smelled of manure. It smelled of the perspiration of tired horses and the wonderful sweet breath of patient cows" (13). A few pages later there is another list of smells, this time of Wilbur's food: "The smell was delicious—warm milk, potato skins, wheat middlings, Kellogg's Corn Flakes, and a popover left from the Zuckermans' breakfast" (22). Once we notice the similarity of these passages, we can realize how often lists occur throughout the book, and we can build consistency by probing the implications of the pattern they create. In doing so, we use the strategy associated with structure.

Structure refers to the way that the various parts of a work relate to each other and form patterns. It depends to a great extent on repetition and variations of the same or similar elements.

As we will see later, the structure of nursery rhymes and many other poems is built on repetition and variations of similar sounds and similar-sounding words, sometimes so much so that the pattern of rhythm and rhyme is more significant than the plot or the message. Repeated words can create repeated pictures or images. The words that describe food in *Charlotte's Web* create pictures—of Wilbur's "skim milk, crusts, middlings, bits of doughnuts, wheat cakes with drops of maple syrup sticking to them, potato skins, leftover custard pudding with raisins, and bits of Shredded Wheat" (25), of Charlotte's "flies, bugs, grasshoppers, choice beetles, moths, butterflies, tasty cockroaches, gnats, midges, daddy longlegs, centipedes, mosquitoes, crickets" (39), of Templeton the rat's "popcorn fragments, frozen custard dribblings, candied apples abandoned by tired children, sugar fluff crystals, salted almonds, popsicles, partially gnawed ice cream cones, and the wooden sticks of lollypops'' (123).

Once we notice how often such images appear, we can both enjoy the rhythmic pattern they produce and build consistency by seeing how they make the book meaningful. These lists all ask us to experience the sensuous pleasure provided by what we would usually think of as ugly or useless—bugs and garbage. The idea that we should accept all things, including the apparently bad things like garbage or bugs or death, as part of the glory that is the world in which we live, is central to the novel—one of its major themes.

But the lists aren't there merely to make us conscious of that message: to some degree, the message is there to create a well-organized structure. The message is neither unusual nor profound: many writers have expressed the same idea in fewer words. It is the way White uses that message as the basis for a complex structure built around descriptive lists, a repeating and varying rhythm of images and ideas, that makes *Charlotte's Web* such a rewarding reading experience.

Point of View: Speakers and Narrators

Implied Speakers. In Chapter 2 we explored how literary texts contain an implied reader, someone with a distinct set of interests and skills whom we are asked to become as we read, in order to best understand and enjoy the experience being offered. If there are implied readers, then it is logical to assume that there are also *implied speakers,* whose personalities are suggested by the words of texts. And just as the readers implied by texts are rarely equivalent to the people who read those texts, the speakers implied by texts are rarely equivalent to the people who write them. In fact, authors carefully control the image their texts present of just who it is that is speaking, in the knowledge that different kinds of speakers provide different sorts of pleasure.

Versions of fairy tales offer a clear example of how texts can imply the personalities of different sorts of speakers. The person telling the story in Charles Perrault's version of ''Sleeping Beauty'' is witty and urbane, and a little supercilious about the unsophisticated qualities of this peasant's tale. Finally, he totally undercuts the story by declaring that its moral is this:

> It seems only logical that a woman should be willing to wait some time for a husband who's rich, gallant and kind. But not many women nowadays would be patient enough to wait for a hundred years. So even though the story shows us that waiting can be a good thing, I'm afraid most young women today yearn too strongly for the joys of marriage to pay much attention to that. (Translation mine)

The speaker of E. Nesbit's version implies a quite different relationship with a reader. This storyteller is a chatty gossip who takes us into her confidence, dwells lovingly on details of clothing and food, and turns the entire story into advice about etiquette:

> Whenever you give a christening party you must always remember to ask all the most disagreeable people you know. It is very dangerous to neglect this simple precaution. Nearly all the misfortunes which happen to princesses come from their relations having forgotten to invite some nasty old fairy or other to their christenings. This was what happened in the case of the Sleeping Beauty. (88)

Since the characters of speakers implied by texts clearly suggest attitudes to the stories they tell, we can build consistency by trying to perceive who they are.

EXPLORATION: Choose (or have children choose) a story or novel, and try to determine what the character, attitudes, and interests of its implied speaker are. In what ways does the text imply these qualities, and how do they affect your understanding and enjoyment of the story?

First-Person and Third-Person Narrators. The speakers implied by texts reveal attitudes not only through their tone and their choices of what is significant or noteworthy in the story they tell, but also by whether the story is narrated in the *first person* or in the *third person.*

A *first-person* narrator reports from his or her own subjective point of view events that he or she has personally experienced. For instance, the main character in Judy Blume's *Are You There God? It's Me, Margaret* speaks directly to readers as she tells her own story.

On the other hand, many narratives are in the *third person;* they present the point of view of someone separate from the events. Sometimes this narrator is an outside observer who reports what happens but who doesn't know what the individual characters think about the events. This tends to be the point of view of the Grimm versions of fairy tales, in which we can only guess about what the characters think from what we are told of their actions. Sometimes third-person narrators are *omniscient.* They know the thoughts of some or all of the characters, and sometimes they may even know more about the characters' feelings than the characters themselves are willing to acknowledge. And sometimes, third-person narrators are similar to first-person narrators: while they are theoretically objective in describing all the characters, in fact they know the thoughts of only one character, and present events from that character's point of view. Narratives of this sort combine the subjectivity of the first person with the objective distance of the third person.

The point of view from which a story is told affects how we understand it. "Sleeping Beauty" would be a different story if told from the viewpoint of the neglected fairy rather than by a third-person narrator. It would be a different story again if told from the viewpoint of the Prince. When we see the events from the viewpoint of an outside observer, we tend not to get too caught up in the specific experience of any one of the characters, but to focus on the meaning of the action rather than on the way individual characters respond to the action. On the other hand, in *Are You There God?* we see things from Margaret's point of view, and for many readers, much of the pleasure of the novel derives from their being able to empathize with her responses to the situations she describes.

EXPLORATION: Explore the effects of a narrator's point of view by considering how a story would be different if told from a different point of view. Choose (or have children choose) a story, and rewrite it; tell a first-person narration from an omniscient narrator's viewpoint, or vice versa. How does the different perspective make the story different?

The basic strategy required in reading *Are You There God?* from Margaret's point of view is to feel sympathy with her interpretation of her story. Such sympathy is often difficult for adult readers, who tend to approach the novel with broader experience than Margaret and readers who identify with her have had, and who tend to have more sophisticated expectations of fiction and more sophisticated strategies for reading it. For sophisticated readers the central pleasure of first-person narratives is often an ability to see through them, to come to an understanding of the events being told that differs from the way in which the narrator perceives them; and writers of such narrations often leave clues that clearly imply the inaccuracy of the words we read. So someone who reads *Are You There God?* with knowledge of the strategies required to read more sophisticated fictions may well see Margaret as a self-pitying and self-indulgent little brat, and believe that Blume has managed to create a "self-portrait" of a typical teenager that cleverly reveals the limited vision of adolescents.

But as a writer for children, Blume probably wanted her readers to see Margaret's point of view as the correct one. We need to have a repertoire of strategies broad enough to cope with nonironic first-person narratives as well as more ironic ones—such as, for instance, the text of Ellen Raskin's picture book *Nothing Ever Happens on My Block,* in which a desperately egocentric narrator's first-person report of his boring life is cleverly undercut by pictures of interesting events taking place behind his back. While intended for an audience younger than that of Blume's novel, this book demands what seems to be a more sophisticated strategy.

The point of view of *Charlotte's Web* is that of a third-person narrator—one who, as we have seen, is especially interested in the ways objects look and feel and smell. Sometimes this narrator merely reports what a careful outside observer would see; for instance, he describes how Fern first meets the pig Wilbur, without saying how she feels about it: "Then she lifted the lid of the carton. There, inside, looking up at her, was the newborn pig. It was a white one" (4). Sometimes, however, this narrator describes how the characters feel; a few pages later, for instance, he knows that Fern is "thinking what a blissful world it was" (7). If we notice when this narrator reports objectively and when he chooses instead to convey characters' feelings, we can take pleasure from the careful way White uses point of view to create moments of suspense and to control our understanding of and attitude toward the events described.

BUILDING THE CONSISTENCY OF TEXTS AS A WHOLE

We have discovered that *Charlotte's Web* has intriguing characters, a suspenseful plot, rich themes, a complex structure, and a variable point of view—and that exploring each of these elements allows us to enjoy different kinds of patterns. While our use of each of these strategies has been rewarded with the satisfaction of a sense of consistency, we won't have achieved the full pleasure of the book unless we put the different strategies into play at the same time. If, as we read a text, we build all five kinds of consistency at once, we can enjoy each one on its own and also, the way they undercut and amplify each other in a complex interweaving.

I said earlier that structure refers to the way that the parts of a text relate to one another. We have explored the structural patterns created by words and by images. But plots also have a structure, a pattern of suspense that leads to a climax; and the structure created by patterns of words and images is different from and cuts across the plot structure. As we read a book, in fact, we find our attention shifting from one to the other: from the question "What happens next" to a descriptive passage that evokes earlier descriptions and points us backward rather than forward.

In other words, what happens next *as we read* is not necessarily the next incident in a sequence of events: it may be a description of a barn or a report of a character's memories. So stories tend to have two plots: the series of actions that make up the events the story narrates and the series of actions that make up the narration of those events.

At the beginning of *Charlotte's Web,* for instance, we learn that Fern hears about the potential death of the runt pig while setting the table for breakfast and rushes outside to plead for its life. These are the events of the story. But we hear about these events by means of a conversation between Fern and her mother, a report of how Fern rushes outside, a description of the grass, and another conversation, this one between Fern and her father. These conversations, reports, and descriptions are the actions of the telling of the story—of what is called the *discourse.*

Discourse

The discourse affects the way in which we understand the events. Sometimes, as in the case of flashbacks, the actions of the discourse don't come in the same order as the actions of the story. In *Charlotte's Web,* for instance, we hear at breakfast that the pigs were born the night before, and thus less emphasis is placed on the birth than if the book began by describing it. White's discourse makes it clear that the birth is less important than Fern's response to it.

The discourse can sum up a number of events in a few words, or occupy many pages with a minute description of one specific event. We would respond to *Charlotte's Web* quite differently if White had simply said, "Once upon a time a girl named Fern was setting the table for breakfast when she heard that her father was about to kill a runt pig. She rushed out to the barn and tried to stop him."

EXPLORATION: Is that statement true? Explore whether your response to this alternate beginning to Charlotte's Web *would be different from your response to the actual beginning, and if so, how.*

Furthermore, the discourse can include many things in addition to the basic events of the story: descriptions of people and places, summaries of character, detailed records of what characters are thinking. It can switch from information about characters to a focus on images, and from descriptions back to actions, in a way that demands our own flexible use of different consistency-building strategies.

Trajectory

The children's novelist Jill Paton Walsh speaks of the discourse as a "trajectory"—"the route chosen by the author through his material. It is the action of a book, considered not as the movement of paraphrasable events in that book but as the movement of the author's exposition and the reader's experience of it" (187–188). Paton Walsh says that "a good trajectory is the optimum, the most emotionally loaded flight path across the subject to the projected end" (188). Inexperienced readers tend to be unconscious of the trajectory, and to read looking for what happens—the events of the story rather than the sequence of the discourse: they tend either to ignore descriptive passages or to assume they are just background information of no significance in understanding the events, too boring to pay much attention to. But the trajectory or discourse of a book has as much effect on our perception of suspense and our interest as does the plot of the story. For instance, the long descriptive list at the beginning of Chapter 6 of *Charlotte's Web,* of the different events of early summer days, comes just after a promise, at the end of the previous chapter, that events will prove Charlotte the spider to be a loyal friend; the passage cleverly builds suspense simply by talking about something completely different from what we have been encouraged to most want to hear about next.

As *Charlotte's Web* reveals, the shifting focus demanded by a complex discourse can create rich reading experiences. Our perception of patterns of images can help us understand the meanings implied by the events of a plot, and vice versa: in *Charlotte's Web* we can see how the lists implying "the glory of everything" help explain the meaning of the saving of Wilbur's life and the death of Charlotte, and how salvation by means of an instrument of death, a spider's web, and then the unavoidable death of the savior, are examples of the paradoxical relations of bad and good that we find in all the lists.

EXPLORATION: Work through (or have children work through) a few pages of Charlotte's Web *or any other children's story or novel. Determine which sort of consistency-building procedure each succeeding sentence or paragraph most clearly relates to, and then consider how the shift between different procedures might help to create the specific effect of the whole. How does a writer use shifts in focus to create suspense and build understanding?*

The connections between the different consistency-building strategies aren't always so clear. In some texts they may undercut rather than support each other, so that their relationship is ironic. That is certainly the effect created by the difference between the narrator's point of view and the information in the pictures of *Nothing Ever Happens on My Block.* But even then, the effect of the whole depends on our perceptions of the way the parts fit together. In the long run, the main strategy implied by consistency building is that the different sorts of consistency are all aspects of and variations on the same central consistency.

In Chapter 8, when we look at postmodern literary theories such as deconstruction, we will discover that some contemporary readers deny the value of looking for this kind of consistency. But even those who doubt the value of consistency building acknowledge that many authors write with the assumption that we will read their texts expecting consistency. Consequently, knowledge of consistency-building strategies remains a significant part of everyone's literary repertoire.

WORKS CITED

Blume, Judy. *Are You There God? It's Me, Margaret.* New York: Bradbury, 1970.

Huck, Charlotte S. *Children's Literature in the Elementary School.* 3rd ed., updated. New York: Holt, Rinehart and Winston, 1979.

Leaf, Munro. *Noodle.* Illus. Ludwig Bemelmans. 1937. New York: Scholastic, 1968.

Lynn, Joanne. "Aesop's Fables: Beyond Morals." *Touchstones: Reflections on the Best in Children's Literature.* Ed. Perry Nodelman. Vol. 2. West Lafayette: Children's Literature Association Publications, 1987.

Munsch, Robert. *The Paperbag Princess.* Toronto: Annick, 1980.

Nesbit, E. "The Sleeping Beauty in the Wood." *The Old Nursery Stories.* 1908. London: Hodder and Stoughton, 1975.

Paton Walsh, Jill. "The Lords of Time." *The Openhearted Audience: Ten Writers Talk about Writing for Children.* Washington: Library of Congress, 1980. 177–198.

Raskin, Ellen. *Nothing Ever Happens on My Block.* New York: Atheneum, 1966.

Scholes, Robert. *Fabulation and Metafiction.* Urbana: U of Illinois P, 1979.

White, E. B. *Charlotte's Web.* 1952. New York: Trophy-Harper & Row, 1973.

CHAPTER 7

The Context of Our Knowledge of Literature

INTERTEXTUALITY

For a young child first hearing "Cinderella," the story of a poor girl magically transformed into a princess is an entirely new experience. Upon later hearing "Snow White," the child might realize that this story also tells of a poor girl magically transformed into a princess; the child will have begun to develop a schema. By the time the child hears "Sleeping Beauty," the schema might be implanted firmly enough so that the child can make sense of the new story in terms of its similarities to the old ones.

The schemata we develop from our previous experience of literature are our most significant contexts for responding to literature, because they provide two sources of understanding and pleasure: the comfort of familiarity, of finding in new experiences elements of ones we've already learned to understand, and the excitement of unfamiliarity, of thinking about the specific details that attract our attention exactly because they don't fit our previously established schemata.

EXPLORATION: Think (or have children think) of another fairy tale about a woman who ends up being transformed into a princess or a queen—perhaps the Grimms' "Frog King" or "Manyfurs." What does it share with the basic pattern underlying such stories? What is unique about it? Is it the similarities or the differences that lead to your pleasure in the story?

Readers can approach a text in terms of what it shares with other texts simply because texts do share so much. Some people assume that each worthwhile story or poem is a separate, unique experience, either emerging exclusively from one person's individual creativity or else inspired by something beyond mere human knowledge—a "muse," perhaps. Certainly every good literary text expresses the unique imagination of its writer; but writers work from their knowledge of previous texts just as much as readers do. The idea of a story about a detective figuring out which suspect committed a crime does not occur independently to each person who writes a mystery novel; most mystery writers have read many such texts before deciding to create their own.

What's true of mystery novels is true of tragedies, novels about talking animals, and the whole range of literary texts. Any given text always has many other texts in its background, and shares many characteristics with them: not just obvious allusions, but also ideas, images, basic story patterns. Finally, all texts—indeed, the many words by which humans communicate their experience in speech, newspapers and letters, on TV and radio as well as in books—are connected with each other. Thus, each book expresses what literary critics call *intertextuality:* the interconnectedness of human language, its patterns, images, and meanings. To focus on a text's intertextuality is to focus on the ways it depends on the reader's knowledge of its connections with other writing.

EXPLORATION: Consider (or have children consider) the intertextuality of any simple poem or story intended for young children. List as many ways you can think of in which it relates to your knowledge of literature and other uses of language.

Because texts share so much, our perception of the distinctness of the texts we read increases in proportion to our overall knowledge of literature: the more we know, the more we see. In this chapter and the next one, we will consider the various ways in which previous experiences of literature can act as schemata that influence our understanding and enjoyment of what we read.

Reading One Work of Literature in the Context of Another

In Hans Christian Andersen's "Princess and the Pea" as in "Cinderella," a prince seeks a bride, and the woman he ends up marrying is an unlikely choice—in this case a stranger who knocks on the palace gate during a rainstorm. Despite her bedraggled appearance, she turns out to be a "real" princess, a fact proven when a pea placed under twenty mattresses and twenty quilts gives her a sleepless night. As in "Cinderella," apparently, true worth triumphs despite appearances, and events lead a prince to a *real* princess even when she's sooty, wet, or otherwise unprincesslike.

But schemata allow us to perceive differences as well as similarities. If we think a little further about "The Princess and the Pea" and "Cinderella," we realize that there are important ways in which they are not alike. In most versions of the story, Cinderella's true worth is her moral goodness; the worth of Andersen's princess is a sensitivity resulting from noble blood. The implication of Andersen's story is that members of the upper classes are inherently more refined than ordinary mortals. The story annoys many readers because they see it as snobbish and undemocratic.

But is it? The princess's ability to feel a single pea through all those mattresses is extreme, and it seems odd that Andersen does not comment on its outlandishness. We might make sense of his not doing so by considering if we have developed any schemata that the story might fit into other than the one about underdogs becoming princesses.

In light of the extreme nature of the princess's sensitivity, I am personally reminded of a poem from my own repertoire of reading: Hilaire Belloc's "Sarah Byng, Who Could Not Read and Was Tossed into a Thorny Hedge by a Bull," in which Sarah's problem develops from her inability to decipher a warning sign. As a result, Sarah learns "to keep away/ From signs, whatever they may say," and is

> Confirmed in her instinctive guess
> That literature breeds distress.

Belloc states this unlikely conclusion with the same calm acceptance with which Andersen tells of the princess's discomfort with the pea. The difference between the accepting tone and the outrageous idea is a source of laughter in the poem. Perhaps Andersen also intends us to laugh at his story; perhaps he is making fun of the supposed superiority of "real" princesses by telling this exaggerated story about one of them, and the story actually means the opposite of what it seems to be saying.

If we reach that conclusion and then think again about "Cinderella," we might see *it* differently also. As members of a society that values kindness, we assume that Cinderella becomes a princess because of her kind heart. But a closer look reveals that Cinderella can be transformed into a princess because she is something like a princess in the first place—the daughter of a nobleman. Perhaps her stepmother's crime is not so much a lack of appreciation for Cinderella's virtue as it is a denial of her rights as the eldest daughter of a rich gentleman; perhaps Cinderella deserved a prince because of her noble blood, no matter how sweet or kind she may have been.

The Context of Other Works by the Same Author

Many readers, both children and adults, seek out further texts by authors they have enjoyed, because they expect a common thread, a consistency of subject and style, in all the texts an author produces. Later, we will explore how some children's writers deliberately produce series of texts about the same characters in similar situations. But because of the consistencies of human personality, texts by the same author usually have a great deal in common, even when their author did not necessarily intend them to. Consequently, knowing that Belloc is being ironic in "Sarah Byng," we suspect he is being equally ironic in a poem called "The Tiger," in which he suggests that tigers make good pets:

> And mothers of large families (who claim to common sense)
> Will find a Tiger well repays the trouble and expense.

And knowing Beatrix Potter's *Tale of Peter Rabbit,* a story about a small animal who loses his clothing in an exciting escape from a farmer's garden, prepares us to focus on the subtleties of Potter's *Tale of Mr. Jeremy Fisher,* in which a frog puts on a mackintosh and a pair of shiny galoshes so that he can go fishing on a rainy day.

But the similarity once again points our attention toward a difference. Peter Rabbit's clothes hinder him, and he can run fast enough to escape from Mr. McGregor only after he gets rid of his shoes; but Jeremy Fisher's clothing saves his life: a trout swallows him, but "was so displeased with the taste of the mackintosh, that in less than half a minute it spat him out again." A perception of similarities can suggest intriguing differences even in two apparently similar texts by the same author.

EXPLORATION: Choose (or have children choose) two texts by an author you admire that strike you as being significantly similar. Does your perception of the similarities also point you toward some interesting differences?

CHILDREN'S LITERATURE AS A GENRE

We can describe certain texts as being mystery novels or children's literature simply because we see them as similar to other texts we have previously labeled as being children's literature or mystery novels. Once we are aware that a number of texts have a good deal in common, we can place them in a category defined by their shared characteristics, and then discover their unique qualities by identifying to what extent the texts match and diverge from that category. Literary specialists call such categories *genres.*

As we saw earlier, the children in the phrase "children's literature" are less significantly the diverse group of real children who might read these texts than the more consistently similar ones implied by the texts themselves. In the next section, we'll consider characteristics that, even though they have emerged from generalizations and assumptions about the needs of children, have resulted in a characteristic implied reader and thus made children's literature a genre—a specific form of literature with its own specific pleasures and problems.

A No-Name Story: The Basic Pattern

The following are descriptions of some children's stories that strike me as typical:

- In Lucy Prince Scheidlinger's *Little Bus Who Liked Home Best,* a municipal bus becomes envious of the "great silver buses" on the superhighway. After joining them, he becomes confused by the traffic, and when he finally finds his way back, he concludes, as the title suggests, that home is best.
- In Leo Lionni's *Fish Is Fish,* a fish is left behind in the pond when his childhood friend becomes a frog and goes off to see the world. When the frog returns

with stories of glamorous sights, the fish resolves to leave the pond. After the frog saves the fish's life by flipping the fish back into the water, the fish concludes that it is better to stay at home.

- In Marjorie Flack and Kurt Wiese's *Story About Ping,* a duck avoids punishment for being the last to return to its home on a boat by staying out on the river. Caught by a boy, the duck is threatened with death. After escaping, he happily returns home despite the inevitable punishment.

While the details change, there is clearly a basic pattern underlying these stories: A young creature, an animal or object with human characteristics, enjoys the security of a comfortable home until something happens that makes it unhappy. The small creature most often leaves home and has exciting adventures; but they turn out to be as dangerous or as discomforting as they are thrilling. Having learned the truth about the big world, the creature finally returns to the security it at first found burdensome, concluding that, despite its constraints, home is best.

EXPLORATION: Browse (or have children browse) through children's books in a library or bookstore to see if you can find examples of this story or stories similar to it. How many stories can you find that are completely different from it?

I believe this story is generic, like the "no-name" canned goods sold in supermarkets. While not identical to it, many other children's stories and poems relate significantly to it. In Munro Leaf's *Noodle,* for instance, a dachshund is concerned with the limitations not of its home, but of its body, and after considering the advantages of the more exotic shapes of animals at the zoo, decides that its original size and shape are ideal: one's own body, like one's own home, is best.

Many interesting and admired children's books follow the same pattern. Beatrix Potter's Peter Rabbit ignores his mother's instructions, has a dangerous adventure away from home, and returns to safety afterward. The title character in Virginia Lee Burton's *Little House* longs for the excitement of the city until the city grows up around her and brings her nothing but noise and neglect. Delighted to be moved back to the country, she vows that she will never again wonder about the city. Maurice Sendak's *Where the Wild Things Are* takes Max from his imposed stay in his own room into an imaginary voyage into wildness, which ends when he decides he wants to return to the comfort of his room. And in Arthur Yorinks and Richard Egielski's *Hey, Al,* a janitor and his dog escape from their boring life by accepting a giant bird's invitation to a paradisal island in the sky. When they start turning into birds themselves, Eddie decides that mopping floors is preferable, and they return to the comforts of home.

Nor is this story pattern restricted to picture books. In Robert Louis Stevenson's *Treasure Island,* Jim Hawkins expresses boredom with the quietness of his home. After his exciting but dangerous experiences with pirates, he returns home convinced that nothing could make him wish for adventure again. In Kenneth Grahame's *Wind in the Willows,* Toad's lust for adventure leads him to prison. At the end he must win back his home, which has been invaded by evil creatures, before he can again experience its comforts. E. L. Konigsburg's *From the Mixed-Up Files of Mrs. Basil E. Frankweiler* describes how a brother and sister seek adventure by running away from home to the safe pleasures of the Metropolitan Museum and then return home again.

Of course, not all children's literature follows this pattern; many stories and poems written for children bear no apparent relationship to it at all. But the fact that the pattern occurs so often is suggestive: its characteristics must satisfy our ideas about what children's literature is or should be.

Furthermore, once we have observed the pattern and are able to use it as a schema, we can read texts that seem different from it as interesting variations on it. For instance, the plot of L. M. Montgomery's *Anne of Green Gables* represents an inversion of the pattern: a child whose life has been filled with troubling adventures arrives at a safe home at the *beginning* of the story.

EXPLORATIONS: (1) Consider (or have children consider) the significance of the generic, "no-name" story. What are its characteristics? Why *do so many texts share these characteristics? What are the implications of these similarities?*

(2) Consider how we can use our knowledge of genre to help us understand a text. Choose (or have children choose) a children's poem or story, and keep it in mind as you think about the characteristics outlined in the next section. Is the text illuminated by these ideas?

CHARACTERISTICS OF THE GENRE

The generic pattern can help us understand the traits that are typical of children's literature as a genre. This section lists and explores some of the implications of these traits.

1. Children's Literature Is Simple and Straightforward

All children's stories and poems are written with the needs of less experienced readers in mind. Many of them, designed for beginning readers, use only a few carefully chosen words.

But that does not mean that children's literature does or should consist *only* of simple words. Potter's *Tale of Peter Rabbit* is basic enough so that most of its language is understandable to children born almost a century after it was written; but it also says, for instance, that the sparrows "implored Peter to exert himself." In *Dr. De Soto,* William Steig rejoices in words that are not only odd but also pretentious—intentionally so, for much of the comedy of the book depends on our awareness of the pomposity of sentences like "The secret formula must first permeate the dentine." Inexperienced readers can understand and enjoy these difficult words because they appear in a context of simpler verbal and pictorial information. In

Charlotte's Web, White provides a more obvious use of fiction as a source of vocabulary enrichment: the spider often provides definitions of the hard words she enjoys using.

The simple language of many children's texts is choppy and graceless; the passages are divided up into short sentences such as "Perry looked. He looked out the window. The window was open." The assumption is that such sentences are easy to read, despite their dissimilarity from the patterns of normal speech. Not surprisingly, many children seem to find them harder to decipher than more conventional sentences.

Language like this might suggest that the characteristic style of children's texts is lack of style. But poems like those by David McCord or Dennis Lee and stories like *Peter Rabbit* or *Charlotte's Web* are not without style. They organize their usually simple words into rhythmic patterns that are pleasing in themselves and add layers of meanings to the words they shape. When Potter tells us that Mr. McGregor had a sieve "which he intended to pop upon the top of Peter," the rhyme of "pop" and "top" and the alliterative p's and t's are musical in themselves and express the abruptness of the action they describe. And when White describes Wilbur eating his slops, the sounds communicate the sensuousness of the experience: "Wilbur grunted. He gulped and sucked, and sucked and gulped, making swishing and swooshing noises, anxious to get everything at once" (75).

2. Children's Literature Focuses on Action

C. S. Lewis once said he was attracted to writing children's books because "this form permits, or compels, one to leave out things I wanted to leave out. It compels one to throw all the force of the book into what was done and said" (236). While children's stories contain descriptions of setting and character, they concentrate on action—on what happens next.

Much adult literature, like spy novels and romances, also focuses on action. In some ways, in fact, a good deal of children's literature is more complicated than many literary texts intended for adults. In spy novels or romances, motivation and meaning are deliberately kept simple so that the pleasure of the chase or the kill isn't diluted by readers being forced to consider moral or emotional implications. But the often complex interpretations of action-oriented texts by writers like Potter and White make it clear that short texts consisting almost entirely of simple words can have profound meanings. As we will see later in this chapter, children's books often have serious educational intentions. As in the stories about little creatures who learn to like home best, children's writers often want both their characters and their readers to focus on the moral or emotional implications of exciting actions. In order to do so, they must find ways of expressing the deeper implications in their apparently straightforward plots.

Sometimes, as in versions of the generic story discussed earlier, the process is obvious: characters merely state what they have learned from their adventures. But in books like *Peter Rabbit* or *Where the Wild Things Are,* complex ideas beneath the surface simplicity are not explicitly stated. Instead, they are implied—shown rather than told. By choosing a series of actions that relate to each other in superficially straightforward but actually complicated ways, Potter and Sendak can both focus on action and imply complex emotional situations. In part, they accomplish that task by expressing subtle emotions in the pictures that accompany their texts. In *Where the Wild Things Are,* for instance, the text itself never explicitly states that Max's visit to the Wild Things might be a complex psychological voyage, in which the Wild Things represent Max's attempt to come to terms with his anger at his mother and his own wildness, but the pictures constantly imply the possibility of that interpretation. For instance, as the book begins, Sendak reveals the constraint Max feels by depicting him in a small picture surrounded by a wide white border, his arms and legs and the ears of his costume an explosion of energetic points that seems to move outward toward that restricting border.

Many longer children's novels offer similarly straightforward narrations of actions that imply subtle psychological events: the maturing of Jim in *Treasure Island,* Wilbur's gradual acceptance of life and death in *Charlotte's Web.*

3. Children's Literature Is about Childhood

While many of the versions of the generic story considered earlier are about humanized objects or animals, their main characters are often described as being young and, in that way, equivalent to the children who read about them. On the other hand, neither Mr. Jeremy Fisher nor the gentlemanly animals of *Wind in the Willows* are young. While the pig Wilbur of *Charlotte's Web* begins as a child, he becomes an adult in the course of the book, and his friend Charlotte eventually dies of old age. Meanwhile, the central characters of many undeniably adult novels—James Joyce's *Portrait of the Artist as a Young Man,* Margaret Atwood's *Cat's Eye*—are children. We can conclude neither that all children's literature is about children nor that all books about children are children's literature.

Even so, children's literature is intended for an audience of children and is supposed to relate to the interests of children. We should thus be able to conclude that it does concern the nature and problems of childhood. The animals and animated toys of many children's stories and poems clearly represent the situation of children. Like human children, Peter Rabbit is torn between the opposing forces of his natural instincts and his mother's wishes—and so, despite his relative maturity, is Mr. Jeremy Fisher. Presumably, too, children can appreciate how the spider Charlotte tricks adult humans because her small size allows children to see themselves in her.

4. Children's Literature Expresses a Child's Point of View

Charlotte and Mr. Jeremy Fisher have more in common with Anne of *Anne of Green Gables* or Sendak's Max than with the children of adult novels—Stephen Dedalus of *Portrait of the Artist* or Elaine Risley of *Cat's Eye.* Not only do both Stephen and Elaine grow up, but in both cases, growing up is defined as the ability to see beyond the limited vision of inexperienced youth. Even as they undergo their youthful adventures, these characters are viewed by their adult selves looking back. We are meant to see through their youthful innocence even as we read about it. But Anne's "limited" vision, her innocent joy, is not a weakness but the source of her superiority to others. Even though Anne grows up, she says "I'm not a bit changed—not really. I'm only just pruned down and branched out. The real *me*—back here—is just the same" (276).

The same is true of most young people in children's books. While characters like Peter Rabbit and Jim Hawkins come to understand more at the end than they did at the beginning, their new knowledge does not undercut or deny the validity of their earlier way of seeing things. They may achieve a wise acceptance of life's limitations, or a mature understanding of the need for a secure if unexciting home. Somehow, though, that doesn't deny the joy of exuberance or the thrill of adventure, or lessen the value of a child's innocent vision. The children's novelist Philippa Pearce says, "Writing about and for children, one should have a view almost from the inside, to re-create—not what childhood looks like now—but what it felt like then" (51).

Although children's books create the effect of being inside a child's mind, Pearce's "almost" is revealing. In an important article, Charles Sarland explores why the work of British children's novelist William Mayne appeals to so few children even though Mayne writes from a small boy's point of view, "recreating for the adult reader that forgotten time when the immediate physical environment was a continual source of interest and even wonder" (218). The trouble is, Mayne does that so successfully that "the reader must forget the action and concentrate instead on the sensations of the moment" (219)—and, as we have already discovered, a focus on action is an equally important characteristic of children's literature. Rather than actually describing how children think, the most characteristic children's books express a childlike point of view *through* what is done and said.

5. Children's Literature Is Optimistic

Because we tend to assume that children are ignorant of pain and suffering and thus see the world without consciousness of the cruelty or suffering within it, we also assume that children's literature expresses that innocent and optimistic way of looking at things. The critic Sarah Smedman says, "Hope is a vital dimension of a children's book, for it recognizes, at least implicitly, that readers are at the beginning of life, in crucial areas still uncommitted, even to their own personalities, and that for such readers growth and change are still to come. In a fictional world which purports to appropriate the world as we know it, the resolution must leave scope for such growth and change" (91–92).

6. Children's Literature Tends toward Fantasy

The fact that children's stories express hope, and therefore typically have happy endings, raises a question about their accuracy and honesty. If we suspect that reality is not always so happy, then we might see the optimism of children's literature as evidence of its lack of realism. We might even say that it tends to be unrealistic.

Children's books are about rabbits who talk, spiders who write, weak children who successfully defeat brawny pirates. Even *Anne of Green Gables,* in which nothing particularly improbable happens, is something of a fantasy: Anne enters the novel as an orphan who is happy and trusting despite the fact that she has been mistreated. While it would be nice to believe that a child could survive such an ugly past in this way, evidence from the real world suggests it would be highly unlikely.

Yet we would like to believe it could happen. As Anne's situation reveals, the details that define children's books as fantasy often imply a symbolic defiance of our knowledge of reality. In fact, the fantastic or utopian realities that children's books depict may purport to represent a *truer* reading of reality than our usual one. Elliott Gose asserts that in children's books, "The reader is invited to share a world of imagination with the implicit offer that he or she may thereby come in contact with a potential that lies below the surface nature of each of us" (15).

7. Children's Literature Is a Form of Pastoral Idyll

Many commentators see the optimistic world typical of children's books as having the same relationship to reality as does the idealized world described in one of the traditional genres of literature—the *pastoral idyll,* a form of poem that celebrates the joys of the rural life, close to nature and in the company of friends. Anita Moss suggests that William Steig's children's novel *Dominic* represents "the pastoral values of childhood" (138). And, according to Geraldine Poss, *Wind in the Willows* is like many children's books in making potentially disturbing events seem safe by placing them "within an innocent pastoral milieu" (84).

8. Children's Literature Views an Un-Idyllic World from the Viewpoint of Innocence

We might wonder if *Dominic, Wind in the Willows,* or other children's books are so purely idyllic, if their happy endings are so unqualified. Typically, as we have discovered, a happy ending in children's literature means a return home to a protective environment. The small creatures involved in these stories had left home to achieve freedom, and they learned the wisdom of not doing so. While they claim to be happy about their discovery that they are not capable of fending for themselves, we might wonder if that joyful acceptance of constraint isn't wish-fulfillment on the part of adult writers who would prefer that children did not in fact wish for more independence. These books confirm the idyllic freedom of weak creatures from the difficulty of the world away from home by forcing them to admit to an inability to deal with the more stressful freedom of that world. Have they happily confirmed an idyllic life or merely been weak enough to accept their repression?

Some children's books are ambiguous enough to raise that question themselves. Unlike the little bus who liked home best, Peter Rabbit never denies the pleasures of the world away from home or promises never to leave again. The happy ending of *Anne of Green Gables* is tinged with irony as Anne faces deep tragedy and retains her idyll only by giving up her plans for a career, and the happy ending of *Charlotte's Web* requires that Wilbur's continuing idyll involve his acceptance of Charlotte's death. At the end of *Treasure Island,* Jim's claim that the treasure he has won has cost him great pain qualifies his bliss. While these endings are happy enough to imply optimism about the idyllic nature of reality, the optimism is muted by the possibility of other interpretations. We might say that while children's literature is written from the viewpoint of innocence, it does not necessarily postulate an innocent or uncomplicated world.

It is no accident, if children's books are like the pastoral idylls of tradition, that the traditional audience of idylls among ancient Greeks or Renaissance Europeans was sophisticated nonrural aristocrats, who enjoyed idylls exactly because they evoked a way of life purer and simpler than their own. Sarah Gilead suggests that even the most idyllic of children's books similarly imply a more painful adult knowledge: "However successfully evoked, the projected child's experiences, mentality or feelings reflect an adult's need for escape from necessity, conflict, or compromise. Determined cheerfulness or confident morality [masks] a gentle poignancy. An ostensibly unambiguous realm, the idyll is filtered by adult intellectuality, by an awareness of irony, sexuality, conflicts, and social power arrangements" (146).

In less interesting children's books, such considerations are merely implied by their absence. The writers of such books have created an idyll by deliberately leaving things out—as Lewis implies. But in more interesting books, the ironies are internal and deliberate, and the result is an ambivalence about the relative values of innocence and experience, the idyllic and the mundane. While it seems likely that in such books an insistence on the knowledge of experience would undercut the claims of innocence, the reverse also takes place. While the ugly truth of reality undercuts the innocent assumptions of characters like Peter Rabbit or Jim Hawkins, their innocence reveals the deficiencies of a cynical acceptance of things as they are. In these richly ambivalent books, the visions and merits of innocence and of experience can be true at the same time. Anita Moss's description of Steig's *Dominic* captures the essence of this ambivalence: "It expresses the wish that human beings may someday attain the fullness of experience and yet retain the innocent sense of newness which assures them that they are at the beginning of a new adventure" (140).

The desire to have both the comfort of home and the danger of adventure, to be both innocent and experienced, to grow up but not grow up, occurs in most children's books. It explains the double appeal of the generic story, in which the excitement of adventure is balanced by the security of a return home—and vice versa, for these texts can be read as merely pretending to accept parental authority as a means of allowing young readers the pleasure of the theoretically dangerous. In fact, such books might be offering children a different message from the one that allows pedagogically minded adults to feel it is acceptable for children to read them.

EXPLORATION: Consider the possibility expressed in the passage above. Explore (or have children explore) a book such as H. A. Rey's Curious George, *which claims to convey the dangers of curiosity by showing the trouble a monkey gets into, but which makes the trouble look like a good deal of fun.*

---

9. Children's Literature Is Didactic

As we have seen, even the idyllic pleasures of children's literature may represent a desire to teach young people—an attempt to educate children into sharing an adult view of the world and of the nature of childhood. Versions of the generic story try to persuade young readers that despite its boredom, home is a better place to be than the dangerous world outside. Less conventional texts also convey messages about behavior and the nature of existence to their young readers. Max's experience in Sendak's *Wild Things* provides readers with a model for dealing with their own wildness, and *Charlotte's Web* not only celebrates the joys of friendship but establishes an attitude of acceptance of "the glory of everything."

That is hardly surprising. As we noted in Chapter 3, children's literature of earlier times was primarily didactic in intent, and most adults still think of it primarily in terms of the educational needs of the audience. The didactic impulse of children's literature creates its most characteristic structures.

10. Children's Literature Tends to Be Repetitious

Because a basic assumption about education is that repeating a task helps us to learn it, another genre trait is repetition. We've discovered that many children's stories involve the same narrative patterns, and we've explored how that repetition allows young readers to develop schemata for making sense of the stories they hear. Individual works of children's literature also contain repetitions.

One common story pattern is the cumulative tale, in which all previous events are repeated after the introduction of each new event:

> This is the house that Jack built.
> This is the malt
> That lay in the house that Jack built.
> This is the rat
> That ate the malt
> That lay in the house that Jack built.

And so on. Like this story, many nursery rhymes and children's poems contain repetitions of words, phrases, and situations. In *The Little House,* for instance, words like "watched" and phrases like "pretty soon" appear often.

But repetition in *Little House* is accompanied by variation. As the text describes, in the same basic verbal pattern, how the seasons pass in the same sequence year after year, the city grows; and thus the almost static situation described at the beginning gradually changes totally. In the pictures, meanwhile, the house is always in the same place, and so are the spiral lines of the surrounding landscape; but the city expands until those spiral patterns finally disappear from view. We have seen how a repeated story pattern allows us to focus on the ways in which individual stories vary from that pattern. *The Little House* reveals how individual works of children's literature contain patterns *within* themselves that enable readers to focus on the significance of variations.

11. Children's Literature Tends to Balance the Idyllic and the Didactic

Some texts for children are purely didactic. They work to counter the limitations of children and have no purpose but to make children better—that is, more like mature adults. But as we saw earlier, some texts for children are purely idyllic, and seek to prevent children from becoming different from what they are already. But whether didactic or idyllic, many children's books can be seen to share a concern with the same sets of opposing ideas, as represented by opposed places or characters. Consider the following list:

Human	Animal
Home	Away
Adult	Child
Maturity	Childishness
Civilization	Nature
Restraint	Wildness
Clothing	Nakedness
Obedience	Disobedience
Imprisonment	Freedom
Boredom	Adventure
Safety	Danger
Calm	Excitement
Acceptance	Defiance
Repression	Expression
Charity	Egotism
Martyrdom	Self-respect
Communal concern	Self-concern
Citizenship	Exile
Companionship	Solitude
Constriction	Liberation
Common sense	Imagination
Sense	Nonsense
Cynicism	Wise innocence
Wisdom	Ignorance
Old ideas	New ideas
Past practice	Future potential
Custom	Anarchy
Conservatism	Innovation
Fable	Fairy tale
Reality	Fantasy
False vision	Reality
Good	Evil
Evil	Good

The list on the left represents values that are boringly repressive or securely safe: a just obedience can be seen as a dangerous repression. The list on the right represents values that are either dangerously rebellious or satisfyingly self-reliant: a dangerous defiance from one point of view is a righteous defiance from the other. What is innocence from one point of view is just ignorance from the other—and thus, words like *reality* and *evil* appear in both lists.

It is possible, of course, that my knowledge of the split in the history of children's literature between idyllic and didactic concerns has given me a schemata for approaching children's literature that amounts to a self-fulfilling prophecy; I may see these oppositions in texts simply because I look for them and expect to find them. Indeed, some feminist theorists believe that dividing up experience into this sort of opposition is a habit of male thinking that helps to repress women. It may not be accidental that traditionalists would tend to identify the positive values on both left and right as masculine, the negative values as feminine.

The danger in doing so is clear. Once we have created these categories and opposed them to each other, we tend to see one as superior to the other. But there is no reason why we need to do so. Indeed, the ability to resist doing so may be evidence of a greater wisdom. That certainly seems to be the case in children's literature, where the less interesting books are often the didactic fables that come down firmly in favor of the values expressed on the left-hand list or the idyllic fantasies that merely pay lip service to the left-hand values as they revel in right-hand values. Meanwhile, as Peter Hollindale suggests, it is "a noticeable feature of some major 'classic' children's books that they test and undermine some of the values which they superficially appear to be celebrating" (20). *Charlotte's Web* preaches acceptance of things as they are but describes how Wilbur learns to change his lot in life. *Peter Rabbit* can be seen as being either about how a bad bunny gets into trouble for disobeying his mother or about how a heroic rabbit gets out of trouble by following his instincts.

Despite the possible dangers, then, I believe that thinking in terms of balanced opposites can be a productive and enjoyable strategy. If we assume that a concern with these matters is characteristic of children's literature, we can productively explore texts in terms of how they express and, often in the most interesting texts, balance these oppositions.

For instance, *Peter Rabbit* and *Jeremy Fisher* involve complications that develop when animals act like humans. Both Peter and Jeremy have enemies who think of them as animals, and therefore believe they have a natural right to attack them: rabbits who steal vegetables from gardens and frogs who get close to trout are asking for trouble. But both Peter and Jeremy behave like human beings, so that their situation is ambiguous in ways which allow these characters to have much in common with the young children who read about them. Parents often call good children "little lambs" or gluttonous ones "little pigs," and the common name for children in our society is "kids." We tend to think of "kids" as basically animal-like savages who must be taught how to act like civilized humans.

For these half animal-half human creatures, clothing is of great significance. It marks them off from the purely animal, from the completely savage creatures who don't wear clothing, but it is often a source of discomfort, something that prevents them from behaving like their natural animal selves. The stories of both Peter Rabbit and Jeremy Fisher explore these interesting contradictions. Both Peter and Jeremy almost die because they act like humans: Peter's shoes and jacket buttons nearly lead to his death, and Jeremy dressed and acting like a human fisherman forgets his frog instincts about avoiding trout. But then both Peter and Jeremy escape disaster because they act like humans—Peter by remembering human words about the dangers of cats spoken by his cousin Benjamin, and Jeremy because his mackintosh tastes so unfroglike.

The balances these books imply between clothing and nakedness, animals and humans, clearly relate to many of the other opposing ideas on the list above; we could easily explore them in terms of other items on the list. Many interesting children's books can be illuminated by similar considerations.

EXPLORATION: Choose (or have children choose) any text intended for children, and explore its characters, actions, and images in terms of the values listed above. Can the text be considered didactic, idyllic, or a balancing of the two? How does (or does not) thinking about opposites help you understand the specific pleasures offered by this text?

GENRE AND FORMULA

We have discovered that children's books tend to have a good deal in common with each other. In fact, the main pleasure offered by the most popular children's books is that they are *not* unique, but similar enough to other books to fulfill young readers' previously developed expectations. Superhero comics and Choose-Your-Own Adventure novels, books about young animals who take trips and learn that home is best, young adult novels about teenagers with physical or emotional handicaps who learn to have more positive self-images—such books offer readers slight variations of a basic formula, without major surprises.

Each of the books about Nancy Drew, for example, describes a mystery that none of the adult authority figures can solve, but they admire Nancy enough to allow her to pursue her investigation. Finally, Nancy figures out the mystery when nobody else can, and, often, the villain is a rough-looking male. If the villain were another young girl, if Nancy couldn't solve the problem but her father or boyfriend could, then readers would rightly be disappointed; the whole point of such books is their confirmation of previous expectations.

Adults tend to look down on these books, to call them "trash" and to believe that they hinder children from learning to enjoy good literature—that is, literature that less obviously fulfills a reader's expectations.

EXPLORATION: Should children read "trash"? Is there any point to reading many similar books by the same author in the same series?

As it happens, I've been told by many people who have become ardent readers of serious literature as adults that they spent part of their childhood absorbing every book about Nancy Drew or a character in a similar series. Young readers of formula books may be learning the basic patterns that less formulaic books diverge from. Perhaps we all must read formula fiction to start with, in order to learn the basic story patterns and formulas that underlie all fiction, and perhaps we cannot appreciate the divergences of more unusual books until we first learn these underlying patterns.

It is certainly no accident that many acclaimed children's books have sequels and appear in a series: extended plots that develop over a number of novels (as in Lloyd Alexander's Prydain series), or groups of novels that describe different characters in similar situations (like Lucy Boston's Green Knowe books), or the same characters in different situations (like Beverly Cleary's books about Ramona). It is also no accident that even highly acclaimed children's novels that stand alone tend to fit into easily identifiable patterns: fantasies about contemporary children who travel into the past or stories about parentless children who manage to survive their loneliness and find happiness.

The fact that even the best children's books are not all that unique does not make them uninteresting. Not only do their repetitions of familiar patterns offer pleasure in themselves, but they often contain striking divergences from these patterns. As complicated variations on a simple schema, they represent a stage beyond the comforting similarities of Nancy Drew books.

WORKS CITED

Andersen, Hans Christian. "The Princess and the Pea." *Hans Andersen's Fairy Tales: A Selection.* Trans. L. W. Kingsland. Oxford: Oxford UP, 1984.

Atwood, Margaret. *Cat's Eye.* Toronto: McClelland and Stewart, 1988.

Belloc, Hilaire. "Sarah Byng" and "The Tiger." *Selected Cautionary Verses.* Harmondsworth, Middlesex: Penguin Puffin, 1964.

Burton, Virginia Lee. *The Little House.* Boston: Houghton Mifflin, 1942.

Flack, Marjorie. *The Story About Ping.* Illus. Kurt Wiese. New York: Viking, 1933.

Gilead, Sarah. "The Undoing of Idyll in *The Wind in the Willows.*" *Children's Literature* 16 (1988): 145–158.

Gose, Elliott. *Mere Creatures: A Study of Modern Fantasy Tales for Children.* Toronto: U of Toronto P, 1988.

Grahame, Kenneth. *The Wind in the Willows.* New York: Scribner, 1933.

Hollindale, Peter. "Ideology and the Children's Book." *Signal* 55 (January 1988): 3–32.

Joyce, James. *A Portrait of the Artist as a Young Man.* 1916. New York: Viking, 1968.

Konigsburg, E. L. *From the Mixed-Up Files of Mrs. Basil E. Frankweiler.* New York: Atheneum, 1967.

Leaf, Munro. *Noodle.* Illus. Ludwig Bemelmans. 1937; New York: Scholastic, 1968.

Lewis, C. S. "On Three Ways of Writing for Children." *Children's Literature: Views and Reviews.* Ed. Virginia Haviland. Glenview: Scott, Foresman, 1973. 231–240.

Lionni, Leo. *Fish Is Fish.* New York: Pantheon, 1970.

Montgomery, L. M. *Anne of Green Gables.* 1908; Toronto: Seal-McClelland and Stewart/Bantam, 1981.

Moss, Anita. "The Spear and the Piccolo: Heroic and Pastoral Dimensions of William Steig's *Dominic* and *Abel's Island.*" *Children's Literature* 10 (1982): 124–140.
Pearce, Philippa. "The Writer's View of Childhood." *Horn Book Reflections.* Ed. Elinor Whitney Field. Boston: Horn Book, 1969. 49–53.
Poss, Geraldine D. "An Epic in Arcadia: The Pastoral World of *The Wind in the Willows.*" *Children's Literature* 4 (1975): 80–90.
Potter, Beatrix. *The Tale of Mr. Jeremy Fisher.* London: Frederick Warne, 1906.
———. *The Tale of Peter Rabbit.* London: Frederick Warne, 1902.
Rey, H. A. *Curious George.* Boston: Houghton Mifflin, 1941.
Sarland, Charles. "Chorister Quartet." *The Signal Approach to Children's Books.* Ed. Nancy Chambers. Metuchen: Scarecrow, 1980. 217–224.
Scheidlinger, Lucy Prince. *The Little Bus Who Liked Home Best.* New York: Fernand & Spertus, 1955.
Sendak, Maurice. *Where the Wild Things Are.* New York: Harper & Row, 1963.
Smedman, Sarah M. "Springs of Hope: Recovery of Primordial Time in 'Mythic' Novels for Young Readers." *Children's Literature* 16 (1988): 91–107.
Steig, William. *Dr. De Soto.* New York: Farrar, Straus and Giroux, 1982.
Stevenson, Robert Louis. *Treasure Island.* 1883. London: Collins, 1953.
White, E. B. *Charlotte's Web.* 1952. New York-Trophy: Harper & Row, 1973.
Yorinks, Arthur. *Hey, Al.* Illus. Richard Egielski. New York: Farrar, Straus and Giroux, 1986.

CHAPTER 8

Literature in Wider Contexts

HISTORY, CULTURE, AND THEORY

The similarities we notice in the texts we read aren't just the ones we can account for by the idea of genre. Texts written at approximately the same time tend to have much in common with one another. So do those written in the same country. If we know something about the events of history or about the traits of a specific culture, we can see how texts relate to the time and place in which they were written—and, also, how these circumstances can throw light on the texts and add to our enjoyment of them. It is also possible to think about a text in the context of literature as a whole—in terms of the essential characteristics of texts as perceived by literary theorists or as suggested by the ideas of thinkers in fields as diverse as psychoanalysis and anthropology. In this chapter, we will consider children's literature in the contexts of history and culture, and in terms of a variety of literary and other theories.

Class and Gender

Beatrix Potter's picture books are a good example of how texts both reveal and are illuminated by the values of their time. Even though her characters are animals, their society resembles the turn-of-the-century England that Potter herself knew. In that society, class distinctions were important, and those who considered themselves gentlemen were people of privilege. Jeremy Fisher is such a gentleman—he's called *Mr.;* he's friends with an alderman, Mr. Ptolemy Tortoise, and even with a member of the aristocracy, *Sir* Isaac Newton; and he wears the clothes of a man of high social standing: a cutaway coat and an embroidered pink vest. If we can see the extent of Jeremy's social pretensions, then the joke of his being merely a frog under his fancy waistcoat, and having to suffer indignities from creatures as insignificant as a water beetle and a stickleback, becomes even funnier.

Jeremy ends his days having dinner with his two male friends. Kenneth Grahame's *Wind in the Willows,* published two years after *The Tale of Mr. Jeremy Fisher,* in 1908, is also about a group of exclusively male, distinctly British animals who spend their time socializing with each other. From the viewpoint of our own time, the absence of females from the group seems odd; it might suggest something about their sexual preferences. Had these two books been written in the 1990s, we might best explain their oddity by assuming that they were designed to give children a healthy attitude toward a homosexual life-style.

But if we have read other works of fiction for both children and adults written around the same time as these two texts, or if we know something from our reading of nonfiction about the social and cultural history of the early 1900s, then we realize that Potter's and Grahame's animals are merely living as conventional young gentlemen did in England at the turn of the century. For audiences of their own time, the behavior of these animals would not necessarily have suggested anything about their sexual preferences. Our knowledge of history and culture can help us understand which of our possible interpretations of a book are the most likely ones.

EXPLORATION: Choose (or have children choose) any other text written for children in an earlier time. In what ways do its assumptions about behavior vary from ones that are currently popular? After doing some historical research, determine to what extent the variations might be accounted for by the circumstances of the time the text was written.

Attitudes toward gender are an interesting aspect of historical and cultural differences. In *The Tale of Peter Rabbit,* Peter's sisters act according to then conventional assumptions about femininity and passively obey their mother's instructions to pick berries, while Peter fulfills traditional stereotypes of male behavior by defying his mother, striking out on his own, and seeking adventure. Other books written at about the same time display similar attitudes. In L. M. Montgomery's *Anne of Green Gables,* published seven years after *Peter Rabbit,* Anne's adventures are relatively minor domestic ones, nothing like the exciting and life-threatening escapades that boys experience in novels like Robert Louis Stevenson's *Treasure Island* (1883) or Rudyard Kipling's *The Jungle Book* (1894).

On the other hand, Anne is more active than Peter Rabbit's sisters, and the millions of female readers who have adored Anne have tended to claim that they admire her for her tomboyish independence more than for the security of her life. Similarly, the millions of girls who have enjoyed reading Louisa May Alcott's *Little Women* have generally singled out the tomboyish Jo as the March sister they most identify with—not the sweet Meg or the saintly Beth, both of whom represent more traditionally desirable feminine traits. Both Anne and Jo represent a blending of traditional ideas of masculinity and femininity; despite their supposed independence of mind, both are willing to accept the restrictions imposed on them by their femininity. From the viewpoint of our own time, Anne and Jo seem to engage in a form of rebellion that, in the end, does not seriously threaten conventional values.

In other words, these books play complex games with conventional notions of gender and with the desire of readers both to accept and to transcend such notions. Once we know something about those conventional ideas, we can enjoy our perceptions of the games.

Nationality

The characters in many American children's novels take it for granted that anyone, no matter how humble, can improve his or her lot in life and achieve a dream. That basic unquestioned assumption defines them as Americans. It is not shared so unquestioningly, however, by the British animals in *Wind in the Willows,* who tend to be content with the ways things are.

I am not suggesting that American novels like *Charlotte's Web* do not support the idea that people should accept their limitations, or that the characters in *Wind in the Willows* have no aspirations. But in American texts, acceptance of limitations often actually allows the characters to aspire toward realistic goals. When Wilbur learns that he can't spin webs like Charlotte, he realizes how much he likes who he is and aspires to stay alive—a goal he can and does reach. On the other hand, the characters in *Wind in the Willows* who aspire to change their lives are merely silly. Rat's wish to travel to foreign lands is seen as a momentary aberration, a lapse from sanity, and Toad's lust for motor cars is shown to be both ridiculous and dangerous. The differences between these books reveal significant differences in national character, ones that can be explored interestingly in numerous other books.

EXPLORATIONS: (1) Read (or have children read) a number of books from another country, such as Canada or Australia. Consider whether they share qualities that might be accounted for by national characteristics.

(2) Or is it dangerous to think that nationalities have *characteristics? Does it encourage stereotyping and lead to bigotry and prejudice?*

READING AGAINST A TEXT

We can focus on the ways in which books express the values of specific historical periods and cultures only if we remain at some distance from them and allow ourselves to think about how the views they present differ from our own. In other words, we must become conscious of what are sometimes called a text's *absences,* the ideas or assumptions it takes for granted and therefore does not actually assert. Our awareness of absences allows both children and adults to enjoy stories written in different times without assuming that sexist or racist or just plain old-fashioned values in the stories are ones we should share.

In order to *surface* absences—that is, bring them to our consciousness—we must first understand that they are in fact merely assumptions. As we discovered earlier in our considerations of history and of toys and TV shows, human beings have generally taken it for granted that the specific values which define their own ideals—their own ideologies—are in fact absolutely and universally true. In *The Tale of Mr. Jeremy Fisher,* for instance, Potter simply assumes the universality of the social hierarchy underlying her characters' motivations and responses. The book does not assert that there is a social scale which places water beetles lower than frogs, but takes for granted that there is such a social scale and that everyone knows it. Because writers assume that their specific view of reality is universal, texts act as a subtle kind of propaganda, and tend to manipulate unwary readers into an unconscious acceptance of their values.

But if we notice the absences in a text and define the ideology they imply, we can protect ourselves from unconscious persuasion. Rather than allowing ourselves to become immersed in a text to the point of accepting its description of reality as the only true one, we can define its values and so arrive at a better understanding of our own. In other words, instead of going along with the values a text implies, we can read *against* it.

Surfacing Political Assumptions

The most obvious way of reading against a text is to approach it from a point of view that questions its political and social assumptions. We do not necessarily have to share the values of the point of view we use in this way; we can merely use it as a device to allow us some distance from our assumptions in order to discover the writer's assumptions.

If we don't share Grahame's assumptions about social hierarchy, for instance, it is not difficult to see how Grahame's *Wind in the Willows* asks readers to take its social hierarchy for granted: the book never questions the assumption of the gentlemanly riverbank animals that the creatures who live in the wild woods are their social and moral inferiors. It would be revealing to think about the events the book describes from the point of view of these citizens of the Wild Woods; in fact, Jan Needle has done just that in his novel *Wild Wood,* which describes how the poverty of the woodland creatures, caused in part by the thoughtlessness of the wealthy Mr. Toad, drives them to rebellion against their supposed superiors; they are not so much thieves and rascals as they are oppressed and deprived. Needle's novel cleverly fills in the absences of Grahame's.

The closer the values of a text come to our own ideologies, the harder it is to read its absences. In some cases it may be impossible. But even then the attempt to do so is worthwhile. We can ask ourselves *why* it is that certain books strike us as being convincingly realistic, and we can help children better understand themselves by encouraging them to do so also.

Surfacing Assumptions about Gender

Another way of reading against a text is to notice its assumptions about gender—as we did in considering the ways in which books by writers like Montgomery and Alcott portray their female characters. As has often been pointed out, gender bias has been so deeply rooted in our culture that words like "he" and "him" traditionally referred to both males and females, but words like "she" and "her" referred only to females. In other words, while a "he" was supposed to be merely a genderless human being, a "she" was specifically female, set apart by gender from the typical state of being human.

Traditionally, writers have assumed that their audience consists of "he's": that is, of either males or females who, while they read, are conscious only of that aspect of their being which is not specifically female—of their basic genderless humanity. But, of course, the "he's" implied as the audience of literature are no more genderless than the "he's" of traditional grammar. In equating the male with the typically human, both literature and grammar suggest that women are less than human, and that femininity is a sign of inferiority.

The extent to which implications of male superiority color literature becomes apparent to anybody who stops reading as a "typical" human being, without consciousness of gender—as a traditional "he"—and tries to read with a consciousness of gender—as a traditional "she." A girl or a woman can read without ignoring her femaleness, as many feminist literary critics do; a boy or a man can read without ignoring the extent to which his responses are governed by the specific limitations of his maleness.

To read in this way is to become conscious of the absences of literary texts that relate specifically to gender. We can see how Anne Shirley's rebellion and ambition in *Anne of Green Gables* are controlled by the need for her to remain acceptably feminine, a good mother and homemaker. Or we can realize how much *Charlotte's Web* asks us to admire the undemanding, selfless, maternal love that Charlotte offers Wilbur: Charlotte devotes herself to Wilbur at the expense of her own needs in a way many people would find less admirable if she were a male and he a female.

EXPLORATION: Try (or ask children to try) reading any children's text "as a woman"—that is, with consciousness of the text's assumptions about gender.

If it is possible to read like a woman, then it should be equally possible to write like one. Feminist literary critics have explored books by women to see if they differ significantly from books by men.

Some critics pursue these investigations from the conviction that women are essentially and inherently different from men, that biological differences create differences in attitude. Others believe that the possibility of differences in attitudes means only that the different experiences society offers women and men have led them to think differently of themselves and of others.

In any case, feminist critics have discovered that women tend not only to write about different aspects of experience—as an obvious example, domestic events rather than adventures in the big world away from home—but also to do so in different ways. For instance, it seems that the way we usually describe the plot of a story or a novel—as a single, unified action that rises toward a climax and then quickly comes to an end—accurately describes the action of many books written by men (and also, of course, of many written by women who have accepted the conventional ideal). But that definition of plot would suggest that the more episodic events of books like *Anne of Green Gables* are amateurish and unexciting; *Anne* has many less intense climaxes rather than one central one, and there's not much unity in its action. Nevertheless, *Anne of Green Gables* is a pleasurable book, even though the pleasure is different from that offered in suspenseful books like *Treasure Island.* Furthermore, many other enjoyable books for both children and adults are similarly episodic—and a large proportion of them are by women. Apparently some women prefer a different kind of pattern of events from the one conventionally assumed to be desirable.

As we saw in Chapter 6, Robert Scholes has likened the pleasure in narrative to that of sexuality. He has suggested that the "archetype of all fiction is the sexual act . . . the fundamental orgastic rhythm of tumescence and detumescence, of tension and resolution, of intensification to the point of climax and consummation" (26). But physiological studies suggest that what Scholes is describing here is typical *male* sexuality—and that female sexuality might just as typically express itself in rhythmic patterns like those of *Anne of Green Gables.* As Beatrice Faust suggests, "Female sexuality can include both intense arousal, which seeks release in orgasm, and a pleasant drift on the plateau level of arousal, which may continue indefinitely" (59).

Furthermore, the fact that the care and education of children have traditionally been the domain of women has meant that a large proportion of the writers and editors of texts for children have been (and continue to be) women. Women have largely been responsible for the development of children's literature, so if this literature has distinct traits, they might well be those that can be identified in women's writing in general. If so, then even male writers who try to satisfy the generic characteristics of children's literature would be writing as women.

In fact, many children's books by males do have an episodic series of minor climaxes rather than one major one. As we discovered, too, many of the genre characteristics we explored in Chapter 7 might be identified as feminine. Perhaps children's literature as a whole is a sort of women's literature. That may explain why so many of the children who are ardent readers are females.

EXPLORATION: Consider (or have children consider) the degree to which characteristics such as repetition or the striking of a balance between the desires of the individual and the needs of the social group might be considered feminine. How might these relate to your own assumptions about female characteristics?

But even if we assume that one sort of plot is inherently male and the other inherently female, we should not conclude that only men can enjoy the more conventional plots, and only women the episodic ones—or that if children's literature is a form of women's writing, only girls should enjoy it. For centuries, women have learned to take pleasure in the kinds of plots that seem to be inherently male. There is no reason why men cannot learn to take pleasure from the kinds of plots that seem to be inherently female—and, thus, if these *are* female plots, to develop some insight into the nature of femininity. A world in which both boys and girls had escaped conventional gender assumptions enough to enjoy, equally, *Anne of Green Gables* and *Treasure Island* would be a healthy one.

Surfacing Assumptions about Race

Just as the texts of a male-dominated society inevitably express a male view as if it were a universal one, and, thus, ask women readers to think like men, the texts of a white-dominated society inevitably express a white view as if it were a universal one—and, thus, ask black or native American readers to think like whites. Consequently, another way of reading against a text is to surface its assumptions about race. To what degree does the behavior of the characters represent racial stereotypes?

As with traditional statements of praise for the nobility of a woman's sacrifice of her own goals in the service of others, racial stereotypes sometimes mask their disdain under apparent praise. Many texts depict nobly innocent natives or blissfully ingenuous blacks whose lack of sophistication prevents them from taking part in white corruption. The apparent nobility is just a polite way of asserting a belittling deviation from white normalcy.

Furthermore, a sense of racial otherness is sometimes so unconscious that it expresses itself in highly subtle ways. A possible example is Paula Fox's award-winning *The Slave Dancer,* a beautifully written book about life on a slave ship, which I had greatly admired. Recently in a children's literature class, however, I was surprised and then convinced by a student's claim that this book expresses a subtle racism. The author has chosen to tell the story of the suffering of captured black slaves from the point of view of a white adolescent who has himself been shanghaied onto the ship, and there seems to be an assumption that young readers of this book would probably identify with such a point of view—not with the blacks who are being so cruelly mistreated, but instead with a white outsider who learns to feel sympathy for their plight. Presumably, then, the audience is white—and perhaps, also, those blacks willing to think about the history of their people from the point of view of a white person.

It is certainly true that the point of view makes the white protagonist's emotional upset at having to observe suffering seem more important than the physical pain he observes. And if we think about the book in this way, we realize that the blacks in the book are left without a voice, and with no way to speak of their own suffering or tell their own story. We are told of only three words spoken by a black; and one of these is mispronounced.

EXPLORATIONS: (1) At this point, I'm confused about my response to The Slave Dancer. *I have no doubt that it is a finely constructed work of art, one that I still find deeply affecting. But I wonder if my saying that means I am somehow accepting these racist implications. You might read the book (or have children read it) and see if you can reach a conclusion about these matters.*

(2) Read some of the critical discussions of the racist implications in children's texts listed under the "Minorities" section of "Contexts of Culture and Ideology" in Chapter 15. Try (or ask children to try) to apply the methods of surfacing racial stereotypes used in these discussions to other children's texts about blacks, Latinos, natives, or other marginalized groups.

READING IN THE CONTEXT OF MYTHS AND ARCHETYPES

Up to this point, we have examined how we can enrich our enjoyment and understanding of a literary text by considering it in relation to other texts it seems similar to: written in the same time or place, by the same author, or in the same genre. It is also possible to think about a text in the context of literature as a whole. Literary theorists try to find patterns that recur in text after text—basic patterns that underlie and give shape and meaning to stories or poems. Different theorists made use of the discoveries of pyschoanalysts, linguists, and others to uncover a fascinating variety of different patterns: symbols, myths, archetypes, motifs, codes, functions. Knowing something about these patterns enables us to identify the place of any specific book in relation to all the books we know.

The sections that follow offer brief introductions to theories that might be useful in a consideration of children's literature. I've included this material as a kind of menu of possibilities, an idea of the kinds of thinking that can be done about literary texts.

You will have learned something important even if you do no more than realize that this variety of possibilities exists. On the other hand, somewhere in this menu of possibilities you might find a way of thinking about literature that satisfies you. If you find your interest sparked by the brief descriptions of any of these theories, I encourage you to pursue your interest in them by reading the works of critical theory listed in Chapter 15.

Psychoanalytical Perspectives

The theories of Sigmund Freud suggest that the motivations for human behavior are often unconscious, buried in parts of our mind about which we have no conscious knowledge. But the material we have buried in our unconscious expresses itself through the images and plots both of dreams and of literature. Equipped with some knowledge of Freudian ideas, we can develop surprising interpretations of the plots and images of even very simple texts. We will examine the Freudian insights of Bruno Bettelheim and Jacques Lacan.

Bettelheim. The American child psychologist Bruno Bettelheim reads "Cinderella" as a story of sibling rivalry and Oedipal jealousy. Children typically believe that their parents prefer their siblings, just as Cinderella's stepmother prefers Cinderella's stepsisters; and the fact that this parent figure is not actually Cinderella's mother represents the Oedipal desire of children to eliminate the parent of their own sex and thus pave the way for the relationship they unconsciously desire with the parent of the other sex. According to Bettelheim, Cinderella's situation at the beginning of the story represents the self-disgust a child feels about his or her desire to be loved by the parent of the opposite sex; "Since the child has such 'dirty' wishes," the child identifies with Cinderella, "who is relegated to sit among the cinders. . . . that is where he also belongs, and where he would also end up if his parents knew of his desires" (243).

Bettelheim explains the events of the story as a working out of these psychological problems. The slipper at the end of the story represents "castration anxiety": "According to Freudian theory the girl's castration complex centers on her imagining that originally all children had penises and that girls somehow lost theirs" (266), just as Cinderella loses her slipper. But it also represents the vagina; the prince "symbolically offers her femininity in the form of the golden slipper-vagina: male acceptance of the vagina and love for the woman is the ultimate male validation of the desirability of her femininity" (271).

Lacan. In recent years, Freud's ideas have been reworked by the French psychoanalyst Jacques Lacan in terms of the findings of structural linguistics. Lacan's writing is complex and often deliberately mysterious; Jane Gallop suggests that Lacan's *Ecrits* are "designed to force the reader into a perpetual struggle of his own with the text" (45). As a result, Lacan's ideas have been applied to literature in a variety of ways; one small example based on just one thread of a complex weaving of ideas can suggest the possibilities.

For Lacan, the "selves" we see ourselves as being are as fictional as the stories of written fiction—limited images like those we see in mirrors when we first become conscious of our separateness—and, so, fiction can be read in terms of the way it echoes our basic human activity of inventing ourselves and then becoming conscious of the limitations of our inventions. All that we usually call reality is in fact fiction, and always less complete than the actual "real," the world outside our consciousness.

A Lacanian reading of a text like "Cinderella" might then turn out to invert its apparent meaning: the "happy" ending transforms Cinderella from a multifaceted being in intimate and intuitive contact with the basic elements of existence, with fire and ash and household dirt, into a fixed and limited creature comfortably placed within the fixed and limited scheme of things. She has become a "subject" in the double sense of the word, not just provided with a specific subjectivity or individuality, but also subject to or dominated by a specific and therefore repressive version of reality. (For Lacan, our "selves" are actually like the grammatical subjects of sentences, apparently in control but with their meaning circumscribed by other components of the entity they are part of. Because we can only speak through a shared language, the "I" who speaks must always express a shared communal vision rather than a unique private one.)

As Cinderella accepts her godmother's transformation of a variety of objects into things of immediate practical use to herself—things that will transform her into the conventional image of an acceptable woman—she becomes for herself what she imagines she should be for others. In terms of Lacan's idea of "the mirror stage," she has imagined her whole self to be as limited as the part of herself that she sees in her mirror and that she imagines others see also. In doing so, she loses touch with the world and with people beyond her own limited imagining. For Lacan, that sort of loss is inevitable. The story of Cinderella shows how human beings develop a sense of something lacking and so inevitably lose wholeness in the process of becoming themselves.

Convincing Interpretations? Interpretations like Bettelheim's and Lacan's do not convince everyone. Many people are repelled by the idea that human minds are so obsessed with sexual concerns, or frightened by the idea that so much that happens to us is beyond our conscious knowledge and control. In fact, the very concepts of a Freudian "unconscious" or a Lacanian "real" that exists beyond our ability to think of it make such interpretations impossible to prove. Because they describe what happens in an area of the mind beyond our rational contact, they are like the beliefs of religious faith, which also transcend rational contact, albeit in a different direction: we can't prove or disprove them, we can merely accept or not accept them.

Even so, these interpretations are thought provoking. Even those who end up rejecting the positions they've considered can learn much from having considered them.

EXPLORATION: After reading a psychoanalytical commentary such as Bettelheim's Uses of Enchantment, *explore your own position on these matters.*

Jung and the Collective Unconscious

Bettelheim's description of the Oedipal content of "Cinderella" relates the story to dream imagery and to many other stories and novels that Freudians would call different versions of the basic family drama of sibling rivalry and sexual jealousy, a drama which all families share but which nevertheless develops independently in each human being. The Swiss psychoanalyst Carl Jung broke with Freud when he decided that the contents of the unconscious transcend the individual experience of separate people. Instead, Jung posited a *collective unconscious,* shared by and present in all humans, and saw the imagery of the collective unconscious, as expressed both in dreams and in literature, as *archetypal.* According to Jung, when we experience the presence of archetypes, "the voice of all mankind resounds in us" (320) and "that is the secret of great art, and of its effect upon us. The creative process . . . consists in the unconscious activation of an archetypal image, and in elaborating and shaping this image into the finished work" (321).

From a Jungian viewpoint, children's fiction can be explored for archetypal plots, such as the recurring story of "the hero with a thousand faces" that Joseph Campbell finds retold in myths from around the world. The basic plot of children's fiction, in which characters leave home to seek adventure and then are sufficiently transformed by their adventure to return home in triumph, is a version of this archetypal plot.

A key Jungian archetype is the *shadow,* which for Jung represents the dark aspects of the personality. In *Mere Creatures,* Elliott Gose sees the Wild Things in Sendak's *Where the Wild Things Are* as the child Max's antisocial tendencies—as his shadow. They are animal-like, for the shadow represents lower aspects of our being that we tend to identify with animals; they are also tricksters, beings like those found in myths around the world which represent the power of anarchic impulse. For Gose, this makes Sendak's picture book into a retelling of a basic Jungian story about how one recognizes and absorbs one's shadow in the process of becoming an integrated, healthy person.

EXPLORATION: Read a Jungian interpretation of a children's text, such as those in Gose's Mere Creatures. *Try (or have children try) to explore a literary text using an approach like Gose's. What does your exploration reveal? Are there important aspects of the text that you have to neglect in focusing on archetypes?*

Frye's Archetypes

While the complex theory of literary classification developed by the Canadian critic Northrop Frye relates closely to Jung's idea of archetypes, Frye limits the scope of the archetypes to literature itself: "I mean by an archetype a symbol which connects one poem with another, and thereby helps to unify and integrate our literary experience" (99). Frye sees literature as a whole as having built up its own archetypal images and patterns of organization over the centuries. He has developed a system for classifying literature by means of these archetypal patterns that throws light on all kinds of literature—on comic books and Nancy Drew novels as well as on recognized classics.

Frye's system places each work of literature at a particular place in an intersecting set of classifications, including differing forms of symbols, differing genres like drama, poetry, and fiction, and differing perspectives from which authors speak. For our purposes, the most interesting of Frye's classifications is *modes:* kinds of relationships between characters and their environments. There are four modes, and the chronological sequence in which they appeared, over time, reveals that each is a *displacement* of the one historically preceding it; that is, each succeeding mode tells the same story in a version less ideal and imaginary and more naturalistic than the mode before it.

The first and purest mode is *myth,* which tells of heroes superior in kind to other humans and to their environment: gods. The second mode, *romance,* tells of heroes superior in degree to other humans and to the environment: not gods, but idealized men and women. There are two modes that describe what is usually called realistic fiction: *high mimetic,* which tells of heroes superior in degree to others but not to the environment, and *low mimetic,* which tells of heroes superior neither to others nor to their environment. The final, and most displaced, mode is the *ironic,* which tells of characters inferior to others in power or intelligence.

A certain kind of children's literature fits into each of these categories. Most obviously, there are many children's versions of traditional myths. Frye himself identifies fairy tales like "Cinderella" and "Snow White" as romance, and high fantasies like Ursula Le Guin's *Wizard of Earthsea* would also qualify. *Charlotte's Web* might be considered to be high mimetic: Charlotte is superior to others, but subject to the forces of nature that bring about her inevitable death. Indeed, most children's novels are to some degree high mimetic, for their main characters do finally triumph over the environment. Nevertheless, some might be considered low mimetic: certainly Laura Ingalls Wilder's Little House books describe ordinary people who rarely master their naturalistic environments. Given the basic optimism of children's literature, we might expect the ironic mode to be the least well represented. But "The Princess and the Pea" and the poems by Belloc we looked at in Chapter 7 describe characters less intelligent than their audience is supposed to be. Indeed, a surprising amount of children's literature is ironic, in that it gives us the pleasure of feeling superior to characters like Simple Simon or the Three Sillies.

EXPLORATION: Consider (or have children consider) which of the modes a particular text falls into.

Just making these classifications isn't particularly interesting. But doing so might offer teachers a way to organize children's reading experiences. According to the critic Virginia Wolf, children's novels imply an increasingly sophisticated audience as they become more displaced, and so confirm "Frye's theory that the cycle of literature from the mythic mode, through the romantic and mimetic modes to the ironic mode requires an increasingly sophisticated reader" (49). If we accept Wolf's conclusion, it provides a logical way of organizing the literary experience of children from least displaced to most displaced, so that previous reading provides a solid base for later reading.

But in terms of our response to individual texts, Frye's classifications are revealing only when we use them as schemata and become conscious of what they leave out of consideration. Each of the works I named as representing a mode can also be seen to contain some characteristics of the other modes. Since there are moments in *Charlotte's Web* that ask us to laugh at Wilbur because we feel superior to him, the text is ironic as well as high mimetic. On the other hand, the very fact that people read "The Princess and the Pea" without consciousness of its irony suggests that it still offers some of the pleasure of the form it parodies. It is a romance as well as a displaced parody of a romance. Meanwhile, the most popular versions of fairy tales tend to be those that place the central romantic story in a displaced ironic context: Disney movies that focus on dwarfs or mice we can feel superior to as well as perfect princes and princesses we can look up to. Even children's versions of myths tend to mix modes: they often add realistic details in order to humanize the heroes and make them seem less distantly ideal. Our consciousness of a classificatory system like Frye's modes allows us not only to consider the significance of these uncharacteristic features but also to perceive what makes distinct works distinct.

READING IN THE CONTEXT OF STRUCTURAL PATTERNS

Frye's classifications focus on the plots of literary works as a whole. Other literary theorists have looked for inherent similarities in the parts that make up those wholes, in order to develop a grammar of stories: a description of the basic elements which are common to all stories but which relate to each other in particular stories in ways that give the stories their distinctiveness. In this context we will consider the work of Claude Lévi-Strauss, Vladimir Propp, and Roland Barthes.

Lévi-Strauss and Structural Analysis

The French anthropologist Claude Lévi-Strauss suggests that all cultures are formed of the same elements, just as all sentences are formed of the same basic parts of speech. The elements of cultures are social groupings—families, clans, classes. The differences in cultures, like the differences in the meanings of sentences, come from the different ways in which these elements are related to each other. If we apply such an idea to literature, we can determine the elements—their central ideas and images—and then explore particular texts in terms of how these elements relate to each other. Such a procedure is a *structural analysis.*

Lévi-Strauss himself asserts that myths represent significant transformations in the cultures that produced them—that myths are stories of the change from one orderly system of relationships to another. If we assume that all stories follow that model, then we can explore one story in order to see how it describes a shifting of relationships. We can determine its essential elements, and then explore how the relationships between the elements shift between the state of equilibrium described at the beginning and the one described at the end.

In the fairy tale "Snow White," for instance, we might identify the characters with elements representing values: the stepmother with aggressiveness and Snow White with passivity. We can then see how the story moves from a state of affairs in which aggressiveness has authority to one in which passivity has authority. We might then also see how the story justifies a conservative attitude, for the independent-minded woman who tries to get her own way is defeated by the woman who accepts what is without question.

The structural analysis I have just done assumes, as all such analyses do, that stories comprise an intellectual debate in which major ideas compete with each other. Seen in this way, the elements of literature are ideas like good and evil, appearance and reality, aggression and passivity, hope and despair, and even more basic oppositions like softness and hardness, cold and warmth, growth and stagnation—oppositions like those we saw as characteristic of children's literature as a genre in Chapter 7. Stories describe how these *binary opposites* conflict with and relate to each other in various ways. Thus "Snow White" is a story of good, identified with softness and passivity, triumphing over evil, identified with hardness and aggression. Because we might not expect weakness to triumph over strength, the story is also about the difference between appearance and reality. The images in the story relate to these ideas: the Queen's magic mirror, suggesting her self-involvement, is contrasted with the open window through which Snow White's mother first sees snow and wishes—not egotistically for beauty, but charitably for the growth of new life. These relationships shift into a new pattern when the Prince sees Snow White neither through a window nor in a mirror, but apparently dead inside a glass coffin.

This kind of focus on basic elements accomplishes two things. It points up the unity of stories by revealing how their parts relate to one another. And as we saw in considering the binary oppositions of children's literature, it shows how a literary work relates to others by describing differing relationships between the same basic elements.

Propp and Functions

Other structural theories focus less on patterns of binary opposites than on the components of plots. According to the folklorist Vladimir Propp, the plots of all the Russian folktales he explored consist of thirty-one basic *functions,* which he listed and numbered. While not all the tales contain all the functions, the functions always appear in the same sequence. The functions are a grammar of actions—an underlying structure of relationships between events that gives coherence to the plots of these and presumably all stories. Consider how stories as diverse as "Cinderella," *Peter Rabbit,* and *Charlotte's Web* express some of this representative group of Propp's functions (the wording is mine):

- **2.** The hero is forbidden to do something.
- **3.** The hero violates the rule.
- **8a.** One member of a family lacks something or desires to have something.
- **9.** Misfortune or lack is made known; the hero is approached with a request or a command and is allowed to go or is dispatched.
- **11.** The hero leaves home.
- **12.** The hero is tested, interrogated, attacked, etc.; the action prepares the way for the hero's receiving either a magical agent or helper.
- **20.** The hero returns.
- **24.** A false hero presents unfounded claims.
- **27.** The hero is recognized.

EXPLORATION: Consider (or have children consider) how one of the texts mentioned or another text of your choice expresses these functions.

If we combine the binary opposites of structuralism with Propp's functions, we can see how each text represents two crosscutting structural patterns: the pattern of ideas and images that make up the binary opposites and the sequenced pattern of events in the plot. These two kinds of patterns are the ones we saw, in Chapter 6, interweaving in our consideration of the discourse of a text.

Barthes and Codes

Roland Barthes has described yet another set of elements of literary works. Working from the ideas of structural linguistics, Barthes believes that any story or poem—or for that matter, any object, any sweater or house or advertisement—is meaningful only because it evokes our previous knowledge of various *codes:* rules or systems of meaning. To give an obvious example: the color red does not inherently mean danger, but drivers stop at a red light because the code ''red light'' has a particular meaning for them. If we apply this idea to literature, we see that our ability to find meaning in stories and poems depends on our knowledge of numerous codes: the dictionary meanings of words, the meanings indicated by the position of words in sentences, the connotations we attach both to words and to the objects they represent, our methods of consistency building, our understanding of story patterns, our expectations of genre, and so on.

In *S/Z,* Barthes suggests that a given work of literature represents the combination and intersection of five basic codes. The codes can be summarized as follows:

- The *proairetic* code, which evokes our knowledge of actions as implied by a text: for instance, what walking or sitting or gossiping is. Decoding a story requires our ability to perceive it as a series of separate but connected actions (the plot).
- The *hermeneutic* code, which defines our expectations of how stories raise questions, create suspense, and provide answers. ''Hermeneutic'' refers to interpretation.
- The code of *semes,* or connotations: the range of associated meanings that the words of a text bring with them beyond their primary, or dictionary, meaning. For instance, the word ''girl'' connotes femininity.
- The code of *symbols:* the meanings the words of a text have as representations of ideas separate from their primary meaning. For instance, in a particular context the word ''path'' might symbolize a person's course of action.
- The *cultural* code, which evokes our knowledge of the values and practices of specific cultures as expressed in a text.

Barthes shows how a text can be broken down into basic units, or *lexis,* each of which evokes a specific code. Using this method, I have developed the following analysis of *Peter Rabbit:*

The Tale of Peter Rabbit[1]

> Once upon a time[2] there were four little bunnies[3] who lived with their mother[4] in a sandy bank under a tree.[5]
>
> [1] The title raises a question that will be answered later: what is Peter Rabbit? A human? An animal? A recipe for preparing rabbit meat? (HERMENEUTIC)

[2] The phrase arouses our knowledge of and expectations for a certain kind of story—the fairy tale. (CULTURAL)
[3] The word "bunnies" has connotations that are different from those of the word "rabbits." It evokes the softness and cuteness of humanized fantasy animals. (SEMIC)
[4] "Mother" evokes our cultural understanding of the roles of mothers in the lives of children (CULTURAL—knowledge of sociology and psychology). Another question is raised. Why just with mother? Where is father? (HERMENEUTIC)
[5] As opposed to bunnies, who live in humanlike houses, real rabbits live in sandy banks, which usually are a good place for fir trees to grow. (CULTURAL—knowledge of zoology and horticulture). This adds another question: how can these "bunnies" also be "rabbits"? (HERMENEUTIC)

UNITY AND DECONSTRUCTION

The various strategies and theories of reading literature that we have considered in Chapters 6, 7, and 8 operate on the same underlying premise. They assume that literary texts have unity or consistency—that is, that all their elements support their central idea, that they are coherent and complete, and that they express coherent visions of the world.

On that assumption, we approach texts as outlined in Chapter 6: with the idea that, for example, the glass objects of "Snow White," the mirrors, windows, coffins—relate meaningfully to each other. Or we try to understand how the many lists in *Charlotte's Web* relate to the story's central concern with "the glory of everything." And once we discover (or, perhaps, create) such relationships in a text, we praise it for its unity.

In recent years, literary theorists have questioned both the possibility and the desirability of unity. Something can be unified only if it is complete. How can a text be complete if its meanings depend on contexts outside itself: on the meanings of the words of which it is composed, on the codes and connotations it evokes, on its relationships to other works of literature? No text is truly closed off.

According to the theorist Jacques Derrida, our sense of the meaning of a word depends on our ability to separate it from all the things it does not mean. Consequently, any given word evokes and depends on meanings unlike or opposite its own. In fact, each word implies the idea of its opposite, and if we explore a text carefully, we will find passages in which that process becomes apparent—where we can perceive what we earlier called absences. We'll discover the cracks in its structure, places where it disguises illogicalities or hides gaps in order to seem complete, or even turns on its apparent meanings and says just the opposite.

This sort of reading is called *deconstruction.* It is not destruction, but an exploration of the constructions of literature to determine the extent of their artificiality, how they *are* constructed or manufactured, and how they work to disguise their own artifice. If we believe that literature represents the real world, we might find it disconcerting to realize how artificial and incomplete are the worlds it describes. But if we believe, with theorists like Barthes, Lacan, and Derrida, that "reality" is itself a series of fictions we create, a set of artificial constructs, then the process of "deconstructing" a text becomes an act of consciousness raising, an insight into the relationships of imagination and logic, fiction and reality.

For instance, we might "deconstruct" *Peter Rabbit* by noticing how it moves against its apparent message. The plot seems to suggest that he who disobeys mother deserves punishment—that mother is always right. But mother, who knows her son well, nearly defies him to disobey her: it is almost as if she encourages his raid on the garden. Peter then has an exciting adventure, whereas his obedient sisters spend a boring day in the heat. Furthermore, Peter survives, despite his mother's warning about his father's death. Perhaps Peter proves his superiority to his father? Perhaps his mother is unconsciously offering him a test to see if he is fit to take charge of the family—a test which he passes? If the story can evoke these possibilities, then the apparent unity with which it supports a message of passive obedience is clearly just an illusion: it can make both that statement and its opposite.

All literature can be seen to make contradictory assertions—and reading with the ingenuity to discover how it does so can be highly enjoyable. This is not to say that anyone can read any text and assume it means anything at all—for meaning depends on context, and in order to persuade others of the meanings we find in literature, we have to explain the contexts that allow us to read as we do. Not any meaning will do, then. But any meaning we can justify and that we can take pleasure in explaining is worthy of consideration.

VALUE IN LITERATURE: THE CANON

The various theories of literature that we have considered raise questions about our conviction that some literary works are better than others, that some texts are trash and others are classics or masterpieces. Frye's archetypes and Barthes's codes can be found in all sorts of literature. They are equally present in Nancy Drew novels and *Charlotte's Web.* If that is true, then how do we determine what makes a literary text worthwhile? What is the difference, if there is any, between good literature and trash?

We tend to assume that good literature is serious—that, unlike trash, it expresses important truths about life. In fact, trashy literature usually says obvious things in obvious ways. Paradoxically, "good" literature seems to be far more open to interpretation than trash is. Its "truths" are elusive; scholars have been finding new ways of reading Shakespeare's *Hamlet*—and Potter's *Peter Rabbit* and White's *Charlotte's Web*—for a long time.

In fact, it is possible that what distinguishes the most important literature is its ability to engender new interpretations by its readers. Frank Kermode suggests that what makes literary texts classics is "an openness to accommodation which keeps them alive under endlessly varying dispositions" (44). What keeps them alive and causes us to consider them great is our ability to keep reading them in new ways, to be continually attentive to the as-yet-unconsidered possibilities of meaning within them.

Whether or not we accept that possibility, the question of literary value remains a contentious one. Even the concept that certain works of literature are the important ones has been called into doubt. Feminists and members of minorities have pointed out the extent to which the texts usually considered worthy of study in schools and universities—the *literary canon*—represent the values and confirm the authority of males of a particular class and color. Much has been done to broaden the canon by rediscovering and revaluing forgotten texts written in the past by women and by members of minorities. These efforts are influencing the way people think about literature. It is not as easy as it once was to take it for granted that Shakespeare's reputation depends on the inherent superiority of his work rather than on the insistence of powerful people and institutions that his work is superior.

Nevertheless, I believe that the concept of a "canon" continues to be useful, and so is the idea that some books are better than others. The process of thinking, of being human, is a matter of valuing some things over others—of making decisions about what foods we eat and what clothes we wear, and even about what principles we choose to live by, on the basis of which ones we believe to be useful, pleasurable, helpful. Knowing what we think is good—and, just as important, trying to understand why we think it is good—we can make thoughtful judgments about our new experiences.

In literature, we can do so by developing our own set of what the poet Matthew Arnold called *touchstones:* texts which have proven to be so satisfying or important to us that we can use them as schemata for judging other books. We can compare other books with them, and in doing so, understand both what makes the touchstones valuable to us and what the other books have to offer.

EXPLORATIONS: (1) What texts would you name as your own touchstones for children's literature? Why?

(2) The literary theories we have considered in this chapter represent different opinions about what matters in literature and about which ways of reading are likely to be most stimulating. My earlier discussions of reading strategies and of the characteristics of children's literature as a genre also represent such opinions, and surely my discussions of these matters reveal my own biases. Having read through the last three chapters, you might go back and consider what my biases are and how my writing reveals them. Which of the theories outlined here do I favor in the approaches I recommend, which ones do I seem to ignore or dislike? To what degree are you willing to share my assumptions and/or conclusions? Why or why not?

WORKS CITED

Alcott, Louisa May. *Little Women.* 1868. Harmondsworth, Middlesex: Puffin Penguin, 1953.

Barthes, Roland. *S/Z.* Trans. Richard Miller. New York: Hill and Wang, 1974.

Bettelheim, Bruno. *The Uses of Enchantment: The Meaning and Importance of Fairy Tales.* New York: Knopf, 1976.

Campbell, Joseph. *The Hero with a Thousand Faces.* New York: Pantheon, 1949.
Derrida, Jacques. *Of Grammatology.* Trans. Gayatri Chakravorty Spivak. Baltimore: Johns Hopkins UP, 1976.
Faust, Beatrice. *Women, Sex, and Pornography.* Harmondsworth, Middlesex: Penguin, 1981.
Fox, Paula. *The Slave Dancer.* New York: Bradbury, 1973.
Frye, Northrop. *Anatomy of Criticism: Four Essays.* Princeton: Princeton UP, 1957.
Gallop, Jane. *Reading Lacan.* Ithaca: Cornell UP, 1985.
Gose, Elliott. *Mere Creatures: A Study of Modern Fantasy Tales for Children.* Toronto: U of Toronto P, 1988.
Grahame, Kenneth. *The Wind in the Willows.* 1908. New York: Charles Scribner's Sons, 1933.
Jung, Carl G. *The Portable Jung.* Ed. Joseph Campbell. New York: Viking, 1971.
Kermode, Frank. *The Classic.* Cambridge: Harvard UP, 1983.
Kipling, Rudyard. *The Jungle Book.* 1894. Oxford: Oxford UP, 1987.
Lacan, Jacques. *Ecrits: A Selection.* Trans. Alan Sheridan. New York: Norton, 1977.
Le Guin, Ursula. *A Wizard of Earthsea.* New York: Parnassus, 1968.
Lévi-Strauss, Claude. ''The Structural Study of Myth.'' *Structural Anthropology.* Trans. Claire Jacobson and Brooke Grundfest Schoepf. Garden City: Doubleday Anchor, 1967. 202–228.
Montgomery, L. M. *Anne of Green Gables.* 1908. Toronto: Seal-McClelland and Stewart/ Bantam, 1981.
Needle, Jan. *Wild Wood.* London: André Deutsch, 1981.
Potter, Beatrix. *The Tale of Mr. Jeremy Fisher.* London: Frederick Warne, 1906.
———. *The Tale of Peter Rabbit.* London: Frederick Warne, 1902.
Propp, Vladimir. *Morphology of the Folktale.* Austin: U of Texas P, 1970.
Scholes, Robert. *Fabulation and Metafiction.* Urbana: U of Illinois P, 1979.
Stevenson, Robert Louis. *Treasure Island.* 1883. London: Collins, 1953.
White, E. B. *Charlotte's Web.* 1952. New York: Trophy–Harper & Row, 1973.
Wolf, Virginia. ''Paradise Lost? The Displacement of Myth in Children's Novels.'' *Studies in the Literary Imagination* 18.2 (Fall 1985): 47–64.

PART FOUR

Kinds of Children's Literature

So far in this book, we have considered schemata of contexts and assumptions that affect all kinds of children's literature, from nursery rhymes to young adult novels. In addition to such overall elements, each type of children's literature has unique characteristics, provides distinct pleasures, and raises specific questions of its own.

The chapters in Part Four explore the characteristics, pleasures, and questions raised by some important kinds of children's literature, in the order that young children might experience them: poetry, picture books, fairy tales, and nonfiction.

The last chapter in the section offers a discussion of qualities specific to children's fiction. But fairy tales, most picture books, and even most poems tell stories, and we will explore the extent to which nonfiction is also fictional. Because almost all children's literature is in some sense fiction, the chapter on fiction also functions as an overview of the characteristics of children's literature in general.

CHAPTER 9

Poetry

THE PLEASURES OF SOUND AND IMAGE

Many children first experience the pleasures of literature in the form of poems: nursery rhymes like this one, recited to them long before they themselves can speak or even understand much language:

> Humpty Dumpty sat on a wall,
> Humpty Dumpty had a great fall.
>   All the king's horses,
>   And all the king's men,
> Couldn't put Humpty together again.

These familiar words are decidedly strange, for they please us even though they do not seem to be very meaningful. Even if we know that the rhyme is a riddle and does make a sort of sense once we realize that Humpty Dumpty is an egg, what matters about "Humpty Dumpty" is less what it means than *how it says what it means:* the sounds of the words and the pictures they evoke rather than the simple idea about eggs that the words express. Not only is that true of all nursery rhymes, I believe it is true of all poetry.

Although poetry stresses sounds and images, it is not meaningless, nor are the meanings of poems insignificant. Even the meaning of "Humpty Dumpty" is significant. But once we've understood that meaning, we aren't likely to forget the words of "Humpty Dumpty." Instead, I think, we tend to go back and reread it, to enjoy the clever way in which these unnecessarily but delightfully complicated words express something so straightforward.

This focus on *how* something is said is most obvious in poems in which the oddities of the specific words draw attention to themselves, as they do in "Humpty Dumpty" or in poems like this one, by Carolyn Wells:

> A tutor who tooted the flute
> Tried to tutor two tooters to toot.
> Said the two to the tutor,
> "Is it harder to toot or
> To tutor two tooters to toot?"

The poem would be much less interesting if it went,

> A couple of flute students
> wondered if their teacher
> found it more difficult
> to play the instrument or
> to teach them to play it.

A little less obviously, the specific words are still an essential part of the pleasure in A. R. Ammons's "Small Song":

> The reeds give
> way to the
>
> Wind and give
> the wind away

This poem hinges on the different meanings of similar-sounding phrases about giving way to something and giving something away; it wouldn't be a poem if it said, "the reeds yield to the wind, and thus reveal it."

The specific words are just as significant a part of the experience of poems which are so insistent on the importance of their meaning that they state it clearly. We know what Langston Hughes wants to tell us in "Dreams" because he proclaims it loudly in the first line:

> Hold fast to dreams
> for if dreams die
> Life is a broken-winged bird
> That cannot fly.
>
> Hold fast to dreams
> For when dreams go
> Life is a barren field
> Frozen with snow.

What is being said here is straightforward, even obvious: don't stop aspiring, or your life will be bleak; without hope, you'll be hopeless. But Hughes makes that obvious statement interesting and important (and a poem) by expressing it in words that do more and say more than the prose version, and say it much more specifically.

His words create patterns of sound: repeating rhythms and repeating rhymes that depend on these exact words being said in this exact order. These words also evoke pictures of a bird and a field that allow us to consider just what it might feel like to be without hope. Furthermore, since birds are meant to fly, Hughes's words say not just that we should aspire, but that humans are meant to aspire, that hopelessness is as uncharacteristic of humans as the inability to fly is of birds. Fields frozen with snow can melt and grow crops; thus, those who learn to aspire can move beyond despair.

Or we might read the poem quite differently: as in many poems, the apparently straightforward meaning may not be so straightforward after all. The "dreams" here might be, not aspirations, but imaginary happenings: daydreams or fantasies. If they are, then holding fast to them is less a matter of hope than of a necessary self-delusion. Hughes may be asking us to realize that life is really bleak and hopeless after all, and that we could not bear the bleakness if we got rid of our illusions; perhaps the truth is that the bird will never fly again, and that life is as barren as that field of snow.

The possibility that we could read the poem in this way may be one of the things that make it a poem. The poem is ambiguous; despite first impressions, its meaning is not straightforward. Rather than merely telling us what to think, the words seem to resonate beyond themselves, to encourage us to consider several possible meanings instead of focusing on the most obvious one.

EXPLORATION: Are other poems also ambiguous or resonant? Choose (or have children choose) a poem and paraphrase it: that is, say what it means to you in your own words. Then reconsider the words of the poem. Do they imply anything more, or different? How are your words different from the words of the poem? Which are more interesting?

A Reading Strategy?

It may be that we just imagine that poems resonate, and so we find meanings in them that we only imagine to be there. Perhaps poems are no different from any other use of language, and their special qualities depend purely on the fact that we think about them differently from the way we think about ordinary conversations or recipes.

We might, for instance, treat the dictionary definition of "egg" as if it were a poem. We could write it out like this:

> the roundish reproductive body
> produced
> by the female
> of animals,
> consisting of
> an embryo
> and
> its envelopes

Now it looks like a poem, and so it is hard not to think of it is as one, not to dwell on the significance of the words in the particular way that we think about words identified as poems.

EXPLORATION: Think (or have children think) about the dictionary definition of "egg" or about some other nonpoetic use of language as if it were a poem. Does your attitude affect the experience of reading the words? How?

Reading the words as if they were a poem, we might conclude that they do not make a very good one—for they don't seem to have the significance we expect of poetry. Or we might decide that they are an exceedingly difficult poem—for we can't figure out what their significance might be. Or we might in fact find something "poetic" about them. We might read them as a description of the planet earth. Or accepting that they do describe eggs, we might see something poetic in the use of the word "envelopes": it might remind us of mailing letters, and perhaps give us the idea that eggs are something like love letters, a blank exterior hiding a soft center of love.

Many poets have taken advantage of the special way of thinking we engage in when we decide that a text is poetry by doing just what I've done here—finding poems in other uses of language. "Found poems," as they are called, can be funny—for example, this poem that John Robert Colombo found in the *Concise Oxford Dictionary:*

FAMILY

Animals of different kinds
In one cage

They can also be startlingly evocative, as this one that a scholar found in the journals of Dorothy Wordsworth, the sister of nineteenth-century British poet William Wordsworth:

The lake was covered all over
With bright silverwaves
That were each
The twinkling of an eye

EXPLORATION: Try (or have children try) to find a poem, in a book or magazine or newspaper. Explore what happens when, after reading the words you have borrowed, you think about them as if they were a poem.

HOW TO EXPERIENCE POETRY

Found poems affirm the extent to which all poetry demands a specific attitude, a playful delight in the ways in which words become interesting in and for themselves. In this section, we will explore eight ways in which we can take that attitude and enrich our response to poems.

1. Paying Attention to the Words Themselves

I comforted my children when they were babies by reciting to them not only nursery rhymes but also poems by W. B. Yeats, T. S. Eliot, and Shakespeare. Shakespeare may not seem to be expressing anything that would appeal to an infant when he says,

> The expense of spirit in a waste of shame
> Is lust in action; and till action, lust
> Is perjured, murderous, bloody, full of blame,
> Savage, extreme, rude, cruel, not to trust. . . .

But to the children the sounds were interesting enough to attract their attention and pleasing enough to soothe them—just as they were soothed by strange sounds like "hickety pickety" and "higglety pigglety" in nursery rhymes.

Words can also be interesting because they are peculiar. This anonymous poem takes advantage of peculiarities of spelling:

> OUGH
>
> As a farmer was going to plough,
> He met a man driving a cough;
> They had words which led to a rough,
> And the farmer was struck on his brough.

And this anonymous rhyme creates pleasure from the fact that the same words can have different meanings:

> Little Willie from his mirror
> Sucked the mercury all off,
> Thinking, in his childish error,
> It would cure his whooping cough.
> At the funeral Willie's mother
> Smartly said to Mrs. Brown:
> " 'Twas a chilly day for William
> When the mercury went down."

2. Paying Attention to the Patterns Words Make

In the Shakespeare poem about "the expense of spirit," the repeated *s* sounds form a pattern and attract our attention. The repetition of consonants is called *alliteration.* The repetition of vowels such as the *a*'s in "a w*a*ste of sh*a*me" is called *assonance.* Repeating sounds are an obvious part of the pleasure of Carolyn Wells's limerick about the flute tutor—and so are repeating words, rhythms, and rhymes. Repetitions of words and rhymes offer a different kind of pleasure in this poem by Gwendolyn Brooks:

WE REAL COOL
THE POOL PLAYERS.
SEVEN AT THE GOLDEN SHOVEL.

We real cool. We
Left school. We

Lurk late. We
Strike straight. We

Sing sin. We
Thin gin. We

Jazz June. We
Die soon.

These short lines focus our attention on the repeated sounds and the rhymes, but not to evoke laughter. The strong repetitions seem inevitable and thus make the sad story the poem tells seem inevitable. The repeated "We" not only reinforces the beat but sets up the significance of its absence in the last line: after "We/Die soon" there is no more "We."

Rhyme. Part of the effect of "We Real Cool" depends on its forceful, obvious rhymes. Rhyme has been a feature of English poetry for centuries, and it is only in the twentieth century that most of the poetry produced has not rhymed. As we saw earlier in our consideration of developmental theories (Chapter 4), it is easy to assume that history represents evolution, and that individual lives duplicate history. As a result, many people believe that nonrhyming poetry, because it came later historically, must be more sophisticated and that, therefore, it is not appropriate for young children.

As a source of repetitive pattern, rhyme is certainly appealing, perhaps in a more obvious and more easily understood way than some other patterns. Like the poems we have considered so far, most of the poems written for children, and most of the poems in anthologies of poems selected for children, do rhyme.

Poems do not have to rhyme, however. Babies will respond to the blank verse of T. S. Eliot's "Waste Land" just as they respond to the rhymes in Shakespeare's "Expense of spirit." Dennis Lee's "Muddy Puddle" creates strong, interesting patterns with almost no rhyme:

I am sitting
In the middle
Of a rather Muddy
Puddle,
With my bottom
Full of bubbles
And my rubbers
Full of Mud,

While my jacket
And my sweater

Go on slowly
Getting wetter
As I very
Slowly settle
To the Bottom
Of the Mud.

And I find that
What a person
With a puddle
Round his middle
Thinks of mostly
In the muddle
Is the Muddi-
Ness of Mud.

Shape. As well as containing repeated *s* and *m* sounds, and similar words, like "middle" and "muddle," Lee's poem has another pattern: its shape on the page. The short lines break up the sentences as we would normally speak them, slow us down, and force our attention to the repetition of the sounds.

The shape a poem takes on the page can become its central focus, as in Colleen Thibaudeau's "Balloon":

as
big as
ball as round
as sun . . . I tug
and pull you when
you run and when
wind blows I
say polite
ly
H
O
L
D
M
E
T
I
G
H
T
L
Y

Conventional Verse Forms. Another sort of pleasure in pattern develops when we become conscious of the history of poems. Carolyn Wells's poem about the flute tutor has the pattern of a standard verse form, the limerick, a form made popular in the nineteenth century by Edward Lear. Once we are aware of this conventional pattern, we can find enjoyment in the pattern itself, and in our ability to recognize it in other poems, such as this one by Lear:

> There was an Old Man in a tree.
> Who was horribly bored by a Bee;
> When they said, "Does it buzz?"
> He replied, "Yes, it does!
> It's a regular brute of a bee."

And our knowledge of the form operates as a schema that teases us when our expectations of it are aroused but then not quite met, as in this poem by W. S. Gilbert:

> There was an Old Man of St. Bees
> Who was stung in the arm by a wasp.
> When asked, "Does it hurt?"
> He replied, "No, it doesn't,
> But I thought all the while 'twas a hornet."

Other conventional forms include the sonnet, a fourteen-line poem with a specific rhyme scheme (the lines from Shakespeare's "Expense of spirit" are the first four lines of a sonnet), and the haiku, a short, three-line poem in which the first line and last line each have five syllables and the middle line has seven syllables, and the last line sums up the essence of the experience expressed in the poem. This is a famous haiku by the master of the form, the seventeenth-century Japanese poet Basho:

> Furuike ya
> Kawazu tobikomu
> Mizu no oto

Or in English, in my own not particularly accurate version,

> A quiet old pond;
> A frog disrupts the surface
> And the splash resounds.

3. Paying Attention to the Pictures Words Make

If we can visualize the situations that carefully chosen words describe, then the words will create imaginary pictures that afford us two kinds of pleasure: having the pictures evoked for us, and perceiving how the words evoke them. Both sources of pleasure are available in Ruth Whitman's "Listening to Grownups Quarrelling":

> standing in the hall against the
> wall with my little brother, blown
> like leaves against the wall by their
> voices, my head like a pingpong ball
> between the paddles of their anger:
> I knew what it meant
> to tremble like a leaf.

Cold with their wrath, I heard
the claws of the rain
pounce. Floods
Poured through the city,
skies clapped over me,
and I was shaken, shaken,
Like a mouse
between their jaws.

There are two kinds of pictures in this poem. The first, the main picture of a child listening to grown-ups quarreling, evokes the child's painful feelings with a clarity that, paradoxically, makes the evocation enjoyable. The second is a series of subsidiary pictures that offer visual equivalents for the child's feelings and help us understand them. These subsidiary pictures, often called *images,* include blowing leaves, a game of Ping Pong, and a thunderstorm. The image of the thunderstorm, which suggests the sounds of the quarrel, is itself evoked in yet another picture, that of a cat, as we hear of "the claws of the rain" pouncing, and guess that the sky that "clapped over me" represents not just a thunderclap but also the action of being struck quickly, as when a cat claps its paws over a mouse. These pictures offer visual parallels for the feelings that the poem is about. As we imagine the pictures, we can recognize their appropriateness as descriptions of a particular situation.

4. Paying Attention to the Patterns of Pictures Words Make

The pictures in "Listening to Grownups Quarrelling" do something else. They create patterns of repetition and variation. The image of leaves blown against a wall is echoed by the image of the head tossed by the Ping Pong paddles, and then by the "claws of the rain."

5. Paying Attention to the Voices Words Create

Like all words, poems imply the voices that speak them—and also, sometimes, the people who might hear those voices. When we read or hear poems, we can think about who might be speaking them, and who their speakers might be speaking to. Walter de la Mare's "Dunce" sums up not just a situation but the personality of the character who tells us about it:

Why does he still keep ticking?
  Why does his round white face
Stare at me over the books and ink,
  And mock at my disgrace?
Why does the thrush call, "Dunce, dunce, dunce!"?
  Why does the bluebottle buzz?
Why does the sun so silent shine?—
  And what do I care if it does?

The poem as a whole gives us enough insight into the character of the person speaking to understand that the strident dismissal of the last line is just boasting, not genuine at all. Many poems give similar insight into characters and their situations by creating distinctive voices, voices like that of the sadly comic speaker in John Cunliffe's "Mutinous Jack in the Box":

> Why should I always jump up
> When they press that stupid button
> always at their call?
> Next time . . . *next* time . . .
> I'll stick my tongue out at them!
> I'll spit!
> I'll shout rude words!
> I'll pull horrid faces!
> I'll make their baby cry
> and turn the milk sour;
> I will!
> Just you wait and see!
> They can't fool me;
> not for ever a slave;
> next time I'll be brave.
>
> B o o o o o o o o o o i i i i i i i n n n n n n n g g g !
>
> Oh dear, I jumped up again,
> Grinning as though I had no brain.
> But . . . just you wait and see,
> Next time I'll do it;
> I will . . . I will . . .

Other poems evoke voices as diverse as the threatened child of "Listening to Grownups Quarrelling" and the annoyed child of "The Muddy Puddle."

The Voices of Children. It is not accidental that these two poems and de la Mare's "Dunce" sound as if they were spoken by children. Many poems written for children, and many other poems selected for inclusion in anthologies of poetry intended for children, imply speakers who are children. Some, like these three, convincingly create childlike moods that are meant to be taken seriously, and that even mature adults can empathize with.

But a number of poems theoretically intended for children seem to adopt a childish voice so that we can see through and feel superior to the speaker's innocence. While this technique might appear to be condescending, poets often have an honorable reason for using it. They want to capture an attitude which they believe to be so exclusively childlike that adults are no longer capable of sharing it; for adults have learned too much to be so joyfully innocent, and have no choice but to admire innocence from a distance. That was probably Robert Louis Stevenson's purpose in writing "My Shadow":

> I have a little shadow that goes in and out with me,
> And what can be the use of him is more than I can see.
> He is very, very like me from the heels up to the head;
> And I see him jump before me, when I jump into my bed.

> The funniest thing about him is the way he likes to grow—
> Not at all like proper children, which is always very slow;
> For he sometimes shoots up taller like an india-rubber ball,
> And he sometimes gets so little that there's none of him at
> all. . . .

But despite its honorable purpose, the poem is still a little condescending—our appreciation of it seems to depend on our own superior knowledge, and thus it seems to be asking us to take pleasure in the child's ignorance. We might wonder what children who share the speaker's ignorance about shadows make of such a poem: does it merely confirm their ignorance? We might also wonder about the effect on inexperienced children of modern poems that revel in similarly immature attitudes, such as Dennis Lee's "Special Person," in which a child innocently describes the future he imagines with his favorite day-care worker:

> I guess I'm going to marry Lynn
> When I get three or four
> And Lynn can have my Crib, or else
> She'll maybe sleep next door.

The main source of pleasure this poem offers is the humor in the speaker's ignorance of the limitations of his own perceptions—a humor other innocents couldn't perceive.

EXPLORATION: Find some poems spoken in the voices of children. Do they allow you to empathize, or does your pleasure derive from the limited understanding of the speaker? If the latter, how might inexperienced children respond to them? Test your own response by sharing the poems with young children.

---

6. Paying Attention to the Stories Words Tell

As well as evoking the voice of a specific character, "The Mutinous Jack-in-the-Box" describes a series of events that have a beginning, a middle, and end. The Jack works himself up to rebellion in a suspense-building set of intensifying statements, after which his jump up is a humorous climax: an event that is surprising in the context of the poem, but also inevitable. In other words, the poem offers the satisfactions of a story.

Many other poems, however, do not so much describe stories as imply them. In responding to "Listening to Grownups Quarrelling" or "The Muddy Puddle" or "We Real Cool," we can imagine the situations that led up to or that are likely to result from the specific events being described. These poems thus present small scenes in ways that allow them to suggest larger and more complicated stories.

7. Paying Attention to the Meanings Words Express

The pleasure in many poems stems from the thoughts they arouse in us. Words are not just sounds, but sounds that have meanings. Many people treasure particular poems that state truths they hold dear, such as, "Hold fast to dreams." And in classrooms in schools and universities, discussions of poems often center on the way we respond to what we are able to summarize of their meaning, so that children read "Dreams" in order to learn the importance of aspirations, and college students read T. S. Eliot to consider his philosophy of life.

This approach to poems has the same limitations as any reading of literature that focuses on its themes: the limitations we considered in Chapter 6. When we focus our attention on the meanings of poems, we shouldn't forget that it is primarily their *way* of expressing meanings that makes them interesting to us. Poems rarely say all that much that is unique or deeply meaningful when considered as philosophy—and almost nothing clear and unambiguous enough to be considered philosophical at all. It is our perception of the rightness of the specific words and images that leads us to treasure poems that express significant truths to us.

Furthermore, as we saw earlier, the words of poems like Hughes's "Dreams" express general truths in ways that provide other, more detailed and more ambiguous meanings. Exploring such meanings is a significant source of our enjoyment of poetry.

EXPLORATION: Consider (or have children consider) whether the poems you like are important for their ideas or for their language. Choose a poem which expresses an idea that is important to you. Is the language in which it expresses the idea a significant part of your appreciation of the poem? Why or why not?

Not all poems make the sort of serious statement about life that a poem like "Dreams" does, but all poems do have meanings and encourage us to think. "Humpty Dumpty" and many other "nonsense" poems cannot give us advice about how to live, but we can think about all the ways in which such poems might possibly be meaningful.

While "Dreams" is organized to encourage us to agree with the ideas it expresses, Hilaire Belloc's "Frog" offers the exact opposite pleasure: if we pay careful attention to it, we will find ourselves thinking about the horrifying but delightful fact that it has manipulated us into thinking the very thoughts and enjoying the very words that the poem itself pretends to be telling us not to enjoy:

Be kind and tender to the Frog,
  And do not call him names,
As "Slimy skin," or "Polly-wog,"
  Or likewise "Ugly James,"
Or "Gap-a-grin," or "Toad-gone-wrong,"
  Or "Billy Bandy-knees":
The Frog is justly sensitive
  To epithets like these.
No animal will more repay
  A treatment kind and fair;
At least so lonely people say
  Who keep a frog (and, by the way,
They are extremely rare).

Poems like "Listening to Grownups Quarrelling" are more serious. But while they encourage serious thought, they don't offer the sort of general statement about life that "Dreams" does. This poem is not about quarreling in general or about parenting in general, but is an evocation of a specific feeling in specific circumstances. As we read it, we may think about the significance of the feeling as it is evoked in the poem; we may wonder whether the feeling speaks to us of our own lives or gives us insight into the lives of others or even into life in general. But we shouldn't confuse those thoughts with the poem itself. A poem is not the memories it evokes for us, nor the thoughts it makes us ponder. It is what evokes those memories and thoughts.

8. Paying Attention to the Patterns of Meanings Words Make

As well as thinking about the meanings of poems, we can also enjoy the patterns those meanings create—the structure of the poem. We can examine, for instance, the ways in which the pictures in "Listening to Grownups Quarrelling" create a shifting pattern of ideas about being battered, or the way in which the sounds and images of Randall Jarrell's "Bird of Night" describe how small creatures like mice and bats might respond to the call of an owl that could kill them. Indeed, Jarrell's poem creates a fascinating pattern of ideas about the relationships of sound waves and waves of water, of the possibility of drowning and the possibility of death, of the word "trying" as meaning "attempting" and as meaning "difficult," of the stillness of death and the act of keeping still in order to prevent death:

A shadow is floating through the moonlight.
Its wings don't make a sound.
Its claws are long, its beak is bright.
Its eyes try all the corners of the night.

It calls and calls: all the air swells and heaves
And washes up and down like water.
The ear that listens to the owl believes
In death. The bat beneath the eaves,

The mouse beside the stone are still as death—
The owl's air washes them like water.
The owl goes back and forth inside the night,
And the night holds its breath.

EXPLORATION: Carefully reread "The Bird of Night," any of the other poems discussed above, or any poem of your choice. Explore (or have children explore) its text in detail, in terms of the eight aspects of poetic response we've considered.

CHILDREN'S POETRY: THE MAKING OF ANTHOLOGIES

As we discovered in our consideration of genre, children's picture books and novels, written expressly for children, have plots, styles, and themes that distinguish them from other kinds of fiction. Throughout this book, I usually assume that children's literature is different enough from other kinds of literature so that it can best be understood by paying attention to the differences.

But when it comes to poetry, the distinctions between children's literature and other sorts of literature get blurry. So far in this chapter, we have considered poems by Dennis Lee, John Cunliffe, and Robert Louis Stevenson that were expressly written for children, and poems by Shakespeare, Langston Hughes, and Ruth Whitman that were originally written for adults. In this way, my selection of poems is like almost all anthologies of selections of poems intended for children.

We mix up adult and children's poetry for a good reason: our faith that poems that adults enjoy can also offer pleasure to children—at least to those children who know how to become the implied readers of poems, and who have learned (or perhaps not yet unlearned) the playful attitudes that allow people of any age to respond positively to poetry. Any group of words on any subject and of any level of subtlety that deserves to be called a poem will appeal to those who have learned how to enjoy the patterns in poetry, even if they are not interested in its subject or don't understand the diction.

Of course, not all adult poems are equally suitable for children. But which ones are? The specific poems each of us thinks suitable for children not only reveal much about our attitudes toward children—how tolerant we think they are of new experiences, what subjects they are interested in or ought to be interested in, what they are capable of understanding—these choices also reveal something of our ideas about what poetry is.

EXPLORATION: Consider (or have children consider) poems by a number of different authors included in any collection of poems intended for children. What kinds of poems are included, and what kinds left out? What do these choices reveal about the anthologizer's attitudes toward children? Toward poetry?

Furthermore, and more significantly, these choices provide children with *their* ideas about what poetry is. The nature of poetry will be defined for them by the qualities of the poems we offer. Some years ago, Kenneth Koch said: "The usual criteria for choosing poems to teach children are mistaken, if one wants poetry to be more than a singsong sort of Muzak in the background of their elementary education. . . . These criteria are total understandability, which stunts children's poetic education by giving them nothing to understand they have not already understood; 'childlikeness' of theme and treatment, which condescends to their feelings and to their intelligence; and 'familiarity,' which obliges them to go on reading the same inappropriate poems their parents and grandparents read" (12).

Many people still use these inadequate criteria, even though they interpret them a little differently. We tend to believe that childhood now is so different from what it was in the past that contemporary children would not find the sweet, gentle poems their parents read either familiar or childlike. What they would be familiar with, and find understandable—and, therefore, what we must think of as being most child-like—are poems meant to be funny and focusing on acts of violence.

Myra Cohn Livingston describes such poems, the work of poets like Jack Prelutsky, Dennis Lee, Roald Dahl, and many others, as a "glorification of the unconscious . . . a sort of 'garbage delight' that assaults literature itself" (157–158; *Garbage Delight* is the name of one of Lee's books of poems). Referring to a poem by Lois Duncan about a girl who teases a dog so unmercifully that it gets mad and eats her up, Livingston writes: "There are some who will say all of this is simply in fun, and children themselves know it is nonsense. . . . But there are others, like myself, who believe that the irresponsible images of the unconscious may be understood by adults, but have no place in the child's world unless there is some helpmeet, some guide, something on which the child may fall back" (159).

EXPLORATION: In the following paragraphs, I express my disagreement with what Livingston says here. Read (or have children read) some poems by Lee or Prelutsky or Dahl or Duncan. Then consider both Livingston's position and mine, and try to determine where you stand on this issue.

If such poems are dangerous, I don't believe that it is because of the irresponsibility of their images. They are, after all, simply in fun, and they merely parallel images and ideas that most young North American children will have experienced already, on TV or in the playground—and usually find funny.

The danger, I think, is in the fact that we tend to give children a steady diet of similar poems, and nothing else—that *all* the poems many children read nowadays are this same sort of funny, anarchic doggerel. While many children do enjoy these poems, some children may come to believe that all poems must rhyme, must have jaunty, obvious rhythms and rhyme schemes, and must focus on the comedy of violence. And this belief might well deprive them of the pleasures of other kinds of poems, such as the thoughtfulness of "Dreams," the evocative painfulness of "Listening to Grownups Quarrelling," the music and terror of "The Bird of Night."

If we wish to help children respond fully to what poetry can offer, then I believe we must expose them to as many different kinds of poems as possible. As parents and educators, we can each develop our own anthologies of poems we enjoy, and that we would like children to be able to enjoy.

EXPLORATION: Read (or have children read) a number of children's poems, and select some—five or six—that are particularly enjoyable, or that you think others ought to experience. Explore why you chose each poem, and what attitudes toward poetry your group of choices might suggest.

WHY MANY PEOPLE DON'T LIKE POETRY—AND WHAT TO DO ABOUT IT

Not everybody likes to ski or to do needlepoint; not everybody likes to read poetry. Nor should they any more than everybody should have to like needlepoint. It is possible to be a happy and complete human being without ever reading a poem. Nevertheless, fewer people enjoy reading poems than might. Often, they dislike poetry because they have never learned *how* to like it.

In primary classrooms, teachers often ask children to sit back and enjoy having poems read to them, without providing them with any understanding of what poems are, or any way of perceiving the technical complexities that make even simple poems work. Even more often, teachers with what I believe to be a misguided faith in the innate creativity of all children ask their students to write their own poems, often without even providing them with a repertoire of poems by others that will enable them to develop schemata for what poetry is or might be.

Furthermore, many people—both teachers and people who write about poetry—believe that it is dangerous for adults to talk with children about their responses to poetry. They claim that our responses to poems are always personal, that all responses to any given poem are equally valid, and that our attempt to discuss children's responses with them is a destructive act of meddling. Such people would agree with Agnes Repplier, who said, "When poetry is in question, it is better to feel than to think" (263).

But with no thought—no discussion of poems, no help in knowing how to make sense of them and enjoy doing so, and thus no sense of the complex craft of poems—children often remain ignorant of the skills that make responding to poetry enjoyable. We need to teach those skills.

Meanwhile, in many high school and university classrooms, the enjoyment of poems is taken for granted, and the focus is on determining poetry's significance. The implication is that, when it comes to poetry, it is better to think than to feel. There is so much discussion of what poems mean that many people come to believe that poetry is purposely obscure—that for no clear reason, poets like to frustrate others by never saying exactly what they mean. According to this common assumption, all poems have "hidden meanings": secret messages that are fairly simple but that poets have concealed under layers of complicated symbols and images. When we read poetry, then, our job is not to explore the meaning of the language of the poem, but, instead, to find the hidden meaning—the one thing the poem does not actually state. The words of poems are just husks—we unwrap them to find the nutritious kernel inside, and then we throw the husks away.

This is frustrating: if the point is the "hidden meaning," then why bother hiding it? Why not just state it and get it over with? This way of thinking about poems prevents many people from getting any enjoyment from them.

Clearly, then, some ways of thinking about poetry make it as unlikable as not knowing how to think about poetry at all. If we want children to enjoy poetry, we need to provide them with knowledge of the possibilities of poetry and of attitudes toward the experience of it, and with techniques and strategies for deriving both understanding and enjoyment from that experience.

WORKS CITED

Ammons, A. R. "Small Song." *The Selected Poems 1951–1977.* New York: Norton, 1977.

Anonymous. "Ough." *A Whimsey Anthology.* Ed. Carolyn Wells. 1906. New York: Dover, 1963.

———. "Little Willie . . . " *The Golden Treasury of Poetry.* Ed. Louis Untermeyer. New York: Golden Press, 1959.

Belloc, Hilaire. "The Frog." *Selected Cautionary Verses.* Harmondsworth, Middlesex: Penguin, 1964.

Brooks, Gwendolyn. "We Real Cool." *Blacks.* Chicago: David, 1987.

Colombo, John Robert. "Family." *Translations from the English: Found Poems.* Toronto: Peter Martin, 1974.

Cunliffe, John. "The Mutinous Jack-in-the-Box." *A Second Poetry Book.* Ed. John Foster. Oxford: Oxford UP, 1980.

de la Mare, Walter. "The Dunce." *Collected Rhymes and Verses.* 2nd ed. London: Faber and Faber, 1970.

Gilbert W. S. "There was an old man." *A Whimsey Anthology.* Ed. Carolyn Wells. 1906. New York: Dover, 1963.

Hughes, Langston. "Dreams." *The Dream Keeper and Other Poems.* New York: Knopf, 1932.

Jarrell, Randall. "The Bird of Night." *The Bat Poet.* New York: Macmillan, 1963.

Koch, Kenneth. *Rose, Where Did You Get That Red? Teaching Great Poetry to Children.* New York: Random House, 1973.

Lear, Edward. "There was an old man." *The Complete Nonsense of Edward Lear.* Ed. Holbrook Jackson. New York: Dover, 1951.

Lee, Dennis. "The Muddy Puddle." *Garbage Delight.* Toronto: Macmillan, 1977.

———. "The Special Person." *Alligator Pie.* Toronto: Macmillan, 1974.

Lear, Edward. "There was an old man." *The Complete Nonsense of Edward Lear.* Ed. Holbrook Jackson. New York: Dover, 1951.

Livingston, Myra Cohn. "David McCord's Poems: Something Behind the Door." *Touchstones: Reflections on the Best in Children's Literature.* Ed. Perry Nodelman. Vol. 2. West Lafayette: Children's Literature Association Publications, 1987. 157–172.

Repplier, Agnes. "The Children's Poets." *Children and Literature: Views and Reviews.* Ed. Virginia Haviland. Glenview: Scott, Foresman, 1973. 263–268.

Shakespeare, William. "Sonnet 129." *The Complete Works of Shakespeare.* Ed. Hardin Craig. Chicago: Scott, Foresman, 1961.

Stevenson, Robert Louis. "My Shadow." *A Child's Garden of Verses.* 1885; Harmondsworth, Middlesex: Penguin, 1952.

Thibaudeau, Colleen. "Balloon." *The New Wind Has Wings: Poems from Canada.* Ed. Mary Alice Downie and Barbara Robertson. Toronto: Oxford UP, 1984.

Wells, Carolyn. "A tutor . . . " *A Whimsey Anthology.* Ed. Wells. 1906. New York: Dover, 1963.

Whitman, Ruth. "Listening to Grownups Quarrelling." *The Marriage Wig and Other Poems.* New York: Harcourt, 1968.

Wordsworth, Dorothy. *The Poetry of Dorothy Wordsworth: Edited from the Journals.* Ed. Hyman Eigerman. Westport: Greenwood, 1970.

CHAPTER 10

Picture Books

THE VISUAL IMAGINATION AND PICTORIAL COMPREHENSION

When most people think of books for children, they think of picture books: short books that tell stories with relatively few words, but with large, usually colorful pictures on every page. Picture books are the most characteristic form of children's literature—indeed, the one literary form that is exclusive to children's literature. While there are both children's stories and adult stories, there are not many stories intended for adults that are told in a few words and with numerous pictures. Why has this particular form of children's book become so popular?

> *EXPLORATION: Before reading what follows, consider (or have children consider) answers to that question. After you have given your response, and then read my answer to the question, consider the implications of the similarities or differences in the two answers.*

There are two common answers to the question of why children's picture books are so popular: children *like* pictures, and children *need* pictures.

Many children do like pictures—for children are human beings, and human beings like pictures. On first picking up a book, people of any age tend to look at the pictures before reading the words. In fact, most of us automatically look at *any* picture we happen to see. As E. H. Gombrich says, "The visual image is supreme in its capacity for arousal" ("The Visual Image" 82). The fact that pictures attract our attention and excite our interest accounts for their presence of pictures in bus and magazine advertising as well as in many children's books. There is no special reason to assume that children like pictures more than adults do.

Children presumably need pictures in books because they find them easier to understand than words, and need pictorial information to guide their response to verbal information. That theory implies two assumptions, one about children and one about pictures. The assumption about children is that their imagination is "visual" in a way that gives them an intuitive ability to understand pictorial information. The assumption about pictures is that they are automatically understandable. Neither of these assumptions is true.

The idea that the imagination of children is qualitatively different from that of adults is no more valid than any other generalization about children. The specific suggestion that children are more visually oriented than adults relates to Piaget's theory that younger children think in more concrete terms: we assume that visual images are more concrete than verbal ones, and that therefore children have a better chance of understanding them. In doing so, we forget that babies respond to voices before they do to pictures, and learn to speak before they learn to draw.

In any case, pictures are no more "concrete" and no less abstract than words are. It is true that, simply because they are attempts to communicate visual information, pictures more obviously resemble the objects they represent than do spoken or written words. Even so, the resemblance is not necessarily apparent to all viewers; a visual depiction understandable to one human being can seem meaningless to another.

In earlier times before Euro-American culture became so pervasive, many anthropologists and explorers showed tribal people in Africa or South America realistic drawings and even photographs. These people, unacquainted with Western culture, were often unable to recognize what the pictures depicted. Because such depictions did not exist in their cultures, they had no strategies for making sense of them.

The pictures that did exist had purposes different from our pictures, and showed the world in a different way. Jan Deregowski reports a study in which some African villagers preferred a split-type drawing of an elephant (showing it from above as if it had been split open, so that all four feet could be seen), while Europeans preferred a top view that did not show the feet. Deregowski says that the different responses come from a different understanding of what pictures are for: "Split-representation drawings develop in cultures where the products of art serve as labels or marks of identification. In the cultures where drawings are intended to convey *what an object actually looks like,* this style is muted and the 'perspective' style is adopted" (187–188).

Even that comment reveals a cultural bias: Deregowski believes he knows "what an object looks like." But the idea that realistic pictures depict objects as seen from a distance from one specific point of view is a relatively new one, having developed only in Europe and only in the last four hundred or so years. To say that the perspective style represents reality more accurately than other styles and that therefore it is readily or even automatically understandable by children may merely reveal our own ideological prejudices.

Like words, in fact, pictures do not convey much meaning until we know the language in which they are expressed. Like words, they are "abstract," in the sense that they exist within systems of learned codes, and thus make little sense to anyone without a previous knowledge of those systems. Because pictures are permeated by the ideological assumptions of their culture, children will not understand pictures until they develop some understanding of the culture.

And that is not all. Children also have to understand the systems of codes and signifiers that are specific to pictures. In *Art and Illusion,* E. H. Gombrich persuasively shows how artists can make visual depictions of objects only in terms of their previous knowledge of earlier visual images—of a repertoire of schemata they have learned from their knowledge of previous art: "Everything points to the conclusion that the phrase the 'language of art' is more than a loose metaphor, that even to describe the visible world in images we need a developed system of schemata" (87). In order to understand such depictions, we must share their visual repertoire.

The fact that so many children *can* interpret pictures at an early age does not mean that understanding pictures is easy. Instead, I believe, it is a tribute to their great flexibility and as great an accomplishment as learning to use spoken language, a skill which children also miraculously teach themselves.

If pictures are not particularly easy for inexperienced minds to make sense of, then why *are* there picture books? There may be no answer to that question but convention. The fact is, picture books do exist. People believe that children like and need pictures, and so publishers can make a profit by providing books to fulfill that perceived need.

But that does not mean that picture books are not a worthwhile form of literature. Some of the most pleasurable experiences offered by children's literature are in picture books. If children may be said to like and need picture books, it is only because they need and ought to like the rich experiences these books can provide.

THE PLEASURE OF PICTURE BOOKS

Because they contain illustrations, picture books offer a form of pleasure different from other types of storytelling. Because they contain words, the pleasure they offer is different from other forms of visual art.

Pictures are inherently different from words, and communicate different sorts of information in different ways. Pictures, which occupy space rather than time, lack an easy means of expressing the temporal relationships of cause and effect, dominance and subordination, and possibility and actuality that the grammar of language so readily expresses because it occupies time rather than space. Meanwhile, words cannot easily communicate the information about the appearance of physical objects that pictures so readily convey. Even a complete verbal description of a face or a setting is more focused on the implications of specific details than is a simple caricature, which readily conveys a sense of a visual whole.

The unique pleasure picture books offer is our perception of the way illustrators make use of these differences between words and pictures. Consider the following examples:

- The text of Margot Zemach's *Jake and Honeybunch Go to Heaven* tells us that "there were angels everywhere." It does not tell us what the pictures do: that the angels are all blacks dressed in glitzy costumes of the 1930s, and that heaven itself is a night club full of exuberant jazz musicians. These images distinguish "heaven" from conventional ideas of it enough to change the meaning of the story significantly.

- The text of Annalena McAfee and Anthony Browne's *Visitors Who Came to Stay* says, " 'Dad, do you see what I see?' asked Katy." The picture changes the significance of her apparently innocuous remark by showing us what she sees: a wildly improbable beach scene that includes a gorilla in a muscleman pose, a woman's foot shaped like a high-heeled shoe, a boy with a fish swimming inside his diving mask.
- The text of one page of *Brian Wildsmith's ABC* says merely "dog DOG." The word could refer to a wide variety of animals of different shapes and sizes, but the pictures show just one, a jowly bassethound. The image changes the vague potential of the original text into a specific, limited image that invites our attention to its specifying details.

HOW PICTURES PROVIDE INFORMATION ABOUT STORIES

In order to notice the distinctions between words and pictures, we need strategies for picture books that are different from our strategies for understanding stories told only in words and that differ also from the ways we often view other pictures. When we look at the pictures in art galleries, we are supposed to absorb and delight in visual impressions. But when we look at the pictures in picture books, we are meant to think about how they relate to the accompanying words, and also to the pictures preceding and following them. In other words, we must consider not only their beauty but also how they contribute to our unfolding knowledge of the story they are part of.

In fact, *everything* in such pictures is less important a source of aesthetic delight than a source of information about a story. Their shape, their style, their composition are means of conveying information about how we are to respond to the story they are part of.

EXPLORATION: As you work your way through this section, explore (or have children explore) how other picture books of your choice make use of the various ways in which pictures provide story information.

Format and First Impressions

Once we have experience in books and reading, visual information directs our response to the story in a picture book before we even open the book. Particular expectations arise from each of the physical qualities of a book: its size and its shape, even the kind of paper it is printed on.

We tend to associate the largest and smallest picture books with the youngest children. In the case of small ones, like Potter's *Peter Rabbit,* that may be because smaller objects seem better suited to the small hands of young readers. In the case of the large ones, like Richard Scarry's *Best Word Book Ever,* it may be that we assume children lack the dexterity to manipulate smaller objects. Such books seem to be large for the same reason that the print in books for the least experienced of readers is large. What is interesting about these assumptions is how directly they contradict each other. That suggests how very much our understanding of these books depends on conventional assumptions, and how conventional and undirected by reason those assumptions are.

Sometimes, though, the effect of a book's physical format on its meaning goes beyond convention: particular physical qualities create real restraints. For instance, even narrow picture books provide illustrators with a wide space to fill, once they are opened. But the human body is relatively tall and narrow, so illustrators are left with a lot of empty space after they draw their characters. They often fill the space by placing the characters in detailed settings. Yorinks and Richard Egielski's *Bravo, Minski* is almost twenty-two inches wide when opened. When Minski gives a demonstration of his singing, he appears in a panoramic scene containing him and more than twenty other people and a dog, each of whom seems to be about the same distance away from us and therefore to be about the same size. (See Figure 1.)

Because we see Minski as a member of a social group, we consider his effect on the group rather than understand him in terms of his own feelings or point of view. Because of their physical form, picture books tend to show characters in wide scenes seen from a distance, and tend to demand less involvement with their characters than stories without pictures.

Covers. As we glance at a book before reading it, the cover is the most significant source of our expectations for it. The picture on a cover or dust-jacket often evokes the essential quality of the story. For instance, Satomi Ichikawa's cover illustration for Patricia Lee Gauch's *Dance, Tanya* shows a young girl in a spotlight against an empty background, both her feet off the floor as she exuberantly swings a piece of cloth through the air: everything is free, open, moving. In contrast, the cover of another book about dancing, Catherine Brighton's *Nijinsky,* consists of a series of constraining boxes, one of which contains a picture of the young Nijinsky manipulating a toy figure of a dancer, just as he himself is made to seem manipulated and constrained in the pictures throughout the book.

Inside a Book. Once we get past a book's cover, other aspects of its design affect our understanding of it. We respond differently to books whose pictures are bordered than we do to those that aren't, to different sizes and kinds of type, to different placements and relationships of pictures and of words.

EXPLORATION: Consider (or have children consider) the effect of aspects of a book's design by imagining how the book would look with a different design. How would you respond to, say, Dance, Tanya *if the text were in Old English type, or to* Where the Wild Things Are *if the words were printed over the surface of the pictures rather than in a white space underneath or beside them?*

Figure 1. Illustration from *Bravo, Minski* by Arthur Yorinks, illustrated by Richard Egielski. Illustration copyright © 1988 by Richard Egielski. Reprinted by permission of Farrar, Straus and Giroux, Inc.

Borders are a particularly interesting example of the effect of design. Events seen through strictly defined boundaries imply detachment and objectivity, a fact that many illustrators of fantasy worlds use to advantage. The white borders in a book like Chris Van Allsburg's *The Polar Express* add a quality of documentary truth to the fantastic events they depict. As in *Nijinsky,* illustrators also use the constraining quality of borders to suggest the tensions of intense activity. Variations in borders suggest shifts in meaning. As Max gets into trouble in *Where the Wild Things Are,* we see his frenzy depicted in small pictures surrounded by a constraining border of white space; but as his imaginative freedom grows, the pictures get larger and the borders smaller.

Mood and Atmosphere

If the words "I fall down the stairs" are said in anguish, the effect is painful, but if they are said with a giggle, we might laugh at them; the specific meaning depends not on the words themselves but on the tone of voice in which they are spoken. The mood of a picture is like the tone of a text: it is an overall quality that affects the meaning and the attitude we take toward it. Illustrators convey mood in a number of ways: through predominating hues, shades, and saturations of colors, through different predominating shapes, and through their choices of media.

Color. *Hues* are classifications of colors, like "red" or "blue," that refer to different parts of the spectrum. Books in which specific hues predominate create different moods for two reasons. The first is that certain hues evoke real objects or settings in which the hues predominate: we see pictures in which greens predominate as restful because we associate green with peaceful forests. The second is that certain hues have conventionally come to signify certain emotions that have no actual relationship to them. Because of its traditional association with the Virgin Mary, for instance, pale blue suggests serenity. For those who know this association, a book like Marjorie Flack and Kurt Wiese's *Story About Ping,* in which blues predominate, evokes a serene mood.

Shades are degrees of brightness and darkness—for instance, light or dark red. We tend to identify darker shades with gloomier subjects, lighter ones with happier subjects. A dark book like *Nijinsky* is somber in mood, while the pastel tones of *Dance, Tanya* seem cheerful.

Saturation is the relative intensity of colors, as when we speak of bright or pale red. More saturated colors seem more intense, less saturated ones more gentle. The intense colors of Marcia Brown's *Shadow* are highly assertive, while the pale tones of her *Cinderella* are quietly elegant; the difference implies her understanding of the mood of two different stories.

Illustrators can also convey meaning by *avoiding* predominating effects. Books that use patches of unrelated colors in shocking combinations share a quality of energy and excitement, whereas more subtle blends of related hues or shades express calm. An illustrator can change the mood within a book by moving from one effect to the other. When we first see Max in his bedroom in *Where the Wild Things Are,* his upset is conveyed by the discordant patches of purple bed and pink bedspread. When he returns to the bedroom at the end of the book, the bed has become a shade of pink, and the more harmonious colors reflect Max's peaceful feeling.

Black and White. Perhaps because of our experience of newspaper photographs and documentary films, pictures in black and white tend to imply seriousness and authenticity. Illustrators often use this quality to underpin the reality of fantasy situations, as in Van Allsburg's black and white depiction of wallpaper coming to life in *The Mysteries of Harris Burdick.* (See Figure 2.)

Shape and Line. We associate rounded shapes with softness and yielding, angular ones with rigidity and orderliness; and we tend to see uncompleted lines as unstable and energetic, while lines that enclose space seem more stable and restful. When one of these possibilities predominates in a book, there is a strong effect on its mood. The story of urban blight told in Virginia Lee Burton's *Little House* never seems particularly sad because nothing in the book, not even the angular apartment buildings, is actually straight-edged—every line in this comforting book is slightly rounded. On the other hand, the incomplete lines in Charles Keeping's spiky drawings make them seem filled with nervous energy. Even when Keeping depicts a corpse, in his version of Alfred Noyes's *The Highwayman,* the explosive lines make the picture disturbingly energetic. (See Figure 3.)

Media. As Gombrich says in "Standards of Truth": "The image cannot give us more information than the medium can carry" (248). Consequently, illustrators' choices of media affect the meanings of the stories they help to tell. For instance, black lines on white paper cannot convey the moods of color; block prints can reveal texture only with difficulty; collage inhibits the creation of depth; and watercolor in its translucency creates the impression of light more readily than tempera does. Furthermore, many media are associated with specific ideas or emotions: we tend to see woodcuts as simple and folk-like, oil paintings as richly elegant. The more we know about media and the conventional uses of them, the richer will be our experience of picture books.

EXPLORATION: Choose (or have children choose) a picture book, and determine what mood its pictures convey. What qualities of these pictures help to convey that mood, and how?

Style

Unlike hue or media, *style* is not a separable quality. It is the effect of all the aspects of a work considered together, the way in which an illustration or text seems distinct or even unique. Style develops from the various choices an artist makes, about both subject and means of presentation. Beatrix Potter's style, for instance, depends not

Figure 2. Illustration from *The Mysteries of Harris Burdick* by Chris Van Allsburg. Copyright © 1984 by Chris Van Allsburg. Reprinted by permission of Houghton Mifflin Co.

just on her use of gently unsaturated watercolors but also on the fact that she depicts small animals in human situations. A book in soft watercolors about a talking elephant would seem as unlike Potter as would a book about a talking rabbit done in saturated reds and oranges.

The styles of picture books can communicate meanings by drawing upon conventions which already have connotations. For instance, even children with little literary

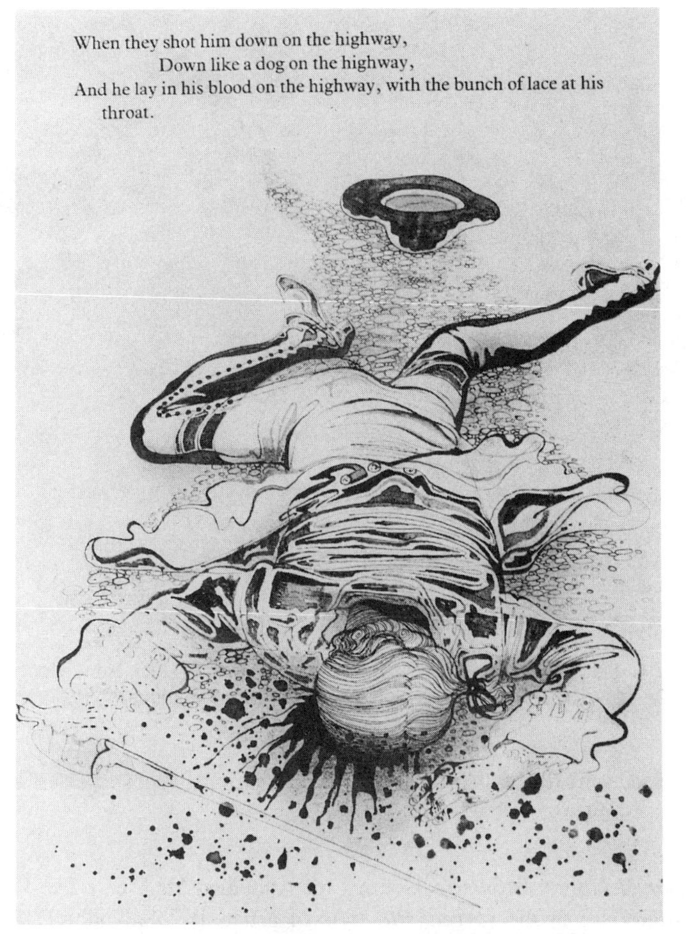

Figure 3. Illustration from *The Highwayman* by Alfred Noyes and Charles Keeping. Copyright © Charles Keeping 1981. Published by Oxford University Press. Reprinted by permission.

experience have learned to expect pictures in the style of cartooning—exaggerated caricatures—to be funny. So we expect humor in Jack Kent's cartoon depictions of fairy tales like "Snow White" and "Cinderella" in his *Happy-Ever-After Book* even before we look closely enough at the pictures to find the humorous details; and we expect anything but humor from the more representational pictures for the same tales by illustrators like Trina Schart Hyman or Marcia Brown. (See Figure 4.)

Reminders of existing styles of art also provide connotations. The theoretically dangerous tale of how a fox stalks a chicken in Pat Hutchins's *Rosie's Walk* becomes humorous because the style of the book evokes the charm of folk art, while the precise black and white drawings in Van Allsburg's *Garden of Abdul Gasazi* make an essentially comic tale seem broodingly serious by evoking the style of documentary photographs.

Figure 4. Illustration from *The Happy-Ever-After-Book* by Jack Kent. Copyright © 1976 by Jack Kent. Reprinted by permission of Random House, Inc.

In the sections that follow, we will look at several types of artistic styles that illustrators might use.

Surrealism. Anthony Browne's pictures for Annalena McAfee's *The Visitors Who Came to Stay* are in the *surrealistic* style of artists like Salvador Dali and René Magritte. They depict unrealistic situations in a highly representational way that makes the impossible seem strangely possible. The book is filled with surrealistic visual puns: as Katy greets her father's visitors, an image of a train in a picture on the wall puffs real smoke that reaches beyond its frame; a bottle and a carrot stand on a shelf beside a half-bottle/half-carrot; and other shelves contain versions of Magritte paintings come to life. (See Figure 5.) These visual puns not only relate to the theme of practical jokes running through the text but also create an eerie atmosphere that, ironically, undermines Katy's insistence that everything is and must remain ordinary.

Impressionism. Whereas surrealism evokes strangeness, *impressionism* tends to be dreamy and romantic. As a result, Sendak's Monet-like impressionist depictions of lushly green landscapes in *Mr. Rabbit and the Lovely Present* alter the effect of Charlotte Zolotow's jaunty staccato text about a little girl seeking help from a giant rabbit in choosing a gift for her mother. In this case, the visual style clearly operates in ironic counterpoint to a text rather than in support of it.

Figure 5. Illustration from *The Visitors Who Came to Stay* by Annalena McAfee and Anthony Browne. Illustrations copyright © Anthony Browne 1984. Reprinted by permission of Hamish Hamilton.

National Styles. Many of the stories in picture books are versions of tales from countries around the world. Illustrators often convey the special atmosphere of these tales by working in styles that reflect their places of origin. Blair Lent's pictures for the Chinese story *Tikki Tikki Tembo,* by Arlene Mosel, are reminiscent of old Chinese watercolors; Barbara Cooney's characters in her version of a Greek legend,

Demeter and Persephone, look like those painted on ancient Greek vases; and Gail Haley's pictures in her version of the English legend *The Green Man* look like the painting on signboards for English inns. Gerald McDermott borrows the style of the wall paintings found in the kivas, or sacred places, of the Pueblos for his retelling of a Pueblo story in *Arrow to the Sun,* and Elizabeth Cleaver's pictures for William Toye's *Mountain Goats of Temlaham* include ceremonial objects in the visual style of the Tsimshian people who originally told this story.

Styles of Individual Artists. Illustrators sometimes even borrow the styles of particular artists. In his various books of magical illusion, Mitsumasa Anno uses techniques of the graphic artist M. C. Escher; in *Stevie,* John Steptoe uses the bright colors and heavy black lines of the French painter Georges Rouault; and in his versions of fairy tales like Perrault's "Cinderella," Errol Le Cain evokes the elegantly decadent style of the British illustrator Aubrey Beardsley.

EXPLORATION: Find pictures of works in the original styles or by the original artist that any of the books mentioned in this section refer to. Compare (or have children compare) the original with the illustrations in the picture book, and explore the significance of similarities and differences.

The Meanings of Borrowed Styles. When styles are borrowed, they rarely mean what they meant to those who created them. Because we see the various styles of art through the filter of history, we interpret them in terms of our own understanding of their times and their makers. For Monet and other impressionists, for instance, the style implied a concern with transient appearances, with the way things momentarily look in particular circumstances of light and shade. But for most people nowadays, impressionist works evoke a more specific meaning: they suggest Monet and his time. They show a preindustrial world of peaceful rural settings that we tend to feel nostalgic about. Thus, when Sendak uses the impressionist style in Zolotow's *Mr. Rabbit and the Lovely Present,* it conveys pastoral calm as much as it does a concern for light and shadow.

The Meanings of Visual Objects

While overall qualities like design and style help convey the mood and meaning of a story, most of the information that pictures provide comes from the specific objects they depict. These objects become meaningful through the contexts they evoke, which relate them to our knowledge and experience of life, literature, and visual art. It is our contextual knowledge that allows us to look at a picture, recognize part of it as a representation of something familiar, and say, "This is a chair," or "This is a Chippendale chair," or even "This is the kind of chair van Gogh shows in his picture of his room at Arles." Our familiarity with a context leads us to focus on specific details—to give them more *weight* in our interpretation of a picture. There are two important ways in which visual objects in pictures develop weight: through symbolism and through codes.

Symbols. Visual *symbolism* is the use of physical objects to represent abstract ideas. When a shadow of a cross appears on the forehead of a boy in Charles Keeping's *Through the Window*, for example, those familiar with Christian imagery will understand the boy's situation differently from those who are not acquainted with such images.

EXPLORATION: The versions of the Grimms' tale "Snow White" by Nancy Ekholm Burkert and Trina Schart Hyman depict many traditional symbols. Look up (or have children look up) the traditional meanings of various objects these books depict—apples, black cats, holly, spiders, bats, dragons, mistletoe, the tarot card for thirteen—and consider what meanings they add to the story.

Freudian Symbols. As we saw in our earlier discussion of literary contexts (Chapter 8), both Freudian and Jungian psychoanalysts invest specific visual images with a deeper unconscious content. Presumably, all productions of the human mind can be read for their unconscious content; it is not difficult to find dark Jungian shadows or pointed Freudian phallic objects in picture books. In William Joyce's *George Shrinks*, for instance, George shoots off a toy cannon strategically placed in front of his lower torso. (See Figure 6.) Not all Freudian imagery is so obvious, but the surprise of finding these implications in apparently innocent pictures is often a source of pleasure.

Codes and Gestures. Some of the more obvious narrative implications of pictures depend not on specific symbols but on basic cultural codes that we tend to take for granted. Because we identify dark with evil and light with goodness, many picture books show evil characters in the shadows and good ones in the sunlight. Similarly, we associate peace and joy with green spaces, and relatively empty, boxlike spaces like Max's bedroom in *Where the Wild Things Are* with sterility. Cultural assumptions also enable us to derive information from the gestures and postures of characters. We understand that upturned heads mean happiness, slumped heads despair, and so on. We also have ideas about the connections between physical appearance and emotions. We know we should dislike the two brothers in Hyman's illustrations in *The Water of Life* because one of them has the sort of narrow, moustached face we associate with devilishness, and the other the thick-necked stolidity we associate with stupidity. Picture books both depend on and teach such conventional assumptions.

Pictorial Dynamics

While the meaning of the objects in pictures depends in part on the external contexts through which we perceive them, much of their significance comes from within a picture itself, particularly in the ways in which the objects relate to one another.

Figure 6. Illustration from *George Shrinks* by William Joyce. Copyright © 1985 by William Joyce. Reprinted by permission of HarperCollins Publishers.

There are two possible forms of relationships: those between objects on the two-dimensional plane of the picture's surface, and those between objects in the three-dimensional space the picture implies.

Two-Dimensional Effects

Shapes. Square shapes are rigid, round ones accommodating. So characters placed inside constricting boxes seem oppressed, and the rounded shape of Peter Rabbit's body escapes constriction as he moves past a severe rectangular picket on his way into Mr. McGregor's Garden.

Certain shapes can also make us pay attention to other shapes. Throughout McDermott's *Arrow to the Sun,* the hero's stylized pointer-like hand points toward the focus of the action throughout the book.

Size. Larger figures tend to have more weight than smaller ones. We realize how threatened Katy feels by the fake monster's hand that Sean wears in *The Visitors Who Came to Stay* because the perspective of the picture puts the hand in the foreground and her in the background, making the hand much larger than she is. But other qualities can give smaller objects more importance: we pay attention to Sendak's little Max among the big Wild Things because there's only one of him and many of them.

The size of characters in relation to their background may imply relationships between character and environment. Characters depicted as small shapes surrounded by forests or large empty rooms seem threatened or lost. But if we enlarged the figure of a character so that it filled the space, the same figure would seem much less bleak.

Location and Composition. The location of an object on the picture plane can give it more or less emphasis. A figure at the center of a picture, like the little house throughout Burton's book, tends to have more weight than those on the sides. This often becomes a problem for illustrators, who wish to attract our attention to figures other than those in the center; they must do so by making use of one or more of the other techniques outlined here.

EXPLORATION: Consider (or have children consider) why our attention is attracted to a certain object and not another. For instance, why do we focus on the figure of God at the edge of the picture of the mule that causes havoc in Jake and Honeybunch Go to Heaven *(Figure 7) rather than to the woman in the center of the picture? Why is our attention directed to Minski in the picture of him singing in Milan in* Bravo, Minski *(Figure 1, page 135), rather than to the woman near the center?*

The layout of the objects in a picture in relation to one another implies invisible shapes: circles, rectangles, squares, or triangles that form the picture's composition. Since these patterns create order and balance, a disruption of them implies disorder. Because the pictures represent the tension in stories, they rarely have

Figure 7. Illustration from *Jake and Honeybunch Go to Heaven* by Margot Zemach. Copyright © 1982 by Margot Zemach. Reprinted by permission of Farrar, Straus and Giroux, Inc.

balanced compositions—consider the many lines and shapes moving discordantly in different directions in the pictures of the mule causing disruption in *Jake and Honeybunch Go to Heaven.* The main exception is often the final picture in a book, depicting the order of a happy ending.

Figure and Ground. Objects in a field of other objects stand out less than isolated ones, and figures sharply isolated from their background stand out more than those that blend in. This is why the important characters in illustrations, unlike the less important ones, are often outlined in black. The dog at the center of the picture of Mama in the arbor in Sendak's *Outside Over There* lacks outlines, for instance, while Mama has them. We also pay more attention in *Dance, Tanya* to Tanya posed alone against a ground of blue carpet than we do to the other members of her family all in a group together. As happens in *Dance, Tanya,* illustrators often show characters against blank grounds when they wish us to focus on the emotional meaning of the figures' gestures and expressions, and against fuller grounds when what's important is the effect of their environment on them.

Left to Right and Top to Bottom. Probably because we expect heavier objects to sink, the bottom of a picture usually suggests more weight than the top. Thus, we become uncomfortable when heavier figures appear in the top half of a picture, a fact that allows many illustrators to convey the sensation of characters, like Jake and Honeybunch, flying. Meanwhile, pictures whose bottom halves are less busy than their top halves often express distress.

We tend to read pictures from left to right, as we have learned to read print. Mercedes Gaffron suggests that pictures contain a "glance curve"—that we look at the figures on the lower left first, and then move our eye in a curve to the upper right. Because we often identify with the first figure we see, the main characters in many picture book stories appear in illustrations on the lower left, and the characters they struggle with on the upper right. A typical example is the picture of Katy meeting her visitors for the first time in *The Visitors Who Came to Stay* (Figure 5, page 141); Katy's father in the upper right greets the visitors as Katy watches from the lower left.

Color. As with the overall effects of predominating colors, the colors of specific objects provide information about those objects. The mere fact that objects are in colors that stand out gives them weight. We focus on one red object in a field of green, or on bright objects like the children in lighted nightclothes in the dark bedroom depicted in Brighton's *Nijinsky.*

Illustrators can also imply relationships between objects of the same or similar colors. In Hyman's illustrations for *The Water of Life,* the dwarf's red hat and green garments reflect the red and green worn by the evil brothers and imply a mysterious connection the brothers ignore. Sendak implies a connection between the moon and Max's wild dance in *Where the Wild Things Are* by making the moon and Max the only white objects in the pictures.

Three-Dimensional Effects

Most picture book illustrations are in some form of representational perspective that implies an imaginary three-dimensional space existing on the other side of the surface of the paper. Thus, as well as being shapes that form patterns on the surface of a picture, the figures that illustrators depict have relationships within this imaginary space. These relationships also contribute to the meaning of a picture.

Perspective. The diagonal lines that create the sense of depth in perspective drawing act like arrows focusing our attention on the objects they lead toward. By using these lines, illustrators can give greater visual weight to small figures. For instance, Anthony Browne uses the perspective lines created by railway tracks to draw attention to the small patch of blue sky seen through a tunnel on an otherwise cloudy day as Katy waits for the train in *The Visitors Who Came to Stay.*

Point of View. We understand events differently when we see them from different points of view. Characters who are seen from below look large and isolated from their backgrounds—we see them against empty skies or ceilings—and seem to be alone and in control of their situations, as is the figure of God throughout *Jake and Honeybunch Go to Heaven.* But when the young dancer falls from a chair in *Nijinsky,* we look down on him from above, falling past a mirror and over a visibly hard bare floor, and that increases the sense of disorder in the picture—the dancer seems trapped by the background. (See Figure 8.) Earlier in the book, however, a picture of the three Nijinsky children seen from above as they sleep on the grass seems comfortingly secure: the background envelops rather than constricts them.

Focus. As in movies, variation in focus also affects the way we respond to a scene. *Long shots,* which show characters surrounded by environment, like most of the pictures in *The Little House,* emphasize the figures' relationship with places and other people, their social situation. *Close-ups* of character's faces tend to make us focus on private feelings. But as we discovered earlier, in exploring the shape of picture books, most of the illustrations in picture books are *middle-distance shots,* showing the characters' entire bodies but within settings, much as we see actors onstage in the theater; the effect is a balance between intimacy and distance.

Overlap. In perspective drawings, the spaces that depictions of objects occupy on the page interfere with or *overlap* each other. Artists can use overlaps to suggest the relationships of the objects they depict. For instance, Katy's feeling of isolation from her visitors as they eat breakfast is amplified by the fact that her face is overlapped and confined by cereal boxes and condiment bottles. Earlier, however, her attachment to her father is revealed by the way her figure overlaps his as they wait for the train.

Figure 8. Illustration from *Nijinsky* by Catherine Brighton. Copyright © 1989 by Catherine Brighton. Used by permission of Doubleday, a division of Doubleday Dell Publishing Group, Inc. and Methuen Children's Books.

Light Sources and Shadows. The light implied by pictures may come from sources both inside and outside the pictures. Like the bright lamps often seen in *Nijinsky,* an actual light source depicted in a picture draws attention both to itself and to what it casts light on. For example, each of the lamps in the scene of a theoretically happy family evening nevertheless lights only one of the Nijinsky children, and so implies their isolation from one another. An implied light from the rear of a picture places characters in front of it in shadow, and Hyman takes advantage of this to place the evil brothers in shadow throughout *The Water of Life* (Figure 9); but when the good brother first meets the dwarf, the light comes from the front and illuminates his face (Figure 10).

We expect light to fall from above, and therefore variations from this convention, like those Van Allsburg uses throughout *The Polar Express,* create an atmosphere of strange mystery.

Blocking. The characters in a picture book often form what directors call stage pictures: they are "blocked"—that is, given positions in relation to each other that imply their social or emotional relationships. In fact, the illustrations in picture books are often much like stage pictures: the characters leave the side of a table closest to us empty so we can see their faces, the central character is often at the apex of

Figure 9. Illustration from *The Water of Life.* Copyright © 1986 by Trina Schart Hyman. Reprinted by permission of Holiday House.

a triangle in relation to less important characters, and the characters overlap each other when the overlapping is meaningful. One of the reasons that picture books seem so capable of telling stories is our usually unconscious assumption that all their characters' positions and gestures do in fact convey information about the events they are taking part in—just as does good staging in the theater.

Movement and Time in Pictures

Since stories are about movements and changes, they necessarily take place in time. But a picture is fixed, and can show only one moment separated from the flow of

Figure 10. Illustration from *The Water of Life.* Copyright © 1986 by Trina Schart Hyman. Reprinted by permission of Holiday House.

time. How then can illustrations imply the passage of time necessary to depict actions and tell stories? Several conventions allow illustrators to suggest movement.

Incomplete Actions. An illustrator can suggest activity by choosing to depict a moment when an action is not complete, thus forcing viewers to imagine its completion. For instance, walking involves moments when the feet are on the floor and moments when they are off it; but since feet on the floor seem to be at rest, an illustrator wishing to depict a character walking would have to show one foot off the ground.

Linear Continuance. We tend to complete the lines in pictures by imagining them extending beyond their depicted length. So when Minski invents the rocket in *Bravo, Minski,* we complete the lines that depict the rocket's flight and so imagine it moving upward. The ''action lines'' used by cartoonists create a similar effect—by echoing the line of an arm or a foot three or four times, these lines invite us to fill the space in between and imagine a continuous movement. Likewise, many lines radiating out from a central point imply explosive activity.

Distortion. Certain forms of distortion suggest movement. When Peter Rabbit runs from Mr. McGregor, he leans forward at an impossible angle with his head shaped like a bullet; the distorted shape implies his speed. (See Figure 11.)

Left-to-Right Movement. We saw earlier that people tend to look at pictures from left to right. As a result, we assume that time passes from left to right—that what happens on the left of a picture happens *before* what happens on the right. When Minski tests his rocket, he stands at the left still holding a lighted match even though the rocket in the middle has already taken off; directly beneath it Minski's father still holds his ears, but by the time our eyes move to the right of the picture the noise of the explosion is over and a group of figures with uncovered ears watches the rocket rise.

Figure 11. Illustration from *The Tale of Peter Rabbit* by Beatrix Potter. Copyright © Frederick Warne & Co., 1902, 1987. Reproduced by permission of Frederick Warne & Co.

Because we assume that time passes from left to right, we assume that characters (and objects like Minski's rocket) are in motion when they point toward the right. And because we are made to feel uncomfortable when characters in motion face toward the left, we assume that they are moving with difficulty. As a result, Jake and Honeybunch always move toward the right; the few times we see Honeybunch pointed to the left, the text tells us she is at rest.

Continuous Narrative. Picture books often use what Joseph Schwarcz calls "continuous narrative"; they show the same character in a number of different poses within the same picture. We are to assume that each of the poses represents one moment out of a series of connected actions, moving in time from left to right. For instance, Ichikawa uses continuous narrative to show Tanya dancing. (See Figure 12.)

Context. The most obvious way in which illustrators can convey the passage of time is simply by counting on our knowledge that a picture is meant to show part of a story. When we understand that, we tend to explore the picture for information about what it does not actually show; we ask what happened to lead up to the situation and what might be the result of it. While any picture provides details that demand explanation, those in picture books are deliberately designed to imply the passage of time by making us ask questions about causes and effects.

The Context of Other Pictures. We have considered how one picture conveys movement. But picture books contain a sequence of pictures, and as we move from one to the next, we imagine what might have happened to change what we see in one picture to what we see in the next. Of course, the words of a text often give us the details about what happens between pictures; but once we have developed the strategy of looking for these connections, we can make them even when there are no words. It is this skill that illustrators depend on when they produce *wordless* picture books—ones that imply stories just by providing a sequence of connected pictures.

EXPLORATION: Consider (or have children consider) the extent to which a wordless book depends on your possession of this skill. Take a wordless book such as Claude Ponti's Adele's Album, *Raymond Briggs's* Snowman, *or Pat Hutchins's* Changes, Changes *and consider the difference between what you actually see and what you guess happens in between the pictures.*

STORYTELLING IN WORDS AND PICTURES

The most obvious context that makes the illustrations in picture books meaningful is the words that accompany them. We can totally change the meaning of a picture simply by putting it in the context of different words. For instance, the picture of

Figure 12. Illustration from *Dance, Tanya,* text copyright © 1990 by Patricia Lee Gauch, illustrations copyright © 1990 by Satomi Ichikawa. Reprinted by permission of Philomel Books.

Nijinsky falling from a chair (Figure 8, page 148) would be different if the text said, "Suddenly everything in the room began to float upward, including the boy," and different again if the text said, "The boy fled in terror as his reflection in the mirror suddenly exploded through the glass and materialized in the room." As these examples reveal, words draw our attention to specific details of pictures and cause us to interpret them in specific ways. At the same time, as we have seen throughout this chapter, the pictures focus our attention on specific aspects of the words and cause us to interpret them in specific ways. As a result, a picture book contains at least three stories: the one told by the words, the one implied by the pictures, and the one that results from the combination of the first two.

EXPLORATION: Explore the extent to which this statement is true by separating the words in a picture book from the pictures, or vice versa. Respond (or have children respond) to a text without seeing the pictures; then reread it with *the pictures and comment on the difference. Or respond to the pictures in a book without reading the words; then look at the pictures while reading the words and comment on the difference. How was the story different without either the words or the pictures? What do these differences tell you about the specific contributions that words and pictures make to picture book storytelling?*

In a discussion of the ways in which various media communicate, Susanne Langer says: "There are no happy marriages in art—only successful rape" (86). Picture books represent this sort of rape. In the most interesting ones, the third story, the one told by the words and pictures together, emerges from the contradictions between the other two stories. Such books take advantage of the essential doubleness of the form by using it for ironic purposes.

For instance, Nigel Gray's text for *A Country Far Away* is the words of a child describing an ordinary day in his life, but Philippe Dupasquier's pictures provide an ironic counterpoint by revealing that the words are actually being spoken by two different boys at the same time, each unconscious of the other. There are two different sets of illustrations, one above the text and one below. While both accurately illustrate the text, one set depicts a suburban child surrounded by the objects of affluence, the other an African in a tribal village. The result is an ironic confrontation of different life-styles. More subtly, the text of *Nijinsky* never suggests what the pictures constantly show us—that even in moments of triumph the young dancer remains sad, that even the flowers and toys thrown at him by happy audiences seem like heavy weapons.

EXPLORATION: Choose (or have children choose) any picture book, and explore whether the difference between the information provided by the words and the information provided by the pictures has ironic implications.

As we shift our attention between the pictures and the text, we must shift between different ways of thinking. The words of a good story are suspenseful; they force us to ask, "And then what happened?" But a good picture is attractive; it forces us to stop and look and absorb its details. As a result, the developing action of the plot is regularly interrupted by our perusals of the pictures.

In less successful picture books, our stopping to examine the pictures makes the text seem choppy. But in good books, it becomes a strength rather than a liability. The text can be divided so that the pauses in the story caused by the presence of illustrations can add to the suspense. The characteristic rhythm of picture books consists of a pattern of such delays counterpointing and contributing to the suspense of the plot.

EXPLORATION: Consider (or have children consider) whether the way the text is divided in a picture book adds to or interferes with the suspense.

While the mere presence of pictures changes the shape of a story, the pictures always depict something. What they depict takes place in only one instant; and even the simplest of actions occur over many instants. As a result, an illustrator must choose which moment to show out of the many possible ones described in even the briefest text. As we have seen, the moments chosen imply what happens before and after them; but the specific moment depicted takes on particular significance, and strongly influences the way we understand a story. For instance, we would see the story as less gloomy if Brighton had chosen to depict Nijinsky perched on top of the pile of chairs, an action also included in the text accompanying the picture of him falling.

PICTURE BOOKS AS PUZZLES

Throughout this chapter, I have assumed that picture books offer the pleasure of stories. But some do not tell a story, and do not seem to be designed primarily to give pleasure: in theory, at least, the purpose of alphabet books and number books is to convey information. If we stop to think about it, however, we may wonder about what kind of information they convey.

EXPLORATION: What information do alphabet or number books convey, and how do they do so?

We usually assume that the purpose of alphabet books is to teach children the letters of the alphabet. Presumably, they see the picture of an apple, name it, and thus learn that the accompanying symbol "A" represents the sound that begins the word "apple." Such a process would work fine if visual symbols directly related to specific words. Unfortunately, they don't. A child might look at the apple and accurately name it "fruit," and another child might accurately label the same picture "Golden Delicious." In fact, rather than using the visual information to help us understand the verbal, most of us treat alphabet books in the opposite way; we use our previous knowledge of the letter as a way of identifying the right word to describe the object. If the apple appears on the A page, then it's an apple; if it appears on the F page, it's a fruit.

The implication of this is that alphabet books are not especially educational: we have to know what they are supposed to be teaching before we can make use of them. Instead, they are a form of puzzle, and pleasurable (and even instructive) for that reason. The same is true of number books. If we already know our numbers, we can have fun counting up the objects in the picture to see if they match that number.

Good illustrators know that such books are enjoyable puzzles, and they create pictures that encourage readers to indulge in this sort of pleasure. For instance, in addition to the main animal depicted on each page of Graeme Base's *Animalia,* there are numerous other objects that begin with the same letter; we can play the game of finding their names.

The fact that even the most practical picture book offers the pleasure of puzzle solving is revealing. In an important sense, all picture books are puzzles. The details of pictures invite our attention to their implications. The unmoving pictures require us to solve the puzzle of what actions and motions they represent. The pictures in wordless books require us to solve the puzzle of what story they imply. In books with text, the words and pictures together tell different stories that require us to solve the puzzle of how to connect them. The pleasure of picture books is not just in the stories they tell but in the game of figuring out what those stories are.

WORKS CITED

Anno, Mitsumasa. *Topsy-Turvies: Pictures to Stretch the Imagination.* New York: Weatherhill, 1970.

Base, Graeme. *Animalia.* Toronto: Irwin, 1987.

Briggs, Raymond. *The Snowman.* London: Hamish Hamilton, 1978.

Brighton, Catherine. *Nijinsky.* New York: Doubleday, 1989.

Brown, Marcia. *Cinderella.* New York: Scribner, 1954.

———. *Shadow.* New York: Macmillan, 1982.

Burton, Virginia. *The Little House.* Boston: Houghton Mifflin, 1942.

Cooney, Barbara. *Demeter and Persephone.* New York: Doubleday, 1972.

Deregowski, Jan B. "Illusion and Culture." *Illusion in Nature and Art.* Ed. R. L. Gregory and E. H. Gombrich. London: Duckworth, 1973. 161–189.

Flack, Marjorie. *The Story About Ping.* Illus. Kurt Wiese. New York: Viking, 1933.

Gaffron, Mercedes. "Right and Left in Pictures." *Art Quarterly* 13 (1950): 312–331.

Gauch, Patricia Lee. *Dance, Tanya.* Illus. Satomi Ichikawa. New York: Philomel, 1989.

Gombrich, E. H. *Art and Illusion: A Study in the Psychology of Pictorial Representation.* New York: Pantheon, 1961.

———. "Standards of Truth: The Arrested Image and the Moving Eye." *Critical Inquiry* (Winter 1980): 237–273.

———. "The Visual Image." *Scientific American* 227 (September 1972): 82–94.

Gray, Nigel. *A Country Far Away.* Illus. Philippe Dupasquier. New York: Orchard, 1989.

Grimm, Jacob and Wilhelm. *Snow White and the Seven Dwarfs.* Illus. Nancy Ekholm Burkert. New York: Farrar, Straus and Giroux, 1972.

———. *Snow White.* Illus. Trina Schart Hyman. Boston: Atlantic–Little, Brown, 1974.

Haley, Gail E. *The Green Man.* New York: Scribner, 1979.

Hutchins, Pat. *Changes, Changes.* New York: Macmillan, 1971.

———. *Rosie's Walk.* New York: Macmillan, 1968.

Joyce, William. *George Shrinks.* New York: Harper & Row, 1985.

Keeping, Charles. *Through the Window.* London: Oxford UP, 1970.

Kent, Jack. *Happy-Ever-After Book.* New York: Random House, 1976.

Langer, Susanne K. *Problems of Art: Ten Philosophical Lectures.* New York: Scribner, 1957.
McAfee, Annalena. *The Visitors Who Came to Stay.* Illus. Anthony Browne. London: Hamish Hamilton, 1984.
McDermott, Gerald. *Arrow to the Sun.* New York: Viking, 1974.
Mosel, Arlene. *Tikki Tikki Tembo.* Illus. Blair Lent. New York: Dutton, 1977.
Noyes, Alfred. *The Highwayman.* Illus. Charles Keeping. Oxford: Oxford UP, 1981.
Perrault, Charles. *Cinderella.* Illus. Errol Le Cain. London: Faber and Faber, 1972.
Ponti, Claude. *Adele's Album.* New York: Dutton, 1988.
Potter, Beatrix. *The Tale of Peter Rabbit.* London: Frederick Warne, 1902.
Rogasky, Barbara. *The Water of Life.* Illus. Trina Schart Hyman. New York: Holiday House, 1986.
Scarry, Richard. *Best Word Book Ever.* Rev. ed. New York: Golden, 1980.
Schwarcz, Joseph H. *Ways of the Illustrator: Visual Communication in Children's Literature.* Chicago: American Library Association, 1982.
Sendak, Maurice. *Outside Over There.* New York: Harper & Row, 1981.
———. *Where the Wild Things Are.* New York: Harper & Row, 1963.
Steptoe, John. *Stevie.* New York: Harper & Row, 1969.
Toye, William. *The Mountain Goats of Temlaham.* Illus. Elizabeth Cleaver. Toronto: Oxford UP, 1969.
Van Allsburg, Chris. *The Garden of Abdul Gasazi.* Boston: Houghton Mifflin, 1979.
———. *The Mysteries of Harris Burdick.* Boston: Houghton Mifflin, 1984.
———. *The Polar Express.* Boston: Houghton Mifflin, 1985.
Wildsmith, Brian. *Brian Wildsmith's ABC.* London: Oxford UP, 1962.
Yorinks, Arthur. *Bravo, Minski.* Illus. Richard Egielski. New York: Farrar, Straus and Giroux, 1988.
Zemach, Margot. *Jake and Honeybunch Go to Heaven.* New York: Farrar, Straus and Giroux, 1982.
Zolotow, Charlotte. *Mr. Rabbit and the Lovely Present.* Illus. Maurice Sendak. New York: Harper & Row, 1962.

CHAPTER 11

Fairy Tales and Myths

UNIVERSALLY KNOWN TALES

For many years, I have asked classes of children's literature students to tell me which fairy tales they know so well that they could tell them to a child without consulting a book. While individual suggestions vary, the classes always end up agreeing on the same eight stories:

"Little Red Riding Hood"
"The Three Little Pigs"
"Goldilocks and the Three Bears"
"Hansel and Gretel"
"Jack and the Beanstalk"
"Snow White and the Seven Dwarfs"
"Sleeping Beauty"
"Cinderella"

Many of us know these same few fairy tales so well that we don't know *how* we know them—where we first heard them. We seem to have always known them. People who produce cartoons and commercials assume that even the youngest children will understand allusions to girls in red hoods or giants who say "Fee fie fo fum." Because these eight tales are an important part of the literary repertoire of our culture, a consideration of their history and their characteristic features should offer insight into our views about fairy tales and into our ideas about stories in general.

EXPLORATION: What is your personal repertoire of fairy tales? List the fairy tales you recall well enough to tell from memory, without consulting a book. Explore the significance of the differences between my students' list and your own.

THE HISTORY OF FAIRY TALES

Oral Stories, or Folktales

The eight tales listed above—indeed all the stories we call fairy tales—are now found in books intended primarily for children, but they were originally what folklorists call "folktales." Some centuries ago, these stories circulated orally. People who could not read remembered them and told them to other people who remembered them and told them again. The fact that these tales had to be remembered without the aid of a written text meant that they would have to have memorable features—features that, as we will see, survive in printed versions.

Other features also survive—features that disturb many adults, like the frightening violence with which wolves threaten Red Riding Hood and the three pigs, or the stereotyping of stepmothers and wolves as evil. Not only do the tales express the conventional assumptions of a different time, but children in earlier times were not singled out as needing a different kind of story than adults. As we saw in Chapter 3, the audience for oral tales would have included both children and adults.

EXPLORATION: Assuming that oral tales preserve the outmoded values of an earlier time, are they suitable literature for children today? Consider (or have children consider) the degree to which fairy tales you know might be communicating attitudes that society no longer considers appropriate.

We are not sure where or how any of the folktales originated. Stories similar to "Cinderella" can be found in historical records from as far back as the seventh century, and from a variety of places around the world. It may be that initially just one inventive person created each of these stories; but the tales grew and changed as they passed from one teller to another. It is still a quality of the fairy tales we tell today that they can be narrated in different ways and yet remain essentially the same story. While the Walt Disney movie version of "Cinderella" differs from the story as told by Charles Perrault, it is still recognizable as "Cinderella," and *Snow White in New York* is still "Snow White" even when Fiona French moves the events to another time and place and turns the seven dwarfs into seven jazz musicians. It is this quality that gives fairy tales their key place in the literature of childhood.

Folktales are so prone to being told differently that folklorists identify them not as individual stories but as types—as similar plots that can be told in different ways.

A system of classification, developed by Antti Aarne and revised by Stith Thompson, divides the stories from oral sources around the world into 2,499 types. For example, "Cinderella" is a subtype of type 510: the story of a girl mistreated by members of her family who receives magical help to get out of trouble and gain the attention of a marriageable male. Tales identifiable as belonging to type 510 include versions from North America and Japan as well as the European story most of us know. The girl can be abused by her mother or her stepmother, and she can be covered in ashes or disguised under animal skins; her helper can be a fairy or a magical tree or a cow; and she can reveal herself to her intended through a glass slipper or a magic ring.

EXPLORATION: Read (or have children read) some of the versions of type 510 included in Cinderella: A Casebook, *ed. Alan Dundes. Why might they be identified as the same type of story? What do they have in common with one another?*

From Oral Tale to Written Story

The tales came to be recorded only when people stopped telling them orally; before that, there was no reason to write them down, for the people who wanted to hear them already had access to them orally and in any case, couldn't read.

The first written records of the tales make it clear they had not originally been intended specifically for children—at least not children with the tastes and interests we usually assume modern children have. In a version of "Sleeping Beauty" recorded in Giambattista Basile's *Pentameron* in 1634, the prince so likes the looks of the sleeping princess that he climbs into bed with her and enjoys "the first fruits of love" (374); then he deserts her, pregnant but still sleeping. She doesn't wake up until one of the twins she has given birth to in her sleep gets hungry enough to suck from her finger the enchanted piece of flax that kept her sleeping.

The First Familiar Tales: Perrault's Versions

Recognizable versions of some of the tales we know first appeared in print in 1697, when Charles Perrault, a man of letters associated with the French court, published a book called *Histoires ou Contes du Temps Passé:* stories of past times. It contained eight tales, including three named by my students: "Little Red Riding Hood," "Cinderella," and a "Sleeping Beauty" in which the pregnancy occurs *after* the awakening.

EXPLORATION: Perrault's versions are recognizable but still different from most current versions of fairy tales. Read (or have children read) accurate translations of Perrault's tales such as those by Angela Carter, and consider what aspects of Perrault's versions surprise you.

When Perrault tells us that the Prince and Sleeping Beauty were married immediately after he awakens her, he then adds that they did not sleep much that night because "the princess didn't seem to feel much need for sleep" (translation mine). For readers nowadays, ironic details like this suggest that Perrault is telling these stories not just for innocent children but also for knowing adults; but it seems more likely that he believed that children were, or ought to be, exactly this knowing. Perrault allows Little Red Riding Hood to go off into the woods without any warning of potential danger—not because her mother thinks there is none, but because she seems to take it for granted that a child capable of surviving in a dangerous world *should* already know about such things. So Little Red, who "didn't realize how dangerous it is to pay attention to wolves," and who later ingenuously accepts the wolf's invitation to take off her clothing and climb into bed with him, is justly rewarded for her ignorance. This is the way the story ends:

> "What big teeth you have, granny!"
> "They're to eat you with!" said the wolf. And he threw himself on Little Red Riding Hood and ate her up. (Translation mine)

And that's it. No being saved either in the nick of time or afterward; the girl is dead and remains so.

But Perrault does add a moral that emphasizes the dangers of ignorance: those girls who are innocent enough to talk to strangers are the ones likely to be devoured by wolves. Furthermore, there are "some very mannerly and apparently tame wolves who follow young girls down the streets and even into their homes; and as everybody knows, alas, these sweet-talking, apparently harmless wolves are actually the most dangerous ones" (translation mine). This implies that young girls who *don't* know that lesson deserve to suffer from their ignorance. It seems likely that Perrault expected the youngsters in his audience to be just as conscious of the irony in his stories as the adults.

The Grimm Versions

The first edition of the next important collection of folktales, by the brothers Jacob and Wilhelm Grimm, appeared in Germany in 1812, and eventually included over two hundred tales. To begin with, it seems, Jacob and Wilhelm Grimm were not interested in an audience of children. What later in the nineteenth century became Germany was then a number of duchies and princedoms, and the Grimms collected folktales with the political purpose of supporting unification by finding evidence of the basic linguistic and cultural oneness of the German people.

Unlike Perrault, then, whose interest in the tales was in their entertainment value, the Grimm brothers were scholars and pioneering folklorists. But while they made great claims for the authenticity of their tales, their methods would not satisfy the more stringent demands of modern folklorists. The Grimms accepted as authentic "folk" tales ones that they heard from literate middle-class sources. As John Ellis shows, there is evidence that the version of "Little Red Riding Hood" they identified as authentically German came from a relative whose French background would have provided access to a printed text of Perrault's version.

Furthermore, while modern folklorists believe that tales should be recorded exactly as told orally by one informant, the Grimms thought they could uncover the most authentic version of a tale by combining the supposed best features of the various versions they heard. But in the process of adding to and deleting from the tales they heard, the Grimms gave preference to events and characterizations that suited their own middle-class, Christian values. For instance, the stepmothers in stories like "Hansel and Gretel" and "Snow White" as the Grimms originally recorded them were birth mothers, an idea that seems to have disturbed the Grimms enough to disguise it.

Despite their original scholarly intentions, the Grimms soon discovered that children could be a significant audience for these stories. The changes they made to the tales from edition to edition imply an attempt to meet the moral needs of children; and in 1825, they published a shorter edition of the tales clearly directed at a popular audience, particularly children. Included in that edition are versions of five of the eight tales my students know best: versions of "Little Red Riding Hood," "Sleeping Beauty," and "Cinderella" different from the ones Perrault told, and two stories first printed by the Grimms, "Snow White" and "Hansel and Gretel."

The Grimms' "Little Red Cap" shows that they or their informants had very different ideas about children than Perrault did. Before the little girl leaves for grandmother's house, her mother gives her many warnings: "Walk properly like a good little girl, and don't leave the path or you'll fall down and break the bottle [of wine that Red Cap is to take to grandmother] and there won't be anything for grandmother. And when you get to her house, don't forget to say good morning, and don't go looking in all the corners" (Manheim 99). Unlike Perrault's mother, this mother believes her daughter is too innocent to look after herself. And she's right; the child does not heed the warnings and is eaten by the wolf.

But since the problem was her disobedience rather than her lack of knowledge, she is allowed a second chance; a hunter comes along and rescues her, and she herself makes the significance of her adventure clear to young readers: "She said to herself, 'Never again will I leave the path and run off into the wood when my mother tells me not to' " (Manheim 101). For Perrault, children should know enough about evil to protect themselves from it; for the Grimms, children need only know how much they *don't* know, so that they can see the wisdom of accepting the wise advice of their parents—and of cautionary fables like this one, which the Grimms made out of a not-necessarily-cautionary oral tale.

EXPLORATION: Few of the over two hundred Grimm tales are widely known. In a complete text like Manheim's, read (or have children read) some of the less familiar tales: stories such as "Clever Hans" (no. 32), "The Robber Bridegroom" (no. 40), "The Two Brothers" (no. 60), "The Glass Coffin" (no. 163), "The Goose Girl at the Spring" (no. 179). In what way do they vary from your expectations of fairy tales? Why might they not have become as popular as the better-known tales?

Fairy Tales after Grimm

The Grimm brothers collection was not widely read until Edward Taylor translated some of the stories into English in 1823. Taylor's *German Popular Stories* was specifically advertised as being for "young minds" (Opie 25) and included comical illustrations by George Cruikshank. It seems to have been the success of this English edition that gave the Grimms the idea of producing the 1825 abridged edition that made the stories popular with German children.

Later in the nineteenth century, when admirers of the Grimm tales in many parts of Europe collected and published tales from their own countries, they took the connection between the tales and children for granted. Fairy tales had achieved the status they still have as children's literature.

The most famous gathering of fairy tales from England, compiled by Joseph Jacobs from a variety of early written sources that claimed oral roots, clearly implies an audience of children, focuses on the entertainment value of mysteries and adventures, ghosts and giantkillers, and offers the pleasure of an energetic writing style. Of the eight best-known tales I listed earlier, three are of English origin and appear in Jacobs: "The Three Little Pigs," "The Three Bears," and "Jack and the Beanstalk."

EXPLORATION: Read (or have children read) a selection of tales from another tradition, such as the Russian tales first collected by Afanas'ev, the Norwegian tales first collected by Asbjørnsen and Moe, or the Italian tales collected by Calvino. What do these tales have in common with the other fairy tales you know? How do they vary?

Tales from Around the World. In this century, as we have developed knowledge of the similarity in folktales told in widely different parts of the world, it has become common to think of the tales as a painless way of encouraging tolerance in children. On the jacket of a typical contemporary collection, Jane Yolen's *Favorite Folktales from Around the World,* Isaac Asimov is quoted as saying, "A book like this is worth a thousand homilies on the brotherhood of humanity. This collection of tales bubbling up from the thoughts and imaginations of ordinary people everywhere in all cultures shows amply the common reservoirs of hopes, fears, love, and rascality that we all share."

I have no doubt that the immense variety of stories from many cultures can be richly satisfying; I personally derive great pleasure from some of the Haitian stories collected by Diane Wolkstein in *The Magic Orange Tree* or the native American stories selected by Richard Erdoes and Alfonso Ortiz.

Not surprisingly, however, my students never mention any stories from other cultures as ones they already know and remember, and they often tell me that they find reading them boring. For those with European backgrounds, stories from Asia or South America can seem disturbingly alien—even though they often represent tale types we are familiar with. My own pleasure in the Haitian tales derives in no small part from their strangeness.

Ironically, furthermore, students from non-European backgrounds *also* often find the versions of stories from their own cultures that are included in children's anthologies equally boring or distressing. The stories have been distorted to suit conventional Euro-American values.

For instance, a student of Chinese background once told me that, while the version of a folktale he had first heard as a child and that was included in Joanna Cole's *Bestloved Folktales of the World* was reasonably accurate, the title given there distorted it. The story is about a woman's conviction that she is meant to marry one specific man, who asks for her hand too late and dies of remorse. On the day of her wedding to another man, she stops the procession, falls on the grave of her true love, and says, "If we were really intended to be man and wife, open your grave three feet wide" (533). The grave opens and the woman leaps into it. Finally, she and her true intended become rainbows. According to my Chinese student, to call this tale "Faithful Even in Death" distorts it to make it fit non-Asian cultural assumptions. That title implies that a woman's faithfulness is a matter of choice on her part and, therefore, a virtue that is being rewarded, whereas the story itself makes it clear that the woman had no choice but to love him whom she was meant to love, and that the situation has nothing to do with virtue or reward. Despite Cole's claim that stories of different cultures "deal with universal human dilemmas that span differences of age, culture, and geography" (xvii), this story expresses a distinctly non-European conception of fate.

EXPLORATION: Read (or have children read) some tales from non-European sources in picture books or in collections of fairy tales from different cultures. Do you find them interesting? Why or why not? To what degree do they vary from traditional European tales? Try to find versions of the same tales in scholarly sources. To what degree have the children's versions been changed to suit our conventional values and assumptions?

ORAL TALES FROM WRITTEN VERSIONS: VARIANT VERSIONS AND CULTURAL VALUES

The way most of us remember fairy tales has little to do with the versions recorded in the pioneering editions. Intriguingly, fairy tales seem to retain the oral characteristic of memorability even for those who first experience them through reading. Once they have been printed, people who read them tend to remember them and then retell them, either orally or in other books. Not surprisingly, the retellings differ from the originals, transformed by the specific values and attitudes of those who tell them.

EXPLORATION: Write down (or have children write down) any or all of the eight popular tales as you already know them yourself. Then look up the versions of these tales by Perrault, the Grimms, and Jacobs, and consider the implications of any differences between your version(s) and the one(s) in the text(s).

The tendency of tales to be modified as they are retold explains why the tales as most people know them now differ from the versions recorded in traditional sources. Nowadays, for instance, we are so fearful of frightening children with the depiction of violence that in many printed versions of the tale, Little Red Riding Hood is not eaten at all; she runs away just in the nick of time, or even beats up the wolf and saves herself. And few contemporary versions record the details of the Grimms' version of "Cinderella," in which the wicked stepsisters cut off their toes and heels in order to fit the shoe, and finally have their eyes pecked out by birds.

This habit of making fairy tales fit patterns we feel comfortable with also explains the peculiarity of "The Three Bears." Who are we supposed to sympathize with, the nice family whose home is invaded or the nice little girl who has to deal with scary bears? The central character in early versions of this story was a nasty old woman, a vagrant who clearly was at fault for breaking into someone else's house. But probably because we expect the main characters in fairy tales to be young innocents, the old woman became a girl; and that change made the tale as ambiguous as it now is, particularly when tales like "Little Red Riding Hood" and "Three Little Pigs" assert the essential villainy of all hairy beasts.

These changes and choices clearly reveal the extent to which our versions of fairy tales express the ideological values of North American middle-class culture: our consciously or unconsciously held attitudes about goodness and justice. They also reveal the extent to which the mass media have created our images of fairy tales: the idea of "love's first kiss" awakening Snow White, rather than the jarring of her glass coffin reported in Grimm, probably comes from the Walt Disney movie, the most widely known version of the story in the fifty years since it first appeared. When we criticize fairy tales for being outmoded, we forget that the archaic sexist or ageist values we assume they express may be those of the United States in the 1930s, not necessarily those of an ancient oral tradition or even those imposed on the tales by writers like Perrault and the Grimms.

EXPLORATION: Compare (or have children compare) a number of current or recent versions of a popular fairy tale with an earlier version by the Grimms, Perrault, or Jacobs. To what degree do the differences represent different cultural assumptions?

WHICH VERSIONS SHOULD CHILDREN READ?

The psychoanalyst Bruno Bettelheim believes that fairy tales in their original versions speak directly to the unconscious concerns of children. Because the tales emerge from an anonymous oral tradition that allows them to express something beyond the limited perceptions of any individual writer, Bettelheim feels they deal with "universal human problems" (6). Bettelheim's position is seriously undermined by his incorrect assumption that the Grimm versions accurately represent the oral tradition; we have already seen that they do not. But there may well be a case for arguing that fairy tales as told by writers like the Grimms and Jacobs *should* be read by children, exactly because their expression of outmoded nineteenth-century values distinguishes them from the literature currently being written for children.

As we saw in Chapter 4, we often assume that children are vulnerable. Because we wish to protect them, the literature we write for them—and the fairy tales we rewrite for them—tend to leave out unsettling ideas and events. Such censoring deprives children of a basic pleasure of literature, the chance to experience painful circumstances without actually suffering from them. It is an opportunity to rehearse difficult situations before having to deal with them in real life.

Older versions of fairy tales, which were not specifically written with the needs of children in mind, offer that opportunity. Furthermore, they do so in terms of richly evocative situations and language that is subtle and often beautiful. Not only will children exposed to a wide variety of new and old stories have access to a variety of enjoyable experiences, but also, I believe, they are not likely to be indoctrinated by the values of any one of them. They will have a large menu from which to choose and thus determine their own values.

Fairy tales are particularly useful in this way, simply because the existence in print of so many different versions of the same tale allows them to act as schemata for one another. The sameness of the shared plot puts the variations, most of which imply different values and assumptions, into sharp relief.

EXPLORATION: There are hundreds of picture book versions of stories like "Cinderella" and "Little Red Riding Hood." Read (or have children read) several different versions of one fairy tale. In what ways do the differences in these versions express different values and ideological assumptions?

CHARACTERISTICS OF FAIRY TALES

Despite their ability to be told in different ways and to convey different values, fairy tales still share many characteristics. We will explore several elements: setting, characters, events, meaning, and structure.

Setting

EXPLORATION: Before reading what follows, explore your answers to the questions I'm considering here. When is "once upon a time"? What did the people wear in fairy tales? What kinds of buildings did they inhabit?

Where and when do fairy tales take place? The phrase, "Once upon a time," evokes a combination of real time and fantasy. Magical things happen: pumpkins turn into coaches, people sleep for a hundred years, pigs and wolves talk. But the settings of fairy tales are not places in which *anything at all* can happen. The talking pigs don't turn into pumpkins; the magic seems restricted to one or two elements in each story; otherwise, things are as they once were in what we assume was the real past of our own real world. Unlike science fiction, which uses fantasy to describe complex future times, fairy tales express nostalgia for a simpler past time.

But "once upon a time" does not refer to any specific time, not Germany in the fifteenth century, or Wales in the seventeenth. When I ask people to explore their mental images of fairy tale settings, they usually describe a vaguely medieval Europe, a place free of the uglier aspects of modern technology.

In the imaginary time and place of fairy tales, the castles are sumptuous, but frighteningly dense woods, where people live in huts, begin just outside the castle walls. There are few "middles," few ordinary houses between the sumptuousness of the castles and the harshness of the huts; the people are usually either incredibly rich or incredibly poor, and the women usually wear either ornately bejeweled gowns or rags.

While the lack of middles makes the fairy tale world seem harsh, it is actually utopian; with none of the confusion caused by reality's complex mixtures of good and bad, problems are easily understood, choices obvious. Adversity is the result of the specific actions of individuals rather than of uncontrollable forces like social inequity or war. People are free to focus on their own problems and even control their own destinies.

Characters

In the clear-cut world of fairy tales, it is easy to figure out whom we should admire and whom we should hate. The distinctions between those who are admirable and those who are hateful are clear from the beginning. Anyone familiar with the pattern of fairy tales expects as soon as a story begins with a description of someone in trouble that that person will end up happily. In fairy tales, in fact, goodness is defined by situation rather than by action: a character who begins in the position of being abused is automatically defined as good.

Some characters do little to deserve their identification as good. While Perrault tells us that Cinderella is kind, the events of the story show her being acted upon by others rather than acting herself; she performs no act that confirms her goodness. Snow White does even less, and Sleeping Beauty does nothing but sleep. On the basis of these characters, we might conclude that goodness in fairy tales consists of passivity, even stupidity: magical assistance comes to those whose lack of abilities puts them most in need of help.

EXPLORATION: Is that statement true? Consider (or have children consider) the goodness of good characters in these or other tales.

Once characters' situations define them as good, furthermore, we continue to consider them good no matter what they do; no bad act seems able to change our judgment of them. Because Jack is in the role of abused victim, we don't seem to care that his exploits in the giant's house are acts of thievery (although some modern versions try to justify his thefts by adding that the giant first stole these objects from Jack's father). And even though the violence directed against characters like Snow White and the Three Pigs first defines them as good, we don't change our minds about their goodness when they perform acts of violence against their enemies.

In order to fill the role of good hero or heroine, a fairy tale character must seem powerless in relation to someone more powerful: someone recognizably evil because he or she has power and misuses it by directing it against someone weaker. The villains of fairy tales have high social status (the queens in "Cinderella" and "Snow White"), or great size and strength (the giant in "Jack and the Beanstalk," the wolves in "Little Red Riding Hood" and "Three Pigs") or great knowledge (the witches of "Hansel and Gretel" and "Sleeping Beauty"). The heroes and heroines are children, poor people, or foolish people like Jack, who sells a cow for a few beans.

Events: A Basic Story Pattern

The movement from the beginning of typical fairy tales to the end is one of the most basic story patterns, one found in numerous other children's stories; the events allow the powerless underdog to exchange places with the character who first had power over him. Usually through some form of magical assistance, the underdog comes to a position of great wealth or social influence, and the previously powerful character dies or becomes an outsider, an underdog. If there were a sequel to "Cinderella" that fulfilled our expectations of fairy tales, Cinderella herself would probably have to be the villain; her marriage has given her the sort of status and power we expect to be a source of evil.

In the real world, underdogs don't often win, for the simple reason that those who are powerful use their power. But the magical elements in fairy tales allow events to take place that could not easily happen in real life. As we saw earlier, the magic in fairy tales is not capricious; in fact, the laws of physics or logic are suspended only to get the "good" characters into trouble or to help them get out of trouble, or both. Pumpkins become coaches only when underdogs like Cinderella are in enough trouble to *need* reality to be suspended; the magic allows her to triumph, and then it stops.

Wish-fulfillment Fantasy. The most significant truth about fairy tales is that they represent things not as they really are, but as we imagine they ought to be. Because their plots offer the satisfaction of an imaginary fulfillment of the wish for power, they are *wish-fulfillment fantasies* for people who perceive or who enjoy pretending to perceive themselves as underdogs. As such, they are emotionally useful stories. Nevertheless, the pleasure fairy tales offer depends on the degree to which we understand that they do represent a wish fulfilled, a distortion of actual reality. Those who question the value of fairy tales for children usually do so because they assume that children cannot distinguish between fantasy and reality and read wish-fulfillment fantasy as a description of the way things actually are.

EXPLORATION: Consider (or have children consider) whether fairy tales are good for children. Can the distortions that allow the tales to act as wish fulfillments—the extremely good heroes and extremely bad villains, the triumph of the weak over the strong—be seen as realistic? Is it bad if they are? Why or why not?

Meaning

Despite the obvious tendencies of fairy tales toward wish fulfillment, most interpreters of fairy tales suggest that they do in fact represent the truth, that the fantasy of the tales is a symbolic depiction of the way things are. As we have seen, Bettelheim called the tales symbolic representations of the truths of the unconscious. From a more mystical perspective, Joyce Thomas identifies the truth of the tales as *the* truth hidden within reality itself, "the unfamiliar asleep within the familiar, the magical housed within the shell of the mundane. . . . This is the world, the tales say, and it is truly marvellous, mysterious, wonder-full" (115). In awakening our sense of wonder, fairy tales teach us to appreciate the mystery of the real world.

Critics like Bettelheim and Thomas find basic "truths" in fairy tales because they wrongly believe that the tales accurately represent an anonymous oral tradition that transcends the distortions of individual retellings. But even critics who understand the degree to which the meanings of tales depend upon the values of a specific teller maintain that they contain deeper truths. In *Fairy Tales and the Art of Subversion,* Jack Zipes says that "the fairy tales we have come to revere as classical are not ageless, universal, and beautiful in and of themselves. . . . They are historical prescriptions, internalized, potent, explosive, and we acknowledge the power they hold over our lives by mystifying them" (11). But Zipes "mystifies" them himself when he insists that the "historical prescriptions" of bourgeois writers like Perrault and the Grimms are distortions of a saner—that is, truer—folk tradition that represents the more radical political values he himself shares; in *Breaking the Magical Spell,* he speaks of "the imaginative motifs and symbolical elements of class conflict and rebellion in the pre-capitalist folk tales" (24). Similarly, Ruth Bottigheimer focuses on the repressive nineteenth-century attitudes imposed on the tales by the Grimm brothers, but discovers a "latent content" hidden within the Grimm versions which she sees as the truth inside the tales and which mirrors her own late-twentieth-century feminist values.

It is interesting that the truths these critics find in the tales seem to represent fulfillments of their personal wishes. The Marxist Zipes finds the truths of Marxism; the feminist Bottigheimer, the truths of feminism. Thus, even for interpreters the tales are wish-fulfillment fantasies.

Even so, the differing interpretations have something in common. In finding an underlying truth, they all imply that in fairy tales, things are not what they seem.

That general idea may actually be the meaning of the tales that most gives us pleasure. Seen from a different point of view, the passivity and stupidity of fairy tale heroes and heroines may be a wise ability to accept that which transcends the limitations of ordinary reason and logic. Cinderella is passive and stupid enough—or wise enough?—to accept the help of her fairy godmother without question. European fairy tales express the paradoxes central to the Christian culture they emerged from: the fool in his folly is wise, and the meek do inherit the earth.

On the other hand, what I've just said may merely be another retelling: my own version of stories whose basic quality is that they are capable of taking on so many different meanings.

EXPLORATION: What do you *think fairy tales mean? Consider (or have children consider) the relative merits of the various theories suggested above, or think through the tales you know in order to develop a theory of your own.*

Structure

If we look at a number of versions of a fairy tale, we can easily distinguish between what varies and what remains the same. What changes are the details that establish an individual storyteller's sense of the meaning of the tale and its function for an audience; what is left after we eliminate the details is a sequence of events that recurs in version after version.

This sequence of events is not itself the authentic or original story; it is merely a basic structural pattern to which details can be added in order to create one of many possible stories. For instance, we can isolate this central sequence of events underlying most versions of "Little Red Riding Hood":

1. Mother gives Little Red instructions and sends her to grandmother.
2. Little Red converses with the wolf.
3. The wolf goes to grandmother (and in most versions, eats her), and then disguises himself as grandmother.
4. Little Red arrives, and the wolf invites her in.
5. Little Red and the wolf discuss his appearance, a conversation culminating in the wolf's threat to eat her.

Beyond that basic structure, various events may occur. What is significant here is that we wouldn't consider a story to be a version of "Little Red Riding Hood" if it did not contain the listed events in the listed order. But we will agree that *any* story that contains these events *is* "Little Red Riding Hood," even if other details are included—for instance, if Little Red meanders through the woods picking flowers or talking to chipmunks between episodes 2 and 3—and no matter what specific instructions Little Red's mother gives her or whether Little Red escapes death at the end.

Many of the best-loved versions of the tales, like those by the Grimms, describe only the central moments in detail and quickly pass over or summarize what happens between them. Rather than the gradually developing plots we conventionally expect of fiction, these versions offer a series of intense moments separated from each other by less intense and more broadly summarized connecting passages.

These central moments have interesting relationships with each other. In ''Snow White'' the picture of a woman looking at herself in a reflecting glass and wishing to be beautiful counterpoints the picture in the previous central moment of another queen looking through clear glass and wishing that someone else be beautiful. The other central moments in the tale also involve looking, often through glass: the huntsman refuses to kill Snow White because he looks at her and finds her beautiful; Snow White looks at the dwarfs' house; the dwarfs look at Snow White asleep; the Queen entices Snow White by talking with her through a window; and the Prince sees and falls in love with Snow White when he sees her through her glass coffin.

Versions that include more details lose the revealing counterpoints that a focus on central moments offers. On the other hand, versions with little detail cannot provide the suspenseful plot and evocation of setting and character that are the basis of our pleasure in other kinds of fiction.

EXPLORATION: Read (or have children read) several different versions of the same tale. Identify the central moments and their relationships with one another. Then compare the degree to which the different versions focus on these central moments. Consider which version satisfies you most, and why.

LITERARY FAIRY TALES

Once fairy tales were collected and retold for children, they became models for writers like Hans Christian Andersen, George MacDonald, and Oscar Wilde, who wished to create similar stories of their own. The sort of story they wrote, based on traditional fairy tales but often substantially different from them, is called a *literary fairy tale.*

In Chapter 7, for instance, we considered Andersen's ''Princess and the Pea,'' a story modeled on traditional fairy tales but with a sophisticated irony unlike the traditional tales. And in his ''Little Match Girl,'' Andersen replaces the traditional happy ending in which an underdog achieves worldly power with something more complex; the underdog dies from cold and hunger, but for those who have eyes to see, the misery is an illusion; she has entered the glory of heaven.

Liberated Fairy Tales

In recent years, in response to the presumed danger of the violence and sexism of traditional fairy tales, a whole body of literature has developed which presents variations of fairy tale situations with more acceptable values—particularly in terms of the way women are portrayed. In Robert Munsch's *Paperbag Princess,* for instance, a determined princess reverses our expectations by using her wits to rescue from a dragon the prince she plans to marry, only to discover that he is too conceited to be worthy of her. In the end, she decides to remain single.

Such stories often strike adult readers as both enjoyable and useful: they are funny, and they present worthwhile role models. What we forget, I think, is the degree to which our own pleasure in these stories depends on our knowledge of all those other stories in which the princes rescue the princesses. Without the outmoded, sexist schema of those stories to compare it with, *Paperbag Princess* loses much of its humor and almost all of its point. If we assume that such stories are good for children, then we must believe one of the following:

- We must first teach children the outmoded traditional role models in order to unteach them.
- Children *already* know these role models. (1) It is natural for children to assume that women are weak and men strong; (2) or else they learn the notion so early in their life that it is firmly established by the time they are old enough to hear simple stories like *Paperbag Princess.*

In any case, all stories reflect the ideologies of their tellers; and if we aren't yet as liberated as we might wish we were, then the stories we tell, despite their good intentions, won't be any more liberated. In "Cinderelma," from *Dr. Gardner's Fairy Tales for Today's Children* by Richard A. Gardner, M.D., a liberated woman still achieves happiness by marrying the man of her dreams. Indeed, marriage is the happy ending of a surprising number of supposedly liberated fairy tales.

In his "Introduction for Adults," Dr. Gardner objects to the happy endings of traditional tales because they misrepresent real possibilities in a way that "contributes to our general dissatisfaction and low frustration tolerance." So after the mistreated Cinderelma realizes there is no such thing as a fairy godmother, makes her own dress and walks to the ball, she rejects the rich prince because she feels she has nothing in common with him; he is enmeshed in the interests of his class. But the story replaces one wish-fulfillment fantasy with another—one that Dr. Gardner so takes for granted as an American that he seems to assume it could not possibly cause dissatisfaction or frustration; Cinderelma falls in love with a man who, like herself, is poor but hardworking, and the two live out the American dream, becoming wealthy through entrepreneurship and diligence.

EXPLORATION: Read (or have children read) some liberated fairy tales, such as those collected in Zipes's Don't Bet on the Prince. *Consider the degree to which they escape repressive, outmoded, or dissatisfying values.*

MYTHS

Folklorists once posited the theory that fairy tales are distorted reminiscences of ancient myths about nature; for instance, the wolf's devouring of Red Riding Hood was supposed to represent the dark of night devouring the sunset. Such theories have been discredited. As far as we know, the tales were always intended to be entertaining stories, even when they were in the oral tradition. But while fairy tales are not myths, many people think that myths can become fairy tales.

Myths as Stories

Myths are stories with a special status. For those who believe in them, they are true—not symbolically true or allegorically true, but absolutely true, a factual accounting of the nature of the world as it is. If we accept their truth, furthermore, myths tell us how to live: what to believe and how to behave. In other words, "myth" is the name we give to stories that express religious truth, when we happen not to believe they are true. For the ancient Greeks, what we call the Greek myths were accurate accounts of real events that not only explained the nature of the world but also defined proper conduct. Similarly, for people who are not Christians, the biblical stories of the creation of the world and the resurrection of Christ are myths.

Nowadays, nobody believes in the literal existence, for example, of Persephone; the particular religious truths in the story of the young woman abducted by Hades have indeed become myths. But the story of Persephone is still a story, even if it is no longer a true one; so it might well be told to those who don't believe its truth for the same reason that we tell fairy tales: for the pleasure it contains.

Anthologies of children's literature contain many stories of this sort—not just Greek and Norse myths, but also stories about supernatural beings from the traditional cultures of native North Americans and other societies around the world. Sometimes these stories are treated as if they were no different from folktales: both Joanna Cole's *Bestloved Folktales of the World* and Jane Yolen's *Favorite Folktales from Around the World* contain not only genuine folktales—stories that started out as entertaining fictional tales—but also a few stories based on godlike beings, such as the Algonquian Glooscap and the Ojibwa Nanabozho, who have the status of myth.

The custom of using myths as entertaining stories raises some provocative questions:

- Can these stories, as some adherents of Carl Jung's teachings believe, convey essential and enduring archetypal truths even to those who don't share the culture they emerged from?
- Separated from their original religious or mythic purposes, are they still good stories?
- More significantly: For those of European background to treat stories of Glooscap or Nanabozho as entertaining literature is exactly like a publisher in Iran producing a book about the magical exploits of the fictional hero Christ for the entertainment of an audience of Muslim children. Even if they are good stories, I believe we need to think about the moral implications of reading what is or once was true and sacred to someone else as just a fiction, as a source not of spiritual truth but of imaginative pleasure.

EXPLORATION: After reading an earlier version of this section, my colleague Mavis Reimer responded this way:

> The logical consequence of the view that we ought *not* to read as a fiction that which is true to someone else is that we finally can read nothing that doesn't confirm our own system of beliefs, a view that is egocentric in the extreme, and a view that you yourself have been urging readers of this book to move past, by unmasking the many different ways we refuse to acknowledge differences in our culture. As a Christian, I have no objection to Iranian children hearing of Christ as a magic hero; I suspect the only Christians who would are extreme fundamentalists. Does the passion with which someone holds a view qualify it as "off-limits" to other readers and writers? That would certainly tend to support the ban on a book such as Salman Rushdie's *The Satanic Verses*. All ideas, ideologies and belief systems must be open to inquiry in a free society—and as you've been suggesting in this book, just such an inquiry is one of the pleasures of reading fiction. Using the texts of people from other cultures in an attempt to access their meanings without having to encounter them as human beings is a deplorable and immoral procedure, and one that we can and should expose; but that's an issue separate from the one you raise here.

Consider (or have children consider) these views. Read Padraic Colum's or Garfield and Blishen's versions of Greek myths or Dorothy Reid's versions of stories about the Ojibwa Nanabozho, and consider their value as fiction. Does the fact that people have believed these stories to represent absolute truth interfere with your pleasure in them? Should it?

Myths and Cultural Education

It is possible to suggest reasons other than just entertainment for children to read myths. As I suggested, Jungians and some religious thinkers believe that myths of all ages and cultures express archetypal knowledge and convey truths even to those who are not members of the culture that produced them; these thinkers would share such stories with children to enable them to experience the archetypal knowledge. Even if we do not accept the existence of archetypes, we might argue that the roots of Western society can be found in the values of ancient Athens, so that reading the Greek myths teaches children something important about the roots of European culture. Or we might say that the Greek myths are still a significant part of the Western cultural repertoire, so that children should learn them as quickly as they can. About stories from non-European cultures like the legends of Nanabozho, we might say that widespread knowledge of these texts can only increase our tolerance and understanding.

Such arguments depend on the assumption that these stories *accurately* represent cultures different from our own—that they are authentic. Unfortunately, as we noticed in regard to folktales, the versions of myths and legends found in books intended for children have almost always been reworked to suit current ideas about what children might enjoy or ought to hear; they represent a form of the "claw back"

I discussed earlier in regard to TV, a version of the alien that makes it more familiar and less frightening.

In a collection not intended for children, such as Richard Erdoes and Alfonso Ortiz's *American Indian Myths and Legends,* it is not surprising to discover that trickster figures like Glooscap or the Sioux Coyote had humorous sexual adventures of the sort that never appear in the stories about them intended for contemporary children. Even the stories that do appear in children's texts have been watered down. In Dorothy Reid's version, Nanabozho flies with geese, then falls into a swamp of oozing mud; in more scholarly versions of this tale, he falls into an enemy camp, where he is tied to a stake and his enemies relieve themselves on him until only his head remains uncovered.

EXPLORATION: Nevertheless, it might be argued that "children's versions" that distort the original tales might have other redeeming educational value for child readers. Explore your own opinion about that.

Furthermore, retelling the stories for children causes differences in style and structure that further distort their meanings. When Christie Harris retells the story "Mouse Woman and Porcupine Hunter," a legend of the Tsimshian people of the North American Northwest coast, she begins the story with the word "once," causing us to expect a fairy tale rather than a description of the sacred activities of divine beings. She then changes the Chief Porcupine, from the divine being in the impressive shape of a human chief who is described in a more authentic version collected by Franz Boaz, into a figure of fun, "near-sighted, solitary, pigeon-toed, bowlegged, slow, and peaceful" (8).

Even stranger, she turns Porcupine Hunter, who is the villain of the original story because he kills too many porcupines, into another figure of fun, a henpecked husband at the mercy of an acquisitive wife. This wife, barely mentioned by Boaz but a central character in Harris's story, is the traditional comic shrew of European tales like "The Fisherman and His Wife"; without knowledge of the original legend, we would have to believe, inaccurately, that the Tsimshian were as sexist as traditional European culture. In retelling the story in the style of a comic European tale, Harris totally misrepresents its tone and its meaning.

EXPLORATION: Jungian thinkers would probably disagree, and say that we gain more by focusing on the archetypal content remaining in new versions of old myths than on the distortions of the rewriting, as I have done here. Explore your response to that possibility by thinking of two different rewritten versions of a myth in terms of how they vary and what they share. Which is more important in your response, the similarities or the differences?

Ironically, perhaps, even when the stories of non-European myths have been watered down or reshaped to fit our conventional expectations, they still express a view of the world different enough to seem alien to many members of the dominant culture. After reading a story about Nanabozho, one of my students described him as "egocentric, cocky, and conceited. I find his character very weak, and I don't have any particular respect for him." This student's European assumption that good is separate from evil and God morally superior to humans prevented her from understanding a godlike figure capable of being both human and divine, helpful and hurtful, good and bad. As Erdoes and Ortiz say, "To those used to the patterns of European fairy tales and folktales, Indian legends often seem chaotic, inconsistent, or incomplete. Plots seem to travel at their own speed, defying convention or at times doing away completely with recognizable beginnings and endings. [The trickster] Coyote is a powerful creature one moment, a snivelling coward the next. . . . To try to apply conventional (Western) logic is not only impossible but unnecessary" (xii).

It may well be that children can benefit from access to myths and legends of different peoples. But as the issues I've raised here suggest, we can't simply assume they will do so without first providing them with some sense of the distinct qualities of this special kind of story.

EXPLORATION: In recent years, native North Americans and members of other minority groups have complained about those in the dominant culture "stealing" their stories, retelling them in ways that change their meaning. Is retelling the story of a culture different from one's own an act of theft? In exploring your response to this question, you might consider the arguments about "the right to represent individuals or topics belonging to a minority culture" (188) reported in Barbara Godard's "Politics of Representation: Some Native Canadian Women Writers."

WORKS CITED

Afanas'ev, Aleksandr. *Russian Fairy Tales.* Trans. Norbert Guterman. New York: Pantheon, 1945.

Andersen, Hans Christian. *Hans Andersen's Fairy Tales: A Selection.* Trans. L. W. Kingsland. Oxford: Oxford UP, 1984.

Asbjørnsen, Peter Christian, and Jørgen Moe. *Norwegian Folk Tales.* New York: Pantheon, 1982.

Basile, Giambattista. *The Pentameron.* Trans. Richard Burton. London: Spring, n.d.

Bettelheim, Bruno. *The Uses of Enchantment: The Meaning and Importance of Fairy Tales.* New York: Knopf, 1976.

Boaz, Franz. *Tsimshian Mythology.* Based on texts recorded by Henry W. Tate. 1916. New York: Johnson Reprint Co., 1970.

Bottigheimer, Ruth. *Grimms' Bad Girls and Bold Boys: The Moral and Social Vision of the Tales.* New Haven: Yale UP, 1987.

Calvino, Italo. *Italian Folktales.* Trans. George Martin. New York: Pantheon, 1980.

Cole, Joanna. *Bestloved Folktales of the World.* Garden City: Doubleday, 1982.

Colum, Padraic. *The Children's Homer.* New York: Collier, 1982.

——. *The Golden Fleece and the Heroes Who Lived Before Achilles.* New York: Collier, 1983.
Dundes, Alan, ed. *Cinderella: A Casebook.* Madison: The U of Wisconsin P, 1982.
Ellis, John. *One Fairy Story Too Many: The Brothers Grimm and Their Tales.* Chicago: U of Chicago P, 1983.
Erdoes, Richard, and Alfonso Ortiz. *American Indian Myths and Legends.* New York: Pantheon, 1984.
French, Fiona. *Snow White in New York.* Oxford: Oxford UP, 1986.
Gardner, Richard A. *Dr. Gardner's Fairy Tales for Today's Children.* Englewood Cliffs: Prentice-Hall, 1974.
Garfield, Leon, and Edward Blishen. *The God Beneath the Sea.* London: Longman, 1970.
——. *The Golden Shadow.* London: Longman, 1973.
Godard, Barbara. "The Politics of Representation: Some Native Canadian Women Writers." *Canadian Literature* 124–125 (Spring-Summer 1990): 183–225.
Grimm, Jacob and Wilhelm. *Grimms' Fairy Tales.* Trans. Edward Taylor. Harmondsworth, Middlesex: Penguin Puffin, 1971.
——. *Grimms' Tales for Young and Old.* Trans. Ralph Manheim. Garden City: Doubleday, 1977.
Harris, Christie. *Mouse Woman and the Mischief Makers.* Toronto: McClelland and Stewart, 1977.
Jacobs, Joseph. *English Fairy Tales.* London: Bodley Head, 1968.
Opie, Iona and Peter. *The Classic Fairy Tales.* London: Oxford UP, 1974.
Munsch, Robert. *The Paperbag Princess.* Toronto: Annick, 1980.
Perrault, Charles. *The Fairy Tales.* Trans. Angela Carter. New York: Bard Avon, 1977.
Reid, Dorothy. *Tales of Nanabozho.* Toronto: Oxford UP, 1963.
Thomas, Joyce. "The Tales of the Brothers Grimm: In the Black Forest." *Touchstones: Reflections on the Best in Children's Literature.* Ed. Perry Nodelman. Vol 2. West Lafayette: Children's Literature Association Publications, 1987. 104–117.
Thompson, Stith. *The Types of the Folktale: A Classification and Bibliography.* 2nd rev. ed. Helsinki: Folk Lore Fellows Communications, 1961.
Wolkstein, Diane. *The Magic Orange Tree.* New York: Knopf, 1978.
Yolen, Jane. *Favorite Folktales from Around the World.* New York: Pantheon, 1986.
Zipes, Jack. *Breaking the Magic Spell: Radical Theories of Folk and Fairy Tales.* Austin: U of Texas P, 1979.
——. *Fairy Tales and the Art of Subversion: The Classical Genre for Children and the Process of Civilization.* London: Heinemann, 1982.
——, ed. *Don't Bet on the Prince: Contemporary Feminist Fairy Tales in North America and England.* New York: Methuen, 1986.

CHAPTER 12

Nonfiction

IS NONFICTION PLEASURABLE?

It may seem strange that a book called *The Pleasures of Children's Literature* includes a chapter on nonfiction. Works of nonfiction—biographies, histories, books about science or architecture—are supposed to communicate facts. Don't the important questions about children's nonfiction concern their usefulness and their accuracy, not the pleasure they might offer?

The most obvious answer I can give to this question is that having knowledge of the fascinating complexity of the world and of people is a pleasure in itself. And it is not just having knowledge that is satisfying: my own experience is that the process of acquiring it, of tracking information down and considering various interpretations of it, can be as much fun as trying to solve a puzzle or a murder mystery.

Nevertheless, nonfictional texts are supposed to represent the truth: unlike fiction or poetry, their main purpose is to communicate knowledge accurately. And that raises another important question: *Is* it possible for a work of nonfiction to be completely true?

Because our knowledge of the world is always expanding, even the most comprehensive informational books eventually become incomplete. Furthermore, I have suggested that making sense of information is something like solving a mystery; but unlike the mysteries of novels, those of reality can be solved in a variety of ways. What is a major turning point in history for some historians has no significance for others. Different scholars may interpret the same information differently and disagree with each other about its implications. These differing interpretations are like the structures of fiction: ways of shaping a body of facts according to patterns that offer the sense of wholeness that fiction does.

The fact that nonfictional texts are never complete, never completely objective, never completely accurate raises further questions. How different is nonfiction from fiction? How different is the pleasure it offers? Do we need to read nonfiction differently from fiction in order to experience the pleasure?

EXPLORATION: Explore (or have children explore) your answers to these questions. Choose some works of nonfiction, and examine whether the pleasures they offer are similar to or different from the pleasures of fiction.

THE FACTS "FOR CHILDREN"

To some degree, the phrase "children's nonfiction" is contradictory. "Nonfiction" implies factual accuracy; but "children's" implies a version of the facts specifically tailored to the needs and interests of inexperienced readers. Works of children's nonfiction tend to eliminate or downplay complications, to focus on obvious generalizations in the faith that such information is all that children can understand. Patricia Lauber expresses a common self-contradictory attitude when she insists that science books for children must be accurate but then adds, "Taking dead aim at some of the concepts and theories of modern science is seldom possible. They are too hard and unfamiliar" (8).

As it happens, however, I've known even very young children who have developed an interest in a particular subject, and who read and understood complex books about it that were intended for adults. Our idea that children won't understand certain concepts because they are "unfamiliar" may be a self-fulfilling prophecy: if we continue to keep children ignorant of these concepts, then of course they'll continue to be unfamiliar. Many people claim to believe that children's minds are more flexible than those of adults. If that is true, then children may actually find it easier to understand ideas that strike adults as unfamiliar and perplexing—but only if we give children access to these ideas.

Depriving children of access to complex knowledge gives them a distorted view of the way things are. For instance, my children inherited a book called *Number* from some older cousins. It informs them that "bi" (as in bicycle) and "pair" (as in a pair of gloves) both mean simply "two," and neglects to mention that "pair" refers to two similar items in a set. Billie Nodelman points out a different sort of distortion by omission when she says that in Sara Stein's *The Science Book,* which claims to be a comprehensive view of all the sciences, "there are subjects not discussed: geology and astronomy, to name two. It seems to me that Stein avoids these topics because they are not within the immediate experience of a child" (182).

A version of the facts intended specifically for children is not merely simpler. As with all children's literature, what children's nonfiction presents is based on assumptions not just about what children can understand but also about what children *should* hear. Aliki's *How a Book Is Made* reveals this sort of assumption when it describes the entire process of the writing, editing, and publishing of a book without reporting a single disagreement. Apparently, young readers aren't supposed to know that adults in the publishing industry do sometimes have arguments. Of course, Aliki may intend an ironic joke in the difference between the dissension or neglect an author often faces in reality and this wish-fulfillment description of a world in which everyone is uncritically enthusiastic, even the reviewers. But since the purpose of the book is to give those without knowledge of publishing some background in the subject, the intended audience could not possibly get the joke.

Sometimes distortions of reality amount to gross misrepresentation. Speaking of her biographical novel about Leonardo da Vinci, E. L. Konigsburg says that the young man whom da Vinci supported for years was probably involved in a homosexual relationship with the great artist. "But . . . I am glad that I write for children. For that explanation of his use of a young boy will never do. It is simply not enough; it is not deep enough" (258). Konigsburg claims that her own interpretation—that da Vinci admired a vitality in the young man that he himself lacked—is more deeply revealing of human nature than the superficial fact of homosexuality; but even if that were true, she still misrepresents by leaving out something she considers inappropriate for children.

In doing so, she discriminates against the considerable number of children who might themselves be beginning to try to understand their own homosexual tendencies or, more immediately relevant, may have a homosexual parent. Deprived of the opportunity to read books describing situations like their own—and as Virginia L. Wolf reports, few such books exist—these children have no choice but to conclude that they are freaks. As Wolf says, "The lack of information available to young people about the gay family is an injustice" (52), especially to the 6 million children of gay parents in the United States.

Our ideas about what aspects of reality children should know have broadened in recent years. Writing in the first issue of *Children's Literature* in 1972, Marilyn Jurich accurately asserted that "some persons are never mentioned, are never subjects, for children's biographies. Those people whose sex lives were 'irregular' are not considered appropriate" (145). Jurich gives as one example the nineteenth-century French writer, George Sand, who defied her society's ideas about behavior proper to women by wearing men's clothing and having a number of tempestuous extramarital relationships. Since 1972, a biography about George Sand intended for young people has appeared. Carol Albanese-Bay says, "Hovey's *A Mind of Her Own* is a fine adolescent-level biography, told from a refreshingly feminist point of view" (61).

Hovey honestly reports many of the controversial aspects of Sand's life. But even this text about a controversial subject does not present children with all the facts. Albanese-Bay also says, "Recent work on Sand has documented her bisexuality, noting her passionate involvement with an actress, Marie Doral. Hovey chooses to ignore this relationship and, instead, waxes eloquent on even the most superficial of Sand's romantic involvements with men. . . . Hovey must have assumed that adolescents would be unable or unwilling to understand such androgyny. She is probably wrong" (60–61).

EXPLORATION: Was Hovey right or wrong? Right or wrong, should she have presented a more complete picture of the truth about Sand's life? Why or why not?

Even when texts of children's nonfiction explore controversial issues, their significance is often distorted, again in order to satisfy widespread assumptions about what children should know of their world. A surprising number of books adopt a superficial version of progress. In his *Medieval World,* for instance, Mitsumasa Anno presents medieval Christianity as a dangerously ignorant set of superstitions that created a dirty and evil-filled world we have, fortunately, grown beyond; he says nothing of the virtues of that less polluted and more stable society that we have lost. Furthermore, Anno views the intolerance of witch hunts and the destructiveness of plagues as evils no longer in existence, a view which ignores aspects of our own world like racial prejudice and AIDS. This sort of misrepresentation of contemporary society seems to be designed to satisfy the belief that children are too weak to cope with depressing facts and need to be shielded from them.

Barbara Harrison suggests that books about the holocaust and nuclear disaster have a similar failing: "Although there is now greater candor in literature for the young than ever before, the one characteristic which adults are reluctant to see diminished in any way is hope, traditionally the animating force in children's books" (69). That insistence on hope isn't necessarily bad—as long as it doesn't depend on the suppression of disturbing facts.

Toshi Maruki's *Hiroshima No Pika,* a controversial picture book for young children that graphically describes the day in the life of a Japanese child on which an atom bomb is dropped on her city, expresses hope in spite of the horror of the destruction it honestly depicts: it ends with its central character, now a deformed adult, insisting that such a catastrophe won't happen again, but only if no one drops a bomb. I personally find the optimism of this book persuasive, because it emerges from and is a response to an unflinchingly honest description of painful events.

Even so, Maruki's book disturbs adults who believe that children are too fragile to cope with such horror. Catherine Studier-Chang says that "*Hiroshima No Pika* has no business in the hands of anyone under the age of twelve" (158). Books that offer children knowledge of potentially disturbing topics may be withheld from them by teachers, parents, librarians, and others. In an interview with Geraldine DeLuca and Roni Natov, the science writer Seymour Simon reports, "I did a book called *Life and Death* which was certainly the poorest selling book I've ever written. It seems that librarians are simply not interested in buying things with death in the title" (22). And many of the students I teach in children's literature courses tell me they would never share a book like *Hiroshima No Pika* with children.

Having read *Hiroshima No Pika* both to preschool children and to university students, I cannot deny its ability to upset audiences both young and not so young. But it seems to me that all human beings *should* be upset about the possibility of nuclear war and that shielding children from such possibility is dangerous. I am convinced that ignorance is always dangerous, even in young children. Knowledge may be painful: but as *Hiroshima No Pika* itself suggests, we can work actively to prevent nuclear disaster only if we are conscious of its possibility.

EXPLORATION: Read Hiroshima No Pika *or another nonfictional work for children that discusses horrific aspects of reality, such as Milton Meltzer's* Never to Forget: The Jews of the Holocaust. *Explore your response, and consider whether you would recommend the book for children. What are the implications of your choice?*

The Misconception of "Making Learning Fun"

Another assumption about childhood that controls the ways in which children are presented with information is the conviction many adults have that children, being fun-loving creatures with little capacity for thought, find information boring. Many writers find ways of "making learning fun"—and in the process, distort what is being taught.

In the supposedly nonfictional *How a Book Is Made,* the writers, editors, and reviewers are all cats who dress and talk like humans. The people in Richard Scarry's *What Do People Do All Day?* are talking hedgehogs and worms. The presence of humanized animals in supposedly factual books is an attempt to make the information painless by burying it in the kind of fictional fantasy we assume children like. While this technique seems harmless, it tends to imply that the real world is a blissful place, the pastoral idyll that much children's fiction and poetry describes.

Texts of children's nonfiction are often filled with riddles, puzzles, and glossy photographs that distort by implying a message opposite the one they are meant to convey. If adults have to work this hard to make information interesting, then surely it must be basically *un*interesting. In believing that we have to *make* learning fun, we may actually be teaching children that it is no fun at all.

EXPLORATION: Is that statement true? Do many children instinctively find information boring, or do we teach them to believe it is boring in the process of trying to persuade them that it is not? Explore your own memories of childhood learning and your experiences as an adult conveying information to children.

In order to make history relevant and interesting for young readers, the vast majority of books about history for children are in fact not nonfiction at all, but "historical fiction" that describes real events in terms of the experiences of imaginary characters. For instance, both Esther Forbes's *Johnny Tremain* and the Colliers' *My Brother Sam Is Dead* place invented characters in the midst of the real events of the American Revolution, and Rosemary Sutcliff describes characters of her own creation in a presumably real Roman Britain in *The Eagle of the Ninth* and *The Lantern*

Bearers. Sutherland and Livingston's *Scott, Foresman Anthology of Children's Literature* sums up the attitude often implied by such books when it says that, "the best historical fiction presents characters and events with an apparent spontaneity that brings them to life so vividly that readers feel no sense of distance" (688).

It seems logical to assume that making history interesting in this way inevitably distorts it. To assume "no sense of distance" is to suggest that people are uninfluenced enough by their times to be basically the same; and I find it hard to accept that possibility.

Fortunately, not all historical fiction is so devoid of a sense of history. But history written with the goal of making the past relevant in this narrow way is, surely, truly fictional.

EXPLORATION: Read (or have children read) works of historical fiction intended for children in order to explore the extent to which they seem believable. Are the characters' values different from our own, or do they have attitudes much like ours? Examine the significance of your conclusion.

IDEOLOGY: NONFICTION AS PROPAGANDA

As we have seen in earlier chapters, assumptions such as the idea that children are inherently optimistic, or inherently resistant to education, or inherently uninterested in people different from themselves, are part of our ideology, our particular way of interpreting the world. We have considered the significance of the fact that we are not often conscious of our ideologies, and usually assume that our version of the truth is an accurate and objective representation of the ways things are. Not surprisingly, then, children's nonfiction unconsciously and inevitably expresses many aspects of our commonly held North American ideology.

In fact—and whether authors are conscious of it or not—children's nonfiction, which claims to be an accurate depiction of reality, often has the express purpose of encouraging children to accept a particular version of reality as the one and only truth. And because readers are persuaded by its claim to objectivity, nonfiction can be an effective form of propaganda.

In order to be effective as propaganda, nonfiction has to put readers in a receptive frame of mind: prepared to accept its accuracy unquestioningly. Nonfiction does so by furnishing the appropriate signals that declare a book to be fact rather than fiction. For instance, we tend to assume that photographs or line drawings are a more accurate representation of how objects look or how they work than impressionistic illustrations; and so the illustrations in much nonfiction are photographs—particularly "serious" black and white photographs—or line drawings. In many books the visual information provided by the pictures is interrupted by a good deal of verbal information: words printed on top of the objects in the pictures, or in white boxes that interrupt the surface of the pictures. This technique creates an atmosphere of scientific seriousness.

Conscious Propaganda

Sometimes the propagandistic elements of nonfictional information are clearly enunciated as being more important than its accuracy. It becomes obvious that the authenticity of the information is less significant than the attitude that exploring the subject is meant to encourage, the ideology that is being reinforced. In elementary school a few years ago, my eldest son learned about a Japan of samurai warriors and teahouses, a Japan without industrialization and with no history of nuclear destruction—a Japan that has not existed for a century. He was being given this inaccurate picture for an excellent reason: he was supposed to be learning tolerance for people different from himself, and it would be harder to make that point about people like the residents of contemporary Japan who dress and eat much like himself, and who live in buildings much like those he is familiar with.

Numerous children's books that claim to be about the lives of people in other countries present similarly inaccurate pictures in order to support the ideology of tolerance. In Peter Spier's *People,* for instance, a page showing people dressed in the traditional costumes of different nations—including a Japanese kimono—says, "People around the world wear different clothes—or none at all." There is no mention of the fact that few people anywhere in the world still wear traditional costumes on a daily basis.

Unconscious Propaganda

Nonfiction is no less ideologically bound even when it does not consciously set out to be propagandistic; it inevitably assumes and reinforces the values of its culture. Even very simple books for babies—those that contain labeled illustrations of common objects—imply an ideology. In books like *Baby's Things,* published by Platt and Munk, the apples in the photographs are shiny and perfect, without flaws or marks or worm holes; the high chairs are clean and freshly painted, without food stains or tooth marks. Everything looks bright and clean and new. These books convey the message that order and cleanliness are desirable qualities, and that material goods are enticing; they introduce babies to the values of a consumer society.

Science as Propaganda

Books about science are particularly prone to expressing ideological assumptions as general truths. By definition, science is an objective and accurate description of reality, and its insistence on careful observation and rigorous testing of hypotheses as the basis for arriving at understanding gives it a kind of objectivity. But we tend to forget that science describes the world only for those willing to accept its assumptions about what reality does and does not consist of and about what means one can and should use in order to understand the world.

People with the conviction that modern science is the only proper way to understand the world tend to be intolerant of those who do not share their conviction: people of earlier times, before the scientific method was established, or contemporary people who prefer to operate by more spiritual or not so conventionally logic-bound definitions of reality.

In his book on the Middle Ages, for instance, Anno makes fun of the ignorance of people who were so "clouded with superstition" that they were unable to discover obvious facts such as the existence of bacteria. As Miriam Youngerman Miller rightly asks, "What is to be gained by criticizing the medieval world for failure to apply the scientific method, when the development of that method still lay centuries in the future?" (169). Anno makes the same unwarranted assumptions that Billie Nodelman claims many scientists do: "Scientists are often true believers in much the same way that fundamental Christians are. They believe they know the Truth and are furious when someone calls that faith into question" (182). Seymour Simon unwittingly offers an example of that point in his interview with Geraldine DeLuca and Roni Natov, when he dismisses the claims of creationists: "I can't believe that saying something as straightforward as 'dinosaurs are several hundred million years old' can become controversial, but among some people, evidently, it is. This is not something that is controversial as far as science is concerned. And if I'm going to do a book about dinosaurs, I'm going to do it from a scientific point of view" (23).

What Simon forgets is that the scientific point of view is one among many. It is a point of view that, as a citizen of the twentieth century, I tend to share myself; I almost always prefer scientific explanations to mystical or spiritual ones. But I also realize that choosing to adopt the scientific perspective is no less a religious act, a matter of faith in one way of seeing things, than choosing to become a Christian or a Buddhist—despite or even because of science's claims to truthfulness.

EXPLORATION: To what extent do you agree with the ideas in the paragraph above? How might your agreement or lack of it affect your judgment of books about science for children?

IDEOLOGY: NARRATIVE AS SELECTIVITY

Not only is choosing to adopt a scientific point of view a religious act: *writing* from the scientific point of view is an act of making fiction—of composing an organized narrative out of the material available. Betty Bacon says, "It is a fallacy of fiction-centered critics that works of nonfiction do not 'tell a story,' do not have a real beginning, middle, and end, that they do not have a climax, and certainly do not have suspense. Proof of the contrary is found in every good book of children's nonfiction" (198).

History as Story

Books of history—even those that are not labeled as historical fiction—are an obvious example of the narrative element in nonfiction. The act of writing about the past is not so much a matter of "sticking to the facts" as of selecting, organizing, and explaining them; and the means by which we select, organize, and explain events almost always relate to the patterns of fictional narrative. Hayden White points out that "the same event can serve as a different kind of element of many different historical stories. . . . The death of the king may be a beginning, an ending, or simply a transitional event in three different stories" (7). In other words, the writing of history is an art of constructing plots, with meanings emerging from the causal connections that the plots create between events.

Henrik Willem van Loon's *The Story of Mankind,* a work of history for children that won the first Newbery Award, in 1922, and is still in print and frequently recommended, is an interesting example. Because we no longer share (or at least no longer publicly admit that we share) van Loon's ideological biases, it is easy for us to see how those biases allow him to provide historical events with a narrative structure.

As its title suggests, this book is very much a story, with the events of history arranged into something like a fairy tale: the history of the world is a story about how good defeats evil, life gets progressively better, and civilization lives happily ever after. Van Loon tells his young readers,

> When you grow up you will discover that many people do not believe in 'progress' and they will prove it to you by the terrible deeds of some of our own contemporaries that 'the world does not change.' But I hope that you will not pay much attention to such talk . . . I do not want to paint too unpleasant a picture. But when you read in the ancient chronicles that the King of France, looking out the windows of his palace, fainted at the stench caused by the pigs rotting in the streets of Paris, when an ancient manuscript recounts a few details of an epidemic of the plague or of the small-pox, then you begin to understand that 'progress' is something more than a catchword used by modern advertising men. (176–177)

Writing from the viewpoint that modern values such as the importance of cleanliness are inherently superior allows van Loon to establish that our particular culture and time is better than any other in history. Finally, the last chapter of the book as he left it (his son Gerard Willem van Loon later added further chapters) offers a happy ending, as it speaks of the "absolute inevitableness" (481) with which something much like the American way of life will become the one glorious civilization of the future. The history of humankind has been turned into a story with a logical sequence of events and a specific central theme.

As is true of much nonfiction, the most significant fiction of history is its claim that it accurately represents the truth. Not accepting that claim allows readers both to investigate the ideological implications of its fictionality and to take pleasure in the fictionality itself. Readers who don't see how much story there is in *The Story of Mankind* will miss out on the fun of thinking about its delightful fictional qualities, its engaging tone, and charming evocation of a genial storyteller.

Biography as Fable

Biographies are even more clearly acts of storytelling. Milton Meltzer, himself a writer of fine biographies, says, "biography is not a compilation of the material you researched. It is a composition of that material" ("Notes" 173). In his own books, Meltzer composes his material with artistry and energy, so that the distinct flavor of his writing reveals the individuality of his subjects. Unfortunately, many biographies intended for children have been composed to accomplish an obviously propagandistic purpose: to provide acceptable role models for young readers. "Biographies for children," says Leonard Marcus, "have a secret subject in addition to the one they are obviously 'about.' That secret subject is the reader. The author, retelling someone else's life, is also to some extent thinking of the reader's own future, of how the reader will be influenced by what the author says" (28). In order to accomplish this goal, which, as we saw in Chapter 6, is exactly the goal of fictional fables, many children's biographies turn the lives of their subjects into fables. It is hard to browse through the biography section of a children's library without coming upon numerous books of this sort.

Charlotte S. Huck suggests that the process of describing lives as worthy of emulation appropriately realizes the purpose of providing biographies for children: "Biography fulfills children's needs for identification with someone 'bigger' than they are. In this day of mass conformity, it may give them new models of greatness to emulate or suggest new horizons of endeavor" (550). Unfortunately, however, many books achieve that purpose by seriously distorting the truth: by leaving out negative facts or information that do not fit the positive values being emphasized. Like all children's nonfiction, then, this sort of biography raises the question of whether accuracy or truthfulness is as significant as the accomplishment of a specific pedagogical purpose. If children learn to believe in themselves by reading a distorted version of the life of Louis Pasteur, does it really matter that the facts have been distorted?

EXPLORATION: Examine that question. How would you answer it? Why?

The difficulty in answering the question might be compounded by a further consideration. If we read biographies—reports of individual lives that have been molded into meaningful stories—primarily as models for our own behavior, then one of the things we may be learning is the idea that we too might be explained in terms of a story—a story we invent to explain ourselves to ourselves. Our conceptions of our own personalities tend to be based on a kind of narrative understanding of our histories; they are a story we tell ourselves, a story about how certain events shaped us and gave our life its central theme or meaning. If our idea of who we are is a form of fiction, then we can hardly be surprised that nonfiction is another form of fiction.

HOW TO READ NONFICTION

The degree to which nonfiction is like fiction—that is, the degree to which it selects, organizes, distorts, and interprets facts—has important consequences both for the ways in which we as adults evaluate nonfiction and the ways in which we can encourage children to respond to it.

- We need to remember that the world is inherently interesting, and having knowledge of it is inherently pleasurable.
- We should encourage children to read books about subjects that may not seem to be immediately relevant. If we persuade children to read history merely to look for people like themselves or biographies merely to look for advice about their future, then we will deprive them of a chance to broaden their knowledge and understanding.
- We need to become conscious of the extent to which nonfiction is fictional, to watch out for the fictional elements, and to evaluate informational books in terms of the degree to which we share their spoken and unspoken assumptions.

EXPLORATION: Read (or have children read) a nonfictional text, and identify the elements of fiction in it. What aspects of its subject does it emphasize? What might it be leaving out? What story patterns does it impose on events or people? It might be useful to consider the degree to which the text expresses the typical characteristics of children's literature as a genre, explored in Chapter 7. Also, if it does express those characteristics, to what extent might they distort the facts?

- Finally and most important, if nonfiction inevitably distorts the truth, then we need to learn to enjoy the distortions: to read nonfiction in much the same way as we read fiction. From both, we should expect insight into reality. But the pleasure of readers in both increases with a consciousness of the patterns (and specific visions of reality) created by the selection and organization of material and the voice that communicates it.

EXPLORATION: Explore (or have children explore) the ways in which the organization and style of a specific work of nonfiction adds to your interest and pleasure in it. After choosing a text, read it in terms of its gaps, and of the ways in which you can fill those gaps by using your repertoire of strategies for building consistency in literary texts in general. (See Chapter 6.)

WORKS CITED

Albanese-Bay, Carol. "Nineteenth-Century Women for Twentieth-Century Teenagers: A Review of Recent Biographies of George Sand and Mary Shelley." *Lion and the Unicorn* 4.1 (1980): 54–70.

Aliki. *How a Book Is Made.* New York: Harper & Row, 1986.

Anno, Mitsumasa. *Anno's Medieval World.* London: Bodley Head, 1980.

Baby's Things. New York: Platt and Munk, n.d.

Bacon, Betty. "The Art of Nonfiction." *Jump Over the Moon: Selected Professional Readings.* Eds. Pamela Petrick Barron and Jennifer Q. Burley. New York: Holt, Rinehart and Winston, 1984. 195–204.

Collier, James Lincoln and Christopher. *My Brother Sam Is Dead.* New York: Four Winds, 1974.

DeLuca, Geraldine, and Roni Natov. "Who's Afraid of Science Books? An Interview with Seymour Simon." *Lion and the Unicorn* 6 (1982): 10–27.

Forbes, Esther. *Johnny Tremain.* Boston: Houghton Mifflin, 1943.

Harrison, Barbara. "Howl Like the Wolves." *Children's Literature* 15 (1987): 67–90.

Hovey, Tamara. *A Mind of Her Own: A Life of the Writer George Sand.* New York: Harper & Row, 1977.

Huck, Charlotte S. *Children's Literature in the Elementary School.* 3rd ed., updated. New York: Holt, Rinehart and Winston, 1979.

Jurich, Marilyn. "What's Left Out of Biography for Children." *Children's Literature* 1 (1972): 143–151.

Konigsburg, E. L. "Sprezzatura: A Kind of Excellence." *Horn Book* 52 (June 1976): 253–261.

Lauber, Patricia. "What Makes an Appealing and Readable Science Book?" *Lion and the Unicorn* 6 (1982): 5–9.

Marcus, Leonard S. "Life Drawings: Some Notes on Children's Picture Books." *Lion and the Unicorn* 4.1 (1980): 15–31.

Maruki, Toshi. *Hiroshima No Pika.* New York: Lothrop, Lee and Shepherd, 1980.

Meltzer, Milton. *Never to Forget: The Jews of the Holocaust.* New York: Dell Laurel Leaf, 1977.

———. "Notes on Biography." *Children's Literature Association Quarterly* 10.4 (Winter 1986): 172–175.

Miller, Miriam Youngerman. "In Days of Old: The Middle Ages in Children's Non-fiction." *Children's Literature Association Quarterly* 12.4 (Winter 1987): 167–172.

Nodelman, Billie. "Science Books, Science Education, and the Religion of Science." *Children's Literature Association Quarterly* 12.4 (Winter 1987): 180–183.

Number. Toronto: Ryerson First Library, 1971.

Scarry, Richard. *What Do People Do All Day?* New York: Random House, 1968.

Spier, Peter. *People.* New York: Doubleday, 1980.

Stein, Sara. *The Science Book.* New York: Workman, 1979.

Studier-Chang, Catherine. "Point of View: *Hiroshima No Pika*—for Mature Audiences." *Advocate* 3.3 (Spring 1984) 158, 166–169.

Sutcliff, Rosemary. *The Eagle of the Ninth.* London: Oxford UP, 1954.

———. *The Lantern Bearers.* London: Oxford UP, 1959.

Sutherland, Zena, and Myra Cohn Livingston. *The Scott, Foresman Anthology of Children's Literature.* Glenview: Scott, Foresman, 1984.

van Loon, Hendrik Willem. *The Story of Mankind.* 1921; New York: Liveright, 1984.

White, Hayden. *Metahistory: The Historical Imagination in Nineteenth Century Europe.* Baltimore: Johns Hopkins UP, 1973.

Wolf, Virginia L. "The Gay Family in Literature for Young People." *Children's Literature in Education* 20.1 (March 1989): 51–58.

CHAPTER 13

Fiction

CHARACTERISTICS OF CHILDREN'S FICTION

Our earlier exploration of the characteristics of children's literature as a genre, in Chapter 7, began with a description of a typical work, a no-name text. Not incidentally, that example was a *story:* a work of fiction. While children's literature includes poems and plays and picture books, its most characteristic mode is fiction, the organization of a series of events into the shape we call a story. As a result, most if not all of the genre characteristics we isolated earlier are significant traits of children's fiction.

Children's fiction consists of novels and stories that are

- simple, but not necessarily simplistic
- action-oriented rather than character-oriented
- about children (or childlike animals or other creatures)
- presented from the viewpoint of innocence
- optimistic, and with happy endings
- didactic
- repetitious in diction and structure
- thematically concerned with opposing or balancing utopian and didactic concerns.

In this chapter, we will explore how these characteristics of children's literature manifest themselves in qualities specific to children's fiction. As well as revealing something about children's fiction, I hope this discussion confirms how we can use our previous general knowledge as a schema for the particular new topics or experiences we encounter.

EXPLORATION: As you read the following sections, explore (or have children explore) the degree to which the general conclusions they offer apply to and/or can help you understand specific texts of your choice. Pay as much attention to departures from my descriptions as to ways in which texts do fulfill them, and consider the extent to which an understanding of what a text shares with others of its kind helps you focus on its distinctive qualities.

Orphans

The main characters in many children's stories and novels are orphans: Anne of Green Gables and a host of other heroines of girls' series books; the pig Wilbur, who is adopted by Fern in *Charlotte's Web;* and characters as diverse as Taran of Lloyd Alexander's Prydain series, Dorothy in Baum's *Wizard of Oz,* and Mowgli of Kipling's *Jungle Book.* Many other characters are partially or temporarily orphaned; Jo and her sisters in Louisa May Alcott's *Little Women,* Jim Hawkins of *Treasure Island,* and Tom of Philippa Pearce's *Tom's Midnight Garden* have been separated from parents either by chance or by choice. The generic children's story I described earlier is about a creature who chooses to orphan itself and then realizes its error.

The prevalence of orphans in children's fiction relates to a central concern with the question of independence and security. Orphans are of necessity independent, free to have adventures without the constraints of protective adults; at the same time, they are automatically faced with the danger and discomfort of lack of parental love. Because we define childhood as that time of life when one needs parental love and control, we believe that the possibility of being orphaned—of having the independence one wants and yet having to do without the love one needs—is an exciting and disturbing idea for children who are not in fact orphans, and a matter of immediate interest for those who are.

EXPLORATION: Is that statement true? Consider (or have children consider) the ways in which texts about orphans may or may not express these ideas.

Alien Environments

The main characters of children's fiction often have to deal with an alien environment, a place as strange and new to them as Green Gables is for Anne, the treasure island is for Jim Hawkins, or the barn is for Wilbur. The fact that children's fiction observes the world from the viewpoint of innocence means that the world itself is a strange place. Children are new to it, and must come to terms with it. So Anne explores her new home, Jim explores the island, the ducks in Robert McCloskey's *Make Way for Ducklings* explore Boston, the Ingalls family explores a series of new homes throughout all of Laura Ingalls Wilder's Little House books; all of these are versions of the generic children's story, in which the young creature learns its limitations by confronting a strange new environment.

This focus on alien environments also helps explain why so much children's fiction is fantasy. Fantasy always describes a place we are not familiar with. The unfamiliar places of children's fantasy often represent the real world that children are unacquainted with and must come to terms with.

For that reason, it seems, many children's fantasies begin in a relatively recognizable world and then take their characters somewhere strange. This "journey" happens in White's *Charlotte's Web,* in Sendak's *Where the Wild Things Are,* in Carroll's *Alice in Wonderland,* in C. S. Lewis's Narnia books, in Alan Garner's *Elidor,* in Susan Cooper's "Dark Is Rising" series. The journey rarely takes place in fantasies for adults, which usually allow us to "suspend our disbelief" precisely by refusing to acknowledge the existence of any world other than the imaginary one in which they occur. In children's fantasy, however, the suspension of disbelief seems to be less significant than the sense that the normal world we live in contains strange and bewildering possibilities: doorways into other worlds.

EXPLORATION: Is that last statement about children's fantasy true? Consider (or have children consider) the ways in which texts about alien environments may or may not express these ideas.

Home/Away/Home Story Patterns

As we have seen, the alien environment occupies only the middle of the generic children's story; the story ends with the main character returning home. Adult fiction that deals with young people who leave home usually ends with them choosing to stay away. As the adult novelist Thomas Wolfe once suggested in the title of one of his books, "You can't go home again." But as happens to Jim in *Treasure Island,* Max in *Where the Wild Things Are,* and Dorothy in *The Wizard of Oz,* characters in children's fiction tend to learn the value of home by losing it and then finding it again. Furthermore, the discovery of a secure home is the central focus of even those books that don't begin with a central character bored by a secure home. Like many books intended specifically for girls, *Anne of Green Gables* begins with Anne's *arrival* at a secure home and describes her happiness there, and many of the best-loved fairy tales describe how a young girl flees an insecure home and eventually finds a safe new home. As Christopher Clausen says, "When home is a privileged place, exempt from the most serious problems of life and civilization—when home is where we ought, on the whole, to stay—we are probably dealing with a story for children. When home is the chief place from which we must escape, either to grow up or . . . to remain innocent, then we are involved in a story for adolescents or adults" (143).

The plot of the generic children's story suggests why the home/away/home pattern is so prevalent. A child or childlike creature, bored by home, seeks the excitement of adventure; but the excitement proves to be dangerous, so the child then seeks the safety of home—which is, of course, boring. We can sum it up this way:

HOME	——→	AWAY
Boring		Exciting
↑BUT↑		↓BUT↓
Safe		Dangerous
HOME	←——	AWAY

If we follow the arrows, we can see how vacillation about the relative pleasures and pains of home and away underpins the ambivalence of much children's fiction: all the characteristic oppositions we considered in Chapter 7 relate to the metaphors of home and away.

By following the arrows in the diagram, we can also see why children's fiction often consists of episodic books and books in series. Home is safe but boring, so one seeks adventure, which is exciting but dangerous: so one seeks home, which is safe but then turns out once more to be boring, thus demanding another adventure, another episode, another sequel.

Theme and Variations

The episodes and sequels of many fine children's stories and novels are not merely repetitions. Because of the didactic impulse that drives all children's literature, stories and novels duplicate similar patterns but in noticeably different ways, and so act as *variations* on the original. Variations can take place within one text, within a series, or in non-series books by the same author.

Variations within One Text. *Charlotte's Web* is an interesting example of how children's fiction operates in terms of theme and variations. It contains two separate but similar plots, the first about how Fern rescues Wilbur from death and the second about how Charlotte rescues Wilbur from death. The first, a realistic story about a little girl and her pet, lasts only for the first few chapters of the novel; the second is a fantasy about talking animals that lasts for the rest of the book. As I discuss in my article "Text as Teacher," the similarities between the two stories make them variations on each other, and allow readers to use the simple and shorter one as a schema to make sense of the complexities of the longer one.

Many other children's books tell what is basically the same story twice, first in a fairly straightforward manner and then with more subtleties.

In *Treasure Island,* there is a short, exciting, but unsettling encounter between Jim Hawkins and the old pirate who stays at his inn, before Jim has the longer, more exciting, and more unsettling encounter with Long John Silver that makes up the bulk of the novel. The first of these encounters, a less complicated version of the story that follows, foreshadows each of its major events.

Similarly, Grahame's *Wind in the Willows* begins with the story of how Mole, unable to resist the temptations of the spring air, leaves its home and the duties of spring cleaning to find a more glamorous life of leisure on the river bank. After that, the book tells story after story of animals tempted to leave home. Those who go suffer for it and those who stay are praised, so that Mole's story exists as a kind of counterpoint to what happens in the rest of the book, a one-sided version of the story of leaving home that acts as a schema for the more complex dilemmas of Rat and Toad.

Anne of Green Gables is like many episodic novels in that each of its chapters tells a similar story: through her childlike exuberance and energy, Anne either charms a repressed adult into the ability to enjoy life for the first time in years or else lands herself in relatively harmless trouble that delights readers. Each chapter is a variation on all the others.

Variations within a Series. Because the episodes described in each chapter of *Anne of Green Gables* are more or less separate, any one of them could be eliminated, or more added, without seriously changing the effect of the novel. In fact, Montgomery could keep adding to the story of Anne until she ended up with six novels. One of the most obvious traits of children's fiction is the proneness of its authors to create variations on their work by writing about the same characters in different but similar situations.

EXPLORATION: After reading this section of the manuscript, my colleague Mavis Reimer asked this provocative question about the tendency of children's writers to place the same characters in similar situations again and again: "In the case of Montgomery, she did so only because she was pressured by her publishers, who were answering the clamor of readers. To what extent can this characteristic of children's literature be seen as a phenomenon of the marketplace?" Another question can be added: Why *do readers clamor for a variation on a pleasurable experience?*

Even those books which are not merely additions to the series but allow different developments to a continuing plot often read like variations of each other. In almost all of the books in Lloyd Alexander's Prydain series, Taran goes on a quest that makes him realize his previous innocence and teaches him important truths about life. While the books as a whole describe how Taran gradually becomes aware of who he is, the individual books are similar enough to one another to be variations not just on that overriding theme but on the other books in the series. It is the repetitiveness of Taran's various quests, the way in which he begins each book in a similar state of mind and then learns variations of the same values, that most clearly defines this series as children's fiction.

Variations in Non-Series Texts. The repetitive nature of children's fiction may be the characteristic of the genre that most draws writers to it. Even when they are not producing series or writing about the same characters, children's writers tend to rework similar themes and ideas. Commenting on his own work, Maurice Sendak has said, "It's not that I have original ideas, but that I'm good at doing variations on the same idea over and over again. . . . That's all an artist needs—one power-driven fantasy or obsession. And to be clever enough to do variations, like a series of variations by Mozart. They're so good that you forget they're based on a single theme" (Lanes 248). Sendak claims that three of his picture books—*Where the Wild Things Are, In the Night Kitchen,* and *Outside Over There*—form a trilogy; in fact, they can be seen to operate as interesting variations on each other. All of them deal in one way or another with ideas and images of windows and walls, eating and being eaten, flying and falling, clothing and nakedness, seeing and speaking, silence and music, lassitude and energy, inside and outside, gender and sexuality, birth and death, seeing and being seen, control and abandon, freedom and responsibility, oneness and multiplicity.

Louise Fitzhugh creates another sort of variation simply because she seems to have been fascinated by children who have wealthy and exceedingly self-centered mothers. The mothers of both Sport in *Sport* and Beth Ellen in *The Long Secret* might almost be the same horrid character, and both operate as variations on Harriet's mother in *Harriet the Spy.* Furthermore, *The Long Secret* describes how Beth Ellen expresses her secret feelings about people in a series of anonymous notes—a variation on the notebook in which Harriet records her impressions in *Harriet the Spy.*

EXPLORATIONS: (1) Consider (or have children consider) the similarities and differences in Sendak's trilogy as discussed in this section. How might they be seen to parallel or counterpoint each other?

(2) Consider (or have children consider) one text, a series, a group of unrelated books by the same author, or an entire subgenre of children's fiction such as school stories or texts about talking mice as a series of variations. How significant is variation as an operative factor in children's fiction?

The Confusion of Eating and Being Eaten

The plots of children's fiction, particularly of stories intended for younger readers, often involve the act of eating. The youthful characters of well-known fairy tales are threatened with being eaten. Little Red Riding Hood brings food to her grandmother, but is threatened with becoming the meal herself; Hansel and Gretel become possible meals after they nibble parts of the witch's house. Peter Rabbit has his dangerous adventure in Potter's *Tale of Peter Rabbit* because he cannot resist Mr. McGregor's vegetables even though his father was made into a pie by Mrs. McGregor. In *Where the Wild Things Are,* Max is sent to his room because he threatens to devour his mother, discovers that the Wild Things want to eat him up because they love him, and is drawn back home by the smell of good things to eat.

While eating is less central in longer works of fiction, it is still an important subject. *The Wind in the Willows* has much to say about the delights of "coldtonguecoldhamcoldbeefpickledgherkinssaladfrenchrollscresssandwichespottedmeatgingerbeerlemonadesodawater." *Charlotte's Web* focuses attention on descriptions of Wilbur's slop, Charlotte's methods of killing her food, and Templeton the rat's pleasure in the feast available at the fair. The sensuous delight of these descriptions of food reveal that in children's fiction, eating seems to occupy the place that sex does in adult fiction.

The fact that children's fiction presents events from the viewpoint of innocence, which we explored in Chapter 7, explains why there is so much preoccupation with eating: from the viewpoint of innocence, sex hardly exists. Either children are not in fact concerned with it or, if Freudians are right, their thoughts about it have been repressed into the unconscious. But food is an intense pleasure. As fairy tales and books like *Peter Rabbit* and *Wild Things* reveal, it is also, like sex, a complex pleasure: the fact that one eats creatures that once lived but were too weak to protect themselves suggests that one—particularly one who is a weak child—might therefore also be eaten.

The concern with eating and being eaten clearly relates to the central concern with animals in children's fiction; both imply a need to determine the degree to which one is a human eater, like one's parents, or an animal-like food, like the "little lambs" and "little pigs" we so often tell children they are. It also relates to the egocentricity of an innocent point of view: the conviction that other people and objects are like oneself and share one's tastes and interests. Innocence confuses (and tries to sort out) subject and object just as it confuses (and tries to sort out) eater and eaten.

EXPLORATION: Is that statement true? Consider (or have children consider) the ways in which texts about eating may or may not express the ideas in the previous paragraph.

Ignorance and Innocence

Many fairy tales are about ingenuously passive girls (such as Cinderella) or the youngest (and dumbest) of three brothers whose ignorance of the ways of the world, lack of self-reliance, and trusting passivity allow him to succeed when his older and wiser brothers fail. Children's fiction often praises ignorance, which it views as a wise innocence.

Characters like A. A. Milne's Winnie-the-Pooh confirm the virtues of ignorance by doing things which are wrong and therefore funny and adorable, charmingly innocent. In *Treasure Island,* the older and theoretically wiser Jim Hawkins who tells us about what happened when he was younger and more ignorant keeps pointing out the folly of his actions on the island. But those who enjoy this book as the adventure it is like the exuberant young Jim who performs these exploits more than the repressive older Jim who disapproves of them. Furthermore, *Treasure Island* lets us know that Jim's ignorant thoughtlessness—for instance, his desertion of his friends that leads him to the marooned Ben Gunn—was actually what won the treasure.

But while children's fiction is written from the viewpoint of innocence, it is written *by* adults, people with more experience than the characters they write about or the audience they write for. Not surprisingly, then, the climax of many children's stories and novels is the main character's realization of his or her ignorance about something: the discovery that innocence has led to danger or despair. In "Hansel and Gretel," the gingerbread house turns out to be a witch's dwelling. In *Treasure Island,* Jim learns he shouldn't have trusted Long John Silver. Both Johnny in Esther Forbes's *Johnny Tremain* and Ged in Le Guin's *Wizard of Earthsea* pay for their egocentric trust in themselves with physical disfigurement, and Harriet in Fitzhugh's *Harriet the Spy* pays for hers with emotional suffering. From the viewpoint of experience, innocence must end, and so the literature of innocence turns out to be about the loss of innocence. While Peter in Barrie's *Peter Pan* and Winnie-the-Pooh in *The House at Pooh Corner* remain innocent, both are deserted by their peers, Wendy and Christopher Robin, who realize that despite the attractions of the idyllic worlds of Peter and Pooh, they themselves must grow up.

But that Peter and Winnie-the-Pooh do remain young forever, and that we are expected to love them for doing so, is a reminder of the essential ambivalence of children's literature—its balancing of opposite values. Much children's fiction deals with attempts to grow up without actually growing up; to mature without losing the joy, optimism, and simplicity of youth; to be neither Peter nor Wendy but some combination of the two. While that sounds impossible, we saw in Chapter 7 that the adult Anne of Green Gables explicitly claims to have done it, and characters like Wilbur and Harriet the Spy seem to manage to do it also.

EXPLORATION: Consider (or have children consider) the endings of some children's novels of your choice. Do their main characters stay innocent, mature, or "grow up without growing up"?

SUBGENRES OF CHILDREN'S FICTION

As I have considered some of the distinguishing characteristics of children's fiction, I have indiscriminately used examples that range from short picture books and fairy tales to comparatively long novels. For all the ways in which Sendak's simple picture book *Where the Wild Things Are* is unlike Alan Garner's complex novel *Red Shift,* they have enough in common to be clearly identified as children's fiction. But despite the overall consistency of all the different kinds of texts we label children's fiction, there are many subgenres: types within the general type with their own specific characteristics.

In this section I discuss a few of the most significant of these subgenres, mainly as examples of the kinds of exploration that might be done of other subgenres. If you wish to try this sort of exploration, you might consider reading and thinking about a group of school stories, of books specifically intended for an audience of girls, of historical novels, of stories of survival in the wilds, of Choose-Your-Own Adventures, of mysteries, of ghost stories; the possibilities are extensive.

Stories about Toys, Dolls, and Other Small Things

Children's literature, as we have seen, often describes humanized animals. Many children's stories are about other humanized characters, from hazelnuts (Norma M. Charles's *Amanda Grows Up*) to toasters (Thomas Disch's *The Brave Little Toaster*). The assumption that children's fiction ought to be about animals or objects with human personalities is so common that many authors apparently take it for granted, without considering the implications of the strange situations they describe. When Hans Christian Andersen reported the life of a toy in "The Steadfast Tin Soldier," he made the toy's inability to move of its own accord central to the story; but when Charles tells the story of a hazelnut in *Amanda Grows Up,* she makes the nut responsible for her actions in a way that raises some questions. Amanda's friends *choose* to jump from the tree, but she herself is afraid to; only when she becomes lonely does she decide to take the plunge. That Amanda actually has this choice raises the question of other choices: Why has she simply accepted the fact that her life thus far has consisted of nothing but hanging from a tree? Why didn't she just jump off earlier and get a job in a laundromat? Or can she choose to jump but not to move? Why? How did she get the human name Amanda in the first place? And how did her friends, also hazelnuts, get the names Phil and Carolyn? Why is it that some of these names are female, some male? In leaving gaps that allow such questions, this story fails to convince; to be convincing, I believe, takes a writer with an imagination literal enough to explore the implications of actually being a hazelnut or a tin soldier or a pig.

EXPLORATION: Choose (or have children choose) a story about an object with human consciousness. To what degree does the story work out the literal implications of the situation? To what degree does its doing so contribute to your enjoyment of the story?

Writers who consider the imaginary situations they describe more literally tend to find implications in their characters' situations that relate to the situations of their readers. Potter and White reveal the metaphoric implications of animals who talk like humans; a number of other writers deal with the metaphoric implications of machines who think like humans.

Even choosing to write a children's story about a machine implies a specific ideal of childhood. When the youthful engine in Gertrude Crampton's *Tootle* makes the mistake of giving in to impulse and jumps the track, we know he is acting in a manner unreasonable for a train. The fact that he is also a child implies that children who read about him are or should also in some way be like trains, and learn as Tootle does to remain on the rails, that is, to act as they've been told to.

Reducing the size of their characters, or bringing miniature objects to life, is another technique children's writers use to create metaphors. In Hans Christian Andersen's "Thumbelina," for instance, a girl as small as a thumb has to cope with a world made for much bigger people. In Lynn Reid Banks's *The Indian in the Cupboard,* a plastic toy comes to life and interacts with a human child. In Mary Norton's *The Borrowers,* small human beings who live within the walls of a normal-size house survive by "borrowing" objects and adapting them to their own use.

These miniature human beings and living dolls and toys are also metaphoric representations of children. Like dogs or pigs or rabbits, the miniature beings are much smaller than the creatures who control them. But unlike animals, toys and miniature humans have no instinctive defenses, no innate ability to cope with the dangers of life in the wild. Thumbelina can be controlled by whatever larger creature comes along, as can the mechanical father and son who are the main characters in Russell Hoban's *Mouse and His Child.* So when these small beings prevail over insurmountable odds, as they always do, they represent a potent version of the wish-fulfillment fantasy: the very small can triumph over the dangerously large, the very powerless over the exceedingly powerful.

Books about miniatures tend to focus on the physical difficulties that their characters face and their ingenious solutions to them. In *Stuart Little,* E. B. White describes his small protagonist's troubles with ordinary toothpaste tubes and drainholes, and in *The Borrowers,* Norton shows how the Clock family adapts postage stamps to wall paintings, spools to chairs, and children's blocks to tables. Much of our pleasure in such books stems from our delight in objects that are just like other objects but on a smaller scale.

Claude Lévi-Strauss suggests the source of that pleasure when he says that the central significance of *all* works of art is that they are miniatures, small-scale versions of larger objects. The objects in paintings are often actually smaller and the ones in literature have fewer attributes than the real objects they represent; and, "being smaller, the object as a whole seems less formidable. By being quantitatively diminished, it seems to us qualitatively simplified. . . . A child's doll is no longer an enemy, a rival, or even an interlocutor. In it and through it a person is made into a subject" (23). The simplification allows us mastery and self-understanding.

In books about miniatures this simplification is itself a central concern. The small creatures of children's fiction tend to express both the virtues and vices of smallness. They are exquisitely delicate but also vulnerable, and often quite small-minded.

The Borrowers are fearful. There's even a suggestion that their ancestors were ordinary-size human beings who produced smaller offspring because of their timidity and lack of emotional magnitude; their outsides diminished to match their state of mind. Many toy characters are egocentric or conservative—"small-minded" in that they have responded to their physical condition by becoming unadventurous and inflexible. If books about animals tend to focus on the ways in which children, in their likeness to animals are more savage than adults, less controlled and more in need of control, books about miniature creatures tend to focus on the ways in which children, in their likeness to toys, are inherently weaker than adults, more prone to give in to their weakness, more in need of resolve and energy. The dispute tends to be not between civility and nature, but between possibility and limitation.

Even the triumphs of miniatures tend to be *little* ones: the Borrowers' epic adventure is a trip out of the house and into the adjoining field. Our consciousness of the relative insignificance of these creatures and their triumphs tends to give an edge of irony to these books: we seem to be expected both to identify with them and to separate ourselves from them, in both cases because of their smallness.

For that reason, perhaps, books about miniatures often give them adult personalities and include normal-size human children for their miniature protagonists to interact with. For instance, Banks's Indian is an adult whose existence depends on a human child. Alternatively, some stories center on a miniature child with an exuberant spirit at odds with its fragile state—like Arietty, the youngest of the Borrowers, or the child in *The Mouse and His Child.* The presence of such children provides a contrast between the timidity or egocentricity characteristic of the little creatures and the greater wisdom of the child. The normal-size child acts with more energy and thoughtlessness than the miniatures, but because of his or her greater size, is also thrust into the role of an adult. For instance, the human boy in *The Borrowers* must take on the parental responsibility of helping the Clock family escape once their presence has been discovered in part through his childish carelessness. The rebellious miniature child tends to share that mixture of childlike innocence and adult responsibility; the mouse child remains optimistic and so can guide his father forward beyond his theoretically mature state of despair.

EXPLORATION: Are the ideas discussed in the previous paragraphs true? Consider (or have children consider) the ways in which other texts about small beings may or may not express these ideas.

Children with Problems

Many works of children's fiction, especially many "young adult" novels intended for readers in their early teens, can be thought of as "problem novels." Their main characters have one specific problem, like obesity or divorcing parents or cancer or a dying grandmother; the plot involves their struggle with and eventual solution of the problem. Such books are an example of the way children's fiction integrates didacticism and wish-fulfillment fantasy.

Like fables, these books are really about how their readers will think and act after finishing the book. For that reason, their central characters are vaguely drawn; they are typical children or adolescents who are so without defining individual qualities that many different readers can identify with them and thus learn from their experience. For instance, Margaret in Blume's *Are You There God? It's Me, Margaret* has all the interests and ideas we assume to be common among twelve-year-olds, and hardly any other attributes at all.

Like fairy tales, however, these books tend to present a wish-fulfillment world in which children and young people are kind and understanding and adults are narrow-minded, repressive hypocrites. One of Margaret's main assumptions is that her friends know better than her elders; and the book doesn't challenge that assumption. If there are good adults in books of this sort, they tend to be young ones, teachers, therapists, or coaches in their early twenties who are close enough to their own youth not to have lost sight of the truth.

The main characters in problem novels are remarkably egocentric. Marcy in Paula Danziger's *The Cat Ate My Gymsuit* admits she isn't suffering from poverty or physical abuse but insists that being "an adolescent blimp with wire-frame glasses, mousy brown hair, and acne" is just as hard to cope with: "Middle-class kids have problems too" (7). In an article titled "Are You There, God? It's Me, Me, ME!" R. A. Siegel calls Blume's character's "self-absorbed" and says, "One of the disturbing results of this preoccupation with the self is the loss of tangible intimacy with any concrete thing or object; the texture of lives lived in a specific, particular place is missing. . . . She creates no place for her characters to inhabit except the self" (75). This sort of isolation is the essence of wish-fulfillment fantasy, for it allows characters absolute confirmation of their opinions and values. Nobody and nothing is seriously allowed to question them.

Given the didactic purpose and fablelike nature of these books, we might expect that their messages would eventually undercut the wish-fulfillment, and guide young readers past their self-absorbed and narrow vision of the way things are. But the messages of many of these books tend to support their wish-fulfillment view of life. The characters learn to accept themselves as they are or to interpret their personal need for self-satisfaction as a way of growing from experience. They learn that the best way to deal with life's problems is to continue to pay close attention to oneself and one's feelings, to interpret the needs of others as attempts at repression, and to put one's own needs first.

I believe that the trouble with such books is that, while they are clearly fantasies, they pretend not only to be realistic but to offer realistic solutions to real problems. Those young readers who actually accept them as real are confirming a dangerous delusion. I suspect, though, that readers who enjoy these books know them for the fantasies they are, and enjoy them for the satisfactions of the wish-fulfillment they offer.

Problem books which clearly announce themselves as fantasies tend to be not only more honest but also more interesting than those that wallow in self-indulgence. Books like Russell Hoban's *How Tom Beat Captain Najork and His Hired Sportsman* and Florence Parry Heide's *The Shrinking of Treehorn* present many of the same ideas in the context of exaggerated fantasy that focuses on the humor of adult repression or insensitivity. Tom lives with his aunt, Miss Fidget Wonkam-Strong, whose character is expressed by the iron hat she always wears, and Treehorn's mother is so worried about her cake falling that she doesn't even hear Treehorn tell her that he's getting smaller. When she finally does hear, she says, "Oh dear. . . . First it was the cake, and now it's this. Everything happens at once." At the other end of the spectrum, books like Robert Cormier's *I Am the Cheese* and William Sleator's *House of Stairs* offer dark fantasies about adults' misuse of power that I personally find more satisfyingly horrific and more emotionally true than supposedly more realistic books.

EXPLORATION: Do you share my feeling that fantasy novels depict problems better than realistic ones? Compare (or have children compare) fantasies like those just mentioned with more realistic books like those by Blume and Danziger. Which seem more convincing? Truer? Why?

Time Fantasies

Many critics of children's literature have named Philippa Pearce's *Tom's Midnight Garden* as the best modern children's novel. Tom, sent to stay with his childless aunt and uncle in a small apartment in a subdivided Victorian house while his brother recovers from an illness, misses the space and freedom of his back garden. Waking in the night, he walks through the door of the house—not into the constricted urban alley he expected, but into the large garden that had been there years before. He has entered the past; in it, he meets and plays with a young girl who is herself a stranger in the house that belonged to her relatives in the earlier time. The friendship of the two children gets them through their feeling of loneliness and exile and ends when they no longer need each other.

A number of critically acclaimed children's novels have a good deal in common with *Tom's Midnight Garden*—so many novels that they have come to form a subgenre of children's fiction with the name *time fantasy*.

The idea of sending children into the past seems to have originated in E. Nesbit's *Story of the Amulet,* first published in 1906; a magic stone allows a family of children to visit ancient Egypt and Rome. In *A Traveller in Time* (1939) Alison Uttley established the pattern followed later by *Tom's Midnight Garden;* a girl of the present visits an old house and enters into its past, where she helps Mary, Queen of Scots in her attempts to flee England. In the Green Knowe series (1954–1976), Lucy Boston continued the pattern by describing encounters between modern children and ones who lived in the same house in several different centuries.

Since *Tom's Midnight Garden* appeared, in 1958, there have been many variations on this idea in books from around the world. Here are just a few examples. Eleanor Cameron's *Court of the Stone Children* tells how a modern child's contact with a girl from eighteenth-century France, whose home has been rebuilt into a museum in San Francisco, helps her to adjust to a new city. Janet Lunn's *Root Cellar* (1980) describes how a lonely girl enters the past, meets people who once lived in her new home, and then travels with a girl from the past to Washington, D.C., to bring a Canadian boy home from the American Civil War. Ruth Park's *Playing Beatie Bow* tells of a modern girl's visit to Victorian Sidney, Australia. Among the many

British time fantasies are William Mayne's *Earthfasts,* in which a boy from the eighteenth century finds himself in contemporary England, and Jill Paton Walsh's *A Chance Child,* in which an abused modern child travels down a canal and backward in time, helping and helped by abused children of earlier generations.

In all these time fantasy novels a child, usually a lonely and isolated one, comes to a new place and there feels exiled from a former home. But in the new place, the child has contact with someone from another time who once lived in that place. Through this contact, the child in the present helps the child of the past, and the child of the past helps the child in the present, to solve a mystery or resolve a problem. Usually, both children first long to be somewhere else, but through their friendship they finally realize they belong in their own time and place.

Why does this sort of story attract so many fine children's writers? I suspect that many children's fiction writers like time fantasies because they represent the essence of children's literature. The focus on the past is one way of expressing the nostalgia inherent in children's fiction—a nostalgia characteristic of adults who feel drawn to produce a literature about a childhood they no longer experience. Furthermore, the move into the past and then beyond it into a better understanding of the present is a way of using wish-fulfillment fantasy as a moral parable: it is another version of the combination of the idyllic and the didactic.

EXPLORATIONS: (1) Does the fact that so many novels have so many similar attributes suggest that a form of plagiarism has taken place? Read (or have children read) a number of different time fantasies and explore your response to their many similarities.

(2) Consider the possible significance of the fact that the authors of most of the time fantasies named—and of most other time fantasies—are women.

CHILDREN'S VERSIONS OF ADULT LITERARY FORMS

Many novels for children belong to two genres. They are not only children's fiction but also historical fiction, or mystery, or science fiction, or romance. Because each of these genres has distinct characteristics, different from and even in some cases opposite to the attributes we expect of children's fiction, novels of this sort often represent interesting balances of differing characteristics. Again, I offer considerations of two such subgenres—science fiction and romance—as examples of the kinds of exploration of other genres that might be interesting.

Science Fiction

Science fiction as a genre focuses on the wonders of the imagination and the vastness of human potential, particularly the exotic futures offered by technology. While much science fiction describes disastrous future results of technological development, it still often expresses optimism about human potential: a bad future represents a bad choice now, when we can still make a different choice leading to a better future. But whereas many children's science fiction novels offer young readers visions of wondrous futures, their attitude toward technological advance is often surprisingly negative.

For instance, many science fiction novels for both adults and children describe characters who escape from stultifying closed cities into a larger and better world outside. But in adult novels like Arthur C. Clarke's *City and the Stars,* the entry into the changing world outside the city leads to grander future possibilities, further evolution. In children's novels like H. M. Hoover's *This Time of Darkness,* Ann Schlee's *Vandal,* and André Norton's *Outside,* however, the move from the technological city is to a nostalgically nontechnological natural utopia, the opposite of evolution. In these children's novels, paradoxically, youngsters assertive enough to defy their conservative elders are rewarded by a conservative vision of paradise. They move forward into the past, in a way that defies our expectations of the non-conservative, proevolutionary bias of much adult science fiction and that makes the genre as nostalgic and as ambivalent about youthful revolutionary fervor as much other children's fiction is.

EXPLORATIONS: (1) Test the difference between science fiction for adults and for children by exploring (or having children explore) some adult science fiction and some children's science fiction—particularly novels about closed cities.

(2) Before reading the following section, read (or have children read) a number of "Sweet Dreams" romances. Have each member of a group read a different book and then have members of the group compare notes. What characteristics do the books share? What are the implications of those shared characteristics?

Teen Romances

Like adult romances, books in teen series like "Sweet Dreams" usually deal with apparently plain but secretly beautiful females who find themselves torn between two older males, one they claim to find attractive but actually feel nothing for and another they at first feel only hostility toward, but end up deeply in love with. A number of commentators have suggested that the hostility the heroines first feel for the men they end up loving is a key to the effect of romance. They must be swept away by love against their will. This accords with the traditional assumption that desirable women are passive, desirable men aggressive, and that therefore men must be aggressive in pursuing the unaggressive women they desire. Romance describes how a powerful male captivates and sometimes even literally captures or imprisons a female, who at first protests but then finds herself a willing victim, pleased by being overpowered and in love with her attacker.

Romance is by far the most widely read form of fiction throughout the world, and it is read almost exclusively by women. In light of its focus on something that sounds so much like victimization, I have to ask why women readers are so fond of romances.

The answer may be that romance offers the same wish-fulfilling pleasures that fairy tales do: both tell how poor or weak people win desirable partners and worldly success by acting passively. Still, I find it frightening that so many female readers find pleasure in the idea that brute force is the essence of romance; it may well suggest the degree to which theoretically outmoded ideas of gender distinctions still hold sway over us.

In *Loving with a Vengeance,* Tania Modleski suggests that there is another side to it. While the male is captivating the female, she is also captivating him. He may first be attracted to the heroine by his physical desire for her, but he soon finds himself caught up in an emotional love against his will. His aggressiveness usually turns out to have been his way of dealing with a passion he can't control and wishes to ignore; but eventually, his love for the female softens him, and he gives in to it just as she gives in to her physical need for him. So what at first seems to be a fantasy about the attractiveness of brute male force is also a typical underdog story in which the weak conquers the strong: in this case, the weak female defeats the powerful male. The only real difference is that the enemy himself is the prize for the victor.

Teen romances express all these ideas, but with significant differences, most of them caused by the difference in the age of the main characters. Adult romances end with marriage; the men and women know they have found the love of their lives, and that justifies the intensity of their feelings for each other. There can be no such justification when we are dealing with teenagers; this love is not *the* love we all expect someday to find, but only an apprenticeship for it. Polly in Elaine Harper's *Mystery Kiss* first fears Ron's kiss because it might mean falling in love and "being stuck with him for life" (18). Of course she does eventually acknowledge her attraction to him, but she makes it clear at the wedding of an older couple that closes the novel that she doesn't want to catch the bouquet because she is too young: "I don't want to catch one of those for a few years yet" (187). A number of teen romances end with the statement about how this particular love is fine for now, but not likely to last forever, nor lead to marriage. Transience replaces commitment.

Furthermore, titillation replaces fulfillment: in the idealized world of young romance there is no sex without marriage. If teen romances are a form of wish-fulfillment fantasy, then the wish they fulfill is an odd one: to think obsessively about sex and romance but never to spoil the obsession by consummating the relationship. In teen romances, the heroines are victims forever.

BEYOND GENRE

Throughout this chapter, I have explored the intense degree to which children's fiction expresses clearly defined characteristics. As Margaret Higgonet suggests, "By virtue of its intensely repetitive forms, children's literature creates clear expectations about how narratives will proceed and particularly about how they will conclude" (37). But I have also tried to show how different kinds of fiction represent variations on the basic characteristics, so that the reading of a varied body of children's stories and novels will not only confirm basic narrative strategies and structures but also encourage use of these basics as a schema to accommodate new forms.

Higgonet points out, moreover, that a number of works of children's fiction, from *Charlotte's Web* to Choose-Your-Own Adventures, disrupt the unified narrative patterns we expect, and in doing so, "open up the space of the child's mental activity. . . . rupture in the narrative line may be recognizable as soon as a child recognizes narrative itself—a stage of awareness that will vary from child to child. Furthermore, the break that at first shocks seems ultimately to produce pleasure, through the processes of rereading, speculation or discussion, and eventual mastery" (51). If we wish to encourage such mastery, then our discussions of fiction with children should center on both the expected patterns and the disruptions of them.

WORKS CITED

(In this list I've provided the name of only the first volume of each of the many series I've referred to in the chapter. Titles of the others volumes can be found in the catalog of any good children's library.)

Alcott, Louisa May. *Little Women.* 1868. Harmondsworth, Middlesex: Puffin-Penguin, 1953.
Alexander, Lloyd. *The Book of Three.* New York: Holt, Rinehart and Winston, 1964.
Andersen, Hans Christian. *Hans Andersen's Fairy Tales: A Selection.* Trans. L. W. Kingsland. Oxford: Oxford UP, 1984.
Banks, Lynn Reid. *The Indian in the Cupboard.* New York: Doubleday, 1981.
Barrie, J. M. *Peter Pan and Wendy.* New York; Scribner's, 1911.
Baum, Frank L. *The Wonderful Wizard of Oz.* Chicago: Hill, 1900.
Blume, Judy. *Are You There God? It's Me, Margaret.* New York: Bradbury, 1970.
Boston, Lucy. *The Children of Green Knowe.* London: Faber and Faber, 1954.
Cameron, Eleanor. *The Court of the Stone Children.* New York: Dutton, 1973.
Carroll, Lewis. *Alice in Wonderland.* 1865. New York: Norton, 1971.
Charles, Norma M. *Amanda Grows Up.* Richmond Hill: Scholastic-TAB, 1976.
Clarke, Arthur C. *The City and the Stars.* New York: Harcourt, 1956.
Clausen, Christopher. "Home and Away in Children's Fiction." *Children's Literature* 10 (1982): 141–152.
Cooper, Susan. *The Dark Is Rising.* New York: Atheneum, 1973.
Cormier, Robert. *I Am the Cheese.* New York: Pantheon, 1977.
Crampton, Gertrude. *Tootle.* Racine: Golden, 1945.
Danziger, Paula. *The Cat Ate My Gymsuit.* New York: Delacorte, 1974.
Disch, Thomas M. *The Brave Little Toaster.* New York: Doubleday, 1986.
Fitzhugh, Louise. *Harriet the Spy.* New York: Harper & Row, 1964.
———. *The Long Secret.* New York: Harper & Row, 1965.
———. *Sport.* New York: Delacorte, 1979.
Forbes, Esther. *Johnny Tremain.* Boston: Houghton Mifflin, 1943.
Garner, Alan. *Elidor.* London: Collins, 1965.
———. *Red Shift.* London: Collins, 1975.
Grahame, Kenneth. *The Wind in the Willows.* 1908. New York: Scribner, 1933.
Harper, Elaine. *The Mystery Kiss.* New York: Silhouette, 1983.
Heide, Florence Parry. *The Shrinking of Treehorn.* New York: Holiday House, 1981.
Higgonet, Margaret. "Narrative Fractures and Fragments." *Children's Literature* 15 (1987): 37–54.

Hoban, Russell. *How Tom Beat Captain Najork and His Hired Sportsman.* London: Cape, 1974.

———. *The Mouse and His Child.* New York: Harper & Row, 1967.

Hoover, H. M. *This Time of Darkness.* New York: Viking, 1980.

Kipling, Rudyard. *The Jungle Book.* 1894. Oxford: Oxford UP, 1987.

Lanes, Selma. *The Art of Maurice Sendak.* New York: Abradale–Abrams, 1984.

Le Guin, Ursula. *A Wizard of Earthsea.* New York: Parnassus, 1968.

Lévi-Strauss, Claude. *The Savage Mind.* Chicago: U of Chicago P, 1966.

Lewis, C. S. *The Lion, the Witch and the Wardrobe.* London: Bles, 1950.

Lunn, Janet. *The Root Cellar.* Toronto: Lester and Orpen Denys, 1980.

Mayne, William. *Earthfasts.* London: Hamish Hamilton, 1966.

McCloskey, Robert. *Make Way for Ducklings.* New York: Viking, 1941.

Milne, A. A. *The House at Pooh Corner.* London: Methuen, 1928.

———. *Winnie-the-Pooh.* London: Methuen, 1926.

Modleski, Tania. *Loving with a Vengeance: Mass-Produced Fantasies for Women.* New York: Methuen, 1982.

Montgomery, L. M. *Anne of Green Gables.* 1908. Toronto: Seal-McClelland and Stewart/Bantam, 1981.

Nesbit, E. *The Story of the Amulet.* London: Unwin, 1906.

Nodelman, Perry. "Text as Teacher: The Beginning of *Charlotte's Web.*" *Children's Literature* 13 (1985): 109–127.

Norton, André. *Outside.* New York: Walker, 1974.

Norton, Mary. *The Borrowers.* London: Dent, 1952.

Park, Ruth. *Playing Beatie Bow.* New York: Atheneum, 1982.

Paton Walsh, Jill. *A Chance Child.* London: Macmillan, 1978.

Pearce, Philippa. *Tom's Midnight Garden.* London: Oxford UP, 1958.

Potter, Beatrix. *The Tale of Peter Rabbit.* London: Frederick Warne, 1902.

Schlee, Ann. *The Vandal.* London: Macmillan, 1979.

Sendak, Maurice. *Where the Wild Things Are.* New York: Harper & Row, 1963.

Siegel, R. A. "Are You There, God? It's Me, Me, ME! Judy Blume's Self-Absorbed Narrators." *Lion and the Unicorn* 2.2 (Fall 1978): 72–77.

Sleator, William. *House of Stairs.* New York: Dutton, 1974.

Stevenson, Robert Louis. *Treasure Island.* 1883. London: Collins, 1953.

Uttley, Alison. *A Traveller in Time.* London: Faber and Faber, 1939.

White, E. B. *Charlotte's Web.* New York: Harper & Row, 1973.

———. *Stuart Little.* New York: Harper & Row, 1945.

Wilder, Laura Ingalls. *Little House in the Big Woods.* New York: Harper & Row, 1932.

PART FIVE

Continuing the Exploration

This book has explored various contexts that might have an effect on our understanding of children's literature, and investigated various questions relating to specific kinds of children's literature. I hope I have managed to persuade readers that children's literature is a source of literary pleasure and intellectual stimulation.

If I have persuaded you, then your interest in children's literature won't end when you put down this book. This last section offers advice about how you might use the understanding and knowledge of children's literature you have developed so far.

The most obvious way to use it is to keep on reading literary texts intended for children, and to share the most stimulating ones with others—especially with children. I hope that you will read children's literature in the context of ideas and expectations you have developed in response to this book, and that doing so deepens your pleasure in the literature.

There are two other ways you can continue your exploration of children's literature: you can teach children some of the strategies you use to derive pleasure from literature; and you can enrich your own understanding and enjoyment by continuing to respond to the opinions of others about the texts you read. The two chapters that follow offer advice to help you in these two areas: first, teaching literary strategies to children, and then, responding to critical discussions of it.

CHAPTER 14

Teaching Children Literature

THE LACK OF LITERARY APPRECIATION

While stories and poems play a prominent role in the education of children, literature itself is rarely the subject of teaching. Young children reading *Charlotte's Web* might be asked to develop their language skills by inserting vocabulary words into webs made of twine and hung in the classroom, or to expand their creativity by exploring what it feels like to try looking radiant, or to build their knowledge by developing an interest in the habits of spiders. But they are seldom asked to consider a text *as* a text—to explore the ways in which it provides its readers with the pleasures of literature.

Even when texts are not being used as the basis for grammar or geography lessons, study of them tends to focus on nonliterary concerns. Standard guides like those by Huck and by Sutherland, Monson, and Arbuthnot define literature as a vicarious experience that offers children insight into the feelings of others, as a transmitter of cultural heritage, and as a resource for the development of cognitive and linguistic skills. These guides say a good deal about the usefulness of literature in teaching these subjects and skills, but surprisingly little about literary appreciation.

In fact, the educational uses of literature recommended in these guides distort the experience of literature in a way that might actually prevent children from enjoying it. Those of us who like reading stories and poems do not do so as a means to investigate geography or to learn how to be more tolerant or more imaginative. We do so because we enjoy the experience.

We might conclude, then, that in order not to interfere with children's pleasure in literature, we should just butt out, and leave them to their own reading. Unfortunately, however, many children *don't* take much pleasure in literature, and left to their own divices they might well choose never to read it al all. That's a pity.

Surely we should at least try to give children access to the pleasures we ourselves experience. This chapter explores ways in which we might accomplish that.

Many of the texts I quote in this chapter focus on the work of classroom teachers and the place of literary study in formal education. But we should not forget the vast potential for education and enrichment outside of school. I hope the various suggestions I make will be used not only in school and not only by teachers, but also in homes and elsewhere, by parents, by grandparents, by librarians—by anyone interested in sharing literary pleasure with children.

IS PLEASURE TEACHABLE?

EXPLORATION: Do you think it is? Before you read the following section, think about your own experiences of studying literature. Have educational experiences (such as reading this book) increased or decreased your pleasure in specific texts? In the process of reading and responding to literature? If so, how? If not, why not?

One of the reasons the focus of our teaching of literature is not on the enrichment of pleasure is the idea that pleasure is private, too dependent on individual tastes and feelings to be teachable. There is no doubt that differences in taste play a large part in our ability to enjoy particular texts, and that is as it should be. Some of us will never enjoy reading the works of James Joyce no matter how persuasively others tell us they like them. We either experience pleasure or we don't. In the words of Peter Neumeyer, "One can't say, 'Have pleasure now, damn it,' as Miss Havisham says to Pip, 'Play, boy' " (146).

But it is also true that many people who might enjoy reading James Joyce simply have not learned the skills necessary to do so. While many people believe that the critical analysis and understanding of literature somehow destroys our pleasure in it, the reverse is more often true. "I think," Neumeyer says, "we simply must have faith that as students understand more, they enjoy more" (147).

Nevertheless, some people who acknowledge that understanding can increase enjoyment still insist that such understanding cannot be actively taught. In *Literature for Young Children,* Joan I. Glazer says that "literature is more *experienced* than *taught*" (51), and according to Huck, "children are developing . . . a way of thinking about books. This should be encouraged but not taught" (707). Why it should *not* be taught is not clear, but the idea seems to relate to various assumptions based on Piagetian theory that we explored in Chapter 4. Perhaps children are too egocentric to develop the distance and objectivity needed for an analytical understanding of literature; perhaps they are at a stage of cognitive development that prevents them from making sense of abstractions; perhaps the imposition of adult language and adult categories interferes with their active learning.

All of these assumptions, we also saw earlier, have been questioned by cognitive psychologists. Children are not necessarily egocentric, not necessarily incapable of dealing with abstractions, not necessarily incapable of learning through conscious instruction.

Furthermore, assuming children will learn literary strategies by themselves merely through exposure to literature leads, generally, to ignorance of these strategies. Many adults emerge from their childhood exposure to literature with simplistic interpretive strategies that prevent them from getting much pleasure from their reading.

EXPLORATION: Again think about your own experience—did you learn literary strategies productive of pleasure by yourself? How did you learn the strategies, consciously or unconsciously? Are you aware of having been taught them? When and by whom?

Meanwhile, there's mounting evidence that the more we talk with children in the language we use in our discussions of literature with other adults, the more we help children develop strategies of understanding and appreciation, the more they can perceive and talk about the subtleties in the books they read, then the more they enjoy literature. Barbara Kiefer describes how young children enjoy their awareness of the subtleties of picture books, and Richard Van Dongen notes children in grade five delight in their consciousness of the artistry of nonfiction. In the symposium on "Teaching Literary Criticism in the Elementary Grades," the editor Jon Stott reports his success in teaching children story patterns, Anita Moss and Norma Bagnall report on successful efforts to introduce young children to various aspects of the critical analysis of literature, and Sonia Landes describes how she provided children in the early elementary grades with strategies for perceiving the structure and subtlety of a picture book. Landes sums up the children's reactions: "The close study of *The Tale of Peter Rabbit* . . . gave them a sense of accomplishment and immense pleasure" (161).

WHAT WE DON'T WANT TO TEACH

If we believe that education works—that children learn from the behavior of their teachers—then we have to acknowledge that much of what they learn is what we have conveyed unintentionally, simply because we have not thought about the implications of our methods. Furthermore, the evidence of many adult's distaste for reading suggests that many conventional methods of teaching children literature are counterproductive—that they produce more despair and uninterest than pleasure. This means we must think about the kinds of attitudes toward literature that particular exercises might produce, and above all, avoid classroom experiences that might turn children away from the pleasures of literature.

Fortunately, we have one infallible principle to guide us. Lola Brown suggests what it is when she says, "The fundamental disharmony between my behaviour as an independent reader and the behaviour of student-readers apparently dictated by classroom conditions is, for me, the starting point in addressing the problem of rendering imaginative literature accessible to *all* young readers" (94). In other words, if we don't want to misrepresent the pleasures of literature, we should avoid *any* practice in the classroom that differs significantly from the practices typical of people who like to read.

There are several things we don't usually do when we read away from classrooms but that teachers often ask children to do:

- As long as we're enjoying what we read, we don't pay much attention to the process of decoding the words, or worry about whether or not we're reading absolutely accurately. We don't interrupt our pleasure in the development of a plot by looking up every single word we're unfamiliar with. Instead, we derive meaning from context as we read. We are often so swept up by the events of a plot that we are content *not* to know the exact meaning of particular words.
- We don't read everything with the same degree of attention; we don't always read closely and analytically; we sometimes just skim through a story or poem. Nor do we keep reading books we hate or find boring just because someone else has decided they're good for us. We feel free to stop reading books we don't like before we've finished them.
- We don't often read with a primary focus on the message or the author's purpose, trying to determine what a story or poem might teach us about or own future behavior. We don't see the reading of literature primarily as a form of self-administered therapy. Nor do we focus on the information about geography or history that novels or poems convey.
- We don't parrot the responses or interpretations provided by other people, particularly those with authority over us, in order to prove that we understood the right things about a book we read.
- We don't express our response to the books we read by involving ourselves in entertaining activities loosely based on them: inventing board games around their events or cooking the foods they describe or making videos in which we imagine ourselves to be reporters interviewing the characters.

When we don't treat our reading in these ways, we are asserting our interest in literature as an experience deserving of attention in and for itself. We're also asserting our control over our own reading—our right to respond to books as we wish and as we actually do, our *ownership* of our own response. If we want children to learn to duplicate the pleasure of our reading experiences, then, we avoid hampering that sort of interest and control. Sutherland, Monson, and Arbuthnot assert, "It goes without saying that any response should be treated with the utmost respect" (502).

Nevertheless, we should remember that respecting the response of others does not necessarily mean not admitting that we disagree with them. To create an environment in which *any* response is appropriate forces us to resign our *own* right to try to dissuade others of those opinions we disagree with, and denies children the pleasures of dialogue about differing responses. It also denies the basic thrust of our effort as teachers: to encourage richer responses.

WHAT WE DO WANT TO TEACH

EXPLORATION: As you read through this section, keep in mind a specific child or group of children you know. To what extent might it be possible to accomplish these goals with this audience? How? Try to think of specific ways in which you might accomplish them.

We can encourage richer responses in a number of ways. We can give children some freedom to choose what literature they'll read and discuss in terms of their own developing tastes and interests. We can offer them ready access to libraries. We can put the children's own responses at the heart of our discussions of literature with them. We can encourage them to see the value and significance of their own responses, and of the ways in which they relate texts to the rest of their experience. In other words, we can encourage the kind of exploration I've encouraged throughout this book. Above all, we can confirm what children who love literature know already: not just that everyone's experiences of it are different but also that these different responses emerge from a shared text and so can be a profitable subject of discussion.

A focus on individual readers' responses suggests specific attitudes and skills we want to help children develop. We want to encourage children to focus their attention away from the products of reading—the ideas or messages they end up with after finishing and thinking about a poem or novel—and onto the processes of reading. Rather than leaving them to imagine that reading is a process of thoughtlessly immersing themselves in a text, we want to encourage them to be conscious of the degree to which they actively intervene in and even manufacture their own reading experiences.

We also want children to become aware of the ways in which texts communicate distinctive experiences, to understand how writers' specific choices of words, phrases, events, and so on work together to create the flavor and meanings of individual texts. Since such an awareness requires the necessary language, we should teach children that language: the words and phrases, like "image," "structure," "gap," "melodrama," or "story pattern," that allow us to formulate and develop understanding of our reading experiences. In her discussion of circular and linear journeys in "Teaching Literary Criticism in the Elementary Grades," Anita Moss reports that "the children eagerly learned the meanings of these words and quickly learned to apply them, not only to stories but also to popular culture and to their own experience" (Stott, "Teaching" 169).

The appropriate language allows us to discuss literature, and fostering an understanding of and enthusiasm for discussion should be a main goal. As Steve Bicknell says, "Literature must be discussed. It is only by discussing with others who have experienced a book that new meaning can be effectively constructed" (Tchudi 45).

To encourage the construction of new meaning, we can also introduce children to the ideas of literary critics. While much literary criticism might seem esoteric for children in elementary school, Linnea Hendrickson describes how she "decided to choose a critical article and consider how its insights might be passed on to preschoolers," and concludes her listing of the insights provided in a complex article about Beatrix Potter that might be transmitted to children by asserting, "The more deeply one delves into criticism, the more ideas one gets" (202).

In addition to placing their response to a text in the context of other readers' responses, we should encourage children to see it in the context of the rest of their experience of literature, and to develop some knowledge of its recurring patterns. In *The Educated Imagination,* Northrop Frye claims that these recurring themes and patterns are the "real subject" of literary study (49): because those themes and patterns represent the ways in which the human imagination has separated itself from, imposed itself upon, and transformed nature, "whatever value there is in studying literature, cultural or practical, comes from the total body of our reading, the castle of words we've built, and keep adding new wings to all the time" (95). Having knowledge of the conventional patterns of genre and structure that critics like Frye speak of will give children entry into a common heritage of literary knowledge beyond their own perceptions, and allow them the pleasure of being able to discuss literature with others who share that heritage.

In order to foster an awareness of the patterns shared even by widely different works of literature, we need to provide children with diverse experiences of literature—with the simple and the complex, the old and the new, the foreign and the domestic, the tragic and the funny—even the good and the bad. Furthermore, we should make both popular literature and TV and movies a significant part of our discussion of literature, in the classroom and elsewhere. As Leslie Stratta and John Dixon say, "Given the fact that students spend more time watching television than they do going to class, it seems suicidal for schools to ignore the media" (175). Rather than ignoring it, we should connect the literature we teach with the rest of the children's experience of narrative. And we should help children develop analytical viewing skills that will protect them from indiscriminate acceptance of hegemonic propaganda. Jo-Anne Everingham says, "My first aim in teaching about television has been to develop the ability to 'read television' by developing the ability to view differently" (67).

We can apply a similar aim to written texts, and work to help children read with a consciousness of ideological implications: of the ways in which texts work to manipulate readers. We might even make children aware of the extent to which their own responses are a product of their culture and their society, and thus allow them greater freedom of choice about accepting ideas they are exposed to.

Ideally, providing children with a variety of literature can help free them from common cultural assumptions about what children can or should like, and develop their willingness to seek pleasure from the new as well as from the familiar. In order to accomplish that, we need the bravery to offer them unusual literary experiences. Candy Carter says, "Somehow in the last decade or so, American teachers got stuck on the idea that students had to 'like' everything, not realizing that part of our job was to help them like it" (59).

HOW TO TEACH LITERARY APPRECIATION

For the most part, assumptions about the limitations of children and the dangers of analytical thinking have meant that teachers have not often even tried to teach children literary skills. As a result, we don't really know that much about how we might do so. Common sense offers the most important guide. We can't teach what we don't know, so anyone who doesn't know how to enjoy reading literature, thinking about it, and entering into dialogues about it shouldn't try to teach these skills. On the other hand, those of us who have these skills need do nothing more than figure out what we ourselves do in the process of enjoying literature and then devise ways of teaching children to follow the same process.

EXPLORATION: Record your thinking as you explore your response to a children's book. Then stand back from what you've written and try to figure out what strategies you were using. How might you go about teaching these strategies to children?

Duplicating the Experiences of Readers

Research into the history of those adults who enjoy reading and responding to literature also suggests some guidelines. The main one is simply that readers tend to come from homes where reading occurs. Their childhood homes contained many books, the adults they lived with read often and enjoyed discussions of books often, the children were often read to by adults who clearly enjoyed doing so, and they had access to a variety of texts, from comic books to sophisticated fiction.

If we want to create readers, we need to duplicate these experiences as much as we can. We can read stories and poems to children as often as possible, and with as much enthusiasm as possible. We can make connections between these texts and other classroom and real-life experiences by reminding students of the ways in which the texts relate to other contexts. We can fill our homes and classrooms with books of all sorts and allow children the freedom to read what they want and to choose which texts they want to discuss in class. We can make ourselves familiar with the books they are reading and the TV programs they are watching and discuss these books and programs with them. And we can do our own reading in the presence of children whenever possible: when students in a classroom are involved in small group discussions, for instance.

Exposure to a Variety of Books

The most successful literature curriculum not only creates situations in which children read copiously but also exposes children to as many different kinds of books as possible: not just "good" literature that we approve of but texts we might consider to be trash; and not just texts that children can easily understand, but more unusual ones. According to Aidan Chambers, "Wide, voracious, indiscriminate reading is the base soil from which discrimination and taste eventually grow. Indeed, if those of us who are avid and committed readers examine our reading history during our childhood and look also at what we have read over the last few months, few of us will be able to say honestly that we have always lived only on the high peaks of literature'' (122). On the other hand, as Candy Carter says, ''No one, not even the most seriously deficient reader, should be denied the opportunity to be exposed to good works of literature. If a student can't handle the vocabulary level, the teacher can put the book on tape; there is no shame in being read to. For a teacher to take it upon himself or herself that a student is too 'slow' a reader to be given a chance to tackle a good book is a serious disservice to another human being'' (58).

The need for variety of types and of levels of complexity means that no graded reader or anthology can encourage literary response. Teachers forced to use such texts should supplement them with other materials. Some enthusiastic teachers go so far as to cut readers up into separate selections, so that each selection becomes an individual pamphlet available for an individual child's reading.

A Consciousness of Response

While exposure to a variety of literature is the best generator of literary pleasure, most classrooms cannot provide the degree of exposure that might create such a response. Children who arrive at school without much familiarity with literature have considerable catching up to do, and the demands of school curricula make it impossible for teachers to spend all day reading to students. We need to develop other ways of teaching literary skills.

The most basic skill is a consciousness of our own response and the responses of others, and of the processes through which we come to understand and enjoy literary texts. Here are some ways to encourage such a consciousness:

- Exercises that focus attention on how we build our responses from the information in texts. For instance, we can read poems or stories the children aren't familiar with a line or a sentence at a time, stopping to allow discussion of the images and ideas that emerge and of how readers confirm or change the expectations these ideas and images arouse.
- Exercises focused on the ways in which we apply our individual expectations to the texts we read, fill in gaps, visualize characters and settings, relate texts to others we've experienced earlier or to patterns we've become conscious of. For instance, we can encourage discussion of what children expect before they begin to read a particular text and how their expectations relate to their previous experiences of literature or life. We can ask for verbal or written descriptions of what gaps children notice and how they fill them, or of their visualizations of characters or settings and what meanings they might imply.
- Group discussions in which children discuss the differences in their responses to a text.
- Journals encouraging children to record their responses and to do exploratory thinking of the sort suggested by the explorations throughout this book.

We can also encourage consciousness of the validity of individual responses by allowing for and encouraging a spectrum of responses to the same text. In Protherough's *Developing Response to Fiction,* Keith Bardgett suggests many activities that children might choose from in terms of their own interests and abilities, including character studies, book reviews, the writing of alternative endings, imaginary interviews with characters, and drawings, in order to fill a wall display ''which would represent all aspects of their responses to the book'' (78).

Nevertheless, such activities become pointless in terms of developing literary pleasure if they draw attention away from literature and the experience of reading it. As Protherough says, ''The work done should not simply start from the book, but should constantly return and refer to it'' (59). We should design activities that, instead of producing substitutes for literary pleasure because we think we ought to make the study of literature fun, show that literature is in and of itself fun.

Focusing on the Text

We want not only to encourage response but also to find ways of helping children develop an understanding of how literary texts engender response. This means we want to focus attention on the texts themselves. Here are some ways of doing so:

- Exercises encouraging awareness of the effect of specific choices of words or patterns or images. For instance, children can rewrite poems in their own words and then consider how the two ways of expressing the same idea are different.
- Exercises, suggested by Sonia Landes, that include ''two simple questions that can be asked over and over again. . . . The first is simply, 'What do you see?' and the child will look closely at the picture and point to things and see what he or she had not seen before. The second is, 'What does the picture tell that the text does not?' and vice versa. This sends the child back and forth between picture and text, responding all the while to the wholeness of the story'' (54).
- Other activities that focus on the ways in which the illustrations in picture books change the meanings of the words, or vice versa. For instance, reading just the written text and asking children to imagine and describe pictures, and then comparing the real pictures with what they imagined; or showing just the pictures and asking children to imagine the words.

Focusing on Connections

We can help children develop knowledge of the interconnectedness of literature by paying careful attention to the sequence in which we introduce texts to children. Protherough says, ''Ideally each new learning situation should incorporate features of earlier learning, provide new ones, and carry the student to a higher level of understanding, skill or appreciation'' (171). We can devise exercises that allow children to compare one poem with another similar one, or to develop an understanding of what limericks have in common with each other, or to perceive how fairy tales share basic story patterns.

As we develop sequences of literature, however, we shouldn't let developmental assumptions prevent us from mixing complex texts with simpler ones. Jon Stott says that "teaching novels in Grade Three, while challenging, is by no means impossible" ("Spiralled Sequence" 159). We should be willing to try it, so that we don't deprive children of the rich diversity that develops skills of literary enjoyment.

We can further develop knowledge of the interconnectedness of literature by encouraging comparisons between TV or movie versions and written texts of the same story, to develop an awareness of how the story differs in the two media. We can show videotapes of TV cartoons and situation comedies and focus on the patterns they share with fairy tales. We can also devise exercises that will make children conscious of the effects on meaning of such factors as camera angle and choice of shots and also of the ideological content of programs and commercials.

Encouraging Dialogue

Since a main pleasure of literature is the dialogues it engenders, we want to encourage dialogue, both among children and between children and ourselves. We can do so by creating the sort of focused but informal atmosphere which makes real dialogue possible. In the classroom, children can explore specific questions and complete specific tasks in groups small enough to allow spontaneous discussion. We should make sure that individual responses are shared: by devising exercises which encourage students to seek out, confront, and make use of each other's responses in developing their own. For instance, children can record their own responses to a text in writing, then read each other's responses and write about the similarities and differences and their possible implications.

We also want to be able to express our own opinions as teachers or parents without turning literary discussion into a spectator sport in which students merely listen to and learn to parrot our responses instead of developing their own. We can participate in discussion without dominating it only if we create an atmosphere in which all opinions are taken seriously enough to be examined, including our own, and in which children develop both the strength of mind to be stimulated rather than hurt by a challenging of their ideas, and the skills of logical argumentation that will allow them to defend themselves. For instance, children can seek the specific details in a text to support their general impression of it, or search for parallels in other texts they already know that might support a particular interpretation.

Surefire Methods?

I realize that most of what I have presented here is general suggestions rather than step-by-step methods of teaching specific texts. I have been vague on purpose. Given the variation in response that makes literary discussion both necessary and enjoyable, there are no surefire methods. Good teaching demands constant attention to what is happening to specific children, and constant resourcefulness in developing ways of responding to problems as they occur.

Nevertheless, even the most resourceful teachers or parents can use some help. For those in search of it, I suggest the following:

1. As more teachers try to teach literary pleasure to children, they are bound to discover that certain methods meet with success. You can learn about such discoveries by reading journals like *Children's Literature in Education* and *Children's Literature Association Quarterly.*

EXPLORATION: Find a discussion of specific methods of teaching children literature in a recent journal, and try what it suggests.

---

2. Good teaching depends on having knowledge of what might be taught. Remember Linnea Hendrickson's suggestion that published literary criticism can engender ideas for teachers.

EXPLORATION: Read any *critical article in a children's literature journal, and think of what in it might be passed on to children, and how.*

---

3. According to Jon Stott, "The gap between what is done in university and school classrooms can be bridged and should be bridged more often" (" 'It's Not What You Expect,' " 161). Thinking about the methods your teachers used to help you develop an understanding and enjoyment of literature may help you develop ways of using the same methods in your own classroom.

EXPLORATION: Has a teacher ever stimulated your appreciation of literature? How? How could you adapt those methods to an elementary classroom?

---

4. Similarly, if you've found any of the ideas or exercises in this book stimulating, children might find them stimulating too. The *Explorations* often suggest thinking that might be done by children, and other ideas in the book could also be the basis for work in elementary classrooms.

EXPLORATION: Choose something in this book that interests you and devise a means of communicating the matters it contains to children.

---

5. Above all else: don't forget the main guideline I suggested earlier, that good teaching of literary pleasure duplicates the practices of ardent readers and avoids anything that ardent readers don't usually do. So read literature yourself, both adult literature and children's literature. Think about your response to what you read, and discuss it with other people. As long as you keep on enjoying these activities, you'll learn more about them that you can pass on to children. And as long as you remember that the pleasure of these activities is what you want to teach, you can devise classroom practices that teach literary pleasure by offering it themselves.

WORKS CITED

Bicknell, Steve. "On Not Teaching Literature and Reading." Tchudi 44–45.

Brown, Lola. "Rendering Literature Accessible." Corcoran and Evans 93–118.

Carter, Candy. "Engaging Students in Reading." Tchudi 57–60.

Chambers, Aidan. *Introducing Books to Children.* London: Heinemann, 1973.

Corcoran, Bill, and Emrys Evans, eds. *Readers, Texts, Teachers.* Upper Montclair: Boynton/Cook, 1987.

Everingham, Jo-Anne. "English and Reading in the New Media." Tchudi 67–71.

Frye, Northrop. *The Educated Imagination.* Bloomington: Indiana UP, 1964.

Glazer, Joan I. *Literature for Young Children.* 2nd ed. Columbus: Merrill, 1986.

Hendrickson, Linnea. "Literary Criticism as a Source of Teaching Ideas." *Children's Literature Association Quarterly* 9.4 (Winter 1984–1985): 202.

Huck, Charlotte S. *Children's Literature in the Elementary School.* 3rd ed., updated. New York: Holt, Rinehart and Winston, 1979.

Kiefer, Barbara Z. "The Child and the Picture Book: Creating Live Circuits." *Children's Literature Association Quarterly* 11.2 (Summer 1986): 63–68.

Landes, Sonia. "Picture Books as Literature." *Children's Literature Association Quarterly* 10.2 (Summer 1985): 51–54.

Neumeyer, Peter. "Children's Literature in the English Department." *Children's Literature Association Quarterly* 12.3 (Fall, 1987): 146–150.

Protherough, Robert. *Developing Response to Fiction.* Milton Keynes, England: Open UP, 1983.

Stott, Jon C. " 'It's Not What You Expect': Teaching Irony to Third Graders." *Children's Literature in Education* 13.4 (Winter 1982): 153–161.

———, ed. "Teaching Literary Criticism in the Elementary Grades: A Symposium." *Children and Their Literature: A Readings Book.* Ed. Jill P. May. West Lafayette: Children's Literature Association Publications, 1983. 160–172.

Stratta, Leslie, and John Dixon. "Writing and Literature: Monitoring and Examining." Corcoran and Evans 174–196.

Sutherland, Zena, Dianne L. Monson and May Hill Arbuthnot. *Children and Books.* 6th ed. Glenview: Scott, Foresman, 1981.

Tchudi, Stephen N., and others, eds. *English Teachers at Work: Ideas and Strategies from Five Countries.* Upper Montclair: Boynton/Cook Publishers, 1986.

Van Dongen, Richard. "Non-fiction, History, and Literary Criticism in the Fifth Grade." *Children's Literature Association Quarterly* 12.4 (Winter 1987): 189–190.

CHAPTER 15

Reading about Children's Literature

CONTINUING THE DIALOGUE

Throughout this book I have tried to encourage readers to enter into a dialogue with my ideas about children's literature and arrive at their own conclusions about the issues I discuss. I have done so because I find this sort of dialogue one of the most pleasurable aspects of my own encounters with literature.

While I enjoy actual conversations about books with other readers, a major part of the dialogue occurs in my reading of books and articles that describe the responses of readers I have never met. When it comes to this sort of critical analysis, I am a distrustful reader; I explore the opinions of others in terms of my own repertoire of experiences and responses, and so I rarely find myself in total agreement with other readers' conclusions about a text as they report them in critical articles or books. But I almost always find myself stimulated by their ideas into thinking new thoughts of my own. Reading critical discussions helps me continue my dialogue with texts and with literature in general.

To encourage other readers to continue their own dialogue in this way, I have provided information in this chapter about further discussions of the topics covered in this book. This is anything but a complete bibliography. These books and articles are the ones I have found most enjoyable, most interesting, most infuriating, most stimulating, or most provocative.

By and large, the structure of what follows mirrors the structure of the book so far; the headings are the titles of the various sections of the book. This means that I list critical texts not in relation to the specific literary texts they discuss, but in terms of the issues they tackle or the theoretical stance they take. I have used abbreviations for the names of some of the journals devoted to children's literature that I find most useful and cite most often. *ChLAQ* is the *Children's Literature Association Quarterly; CLE* is *Children's Literature in Education; Children's Literature* is *CL;* and *LU* is *The Lion and the Unicorn.*

PART ONE: WRITING AND READING

Writing

There is more discussion of the kind of exploratory writing I recommend in Chapter 1 in William Zinsser's *Writing to Learn* (New York: Perennial Library-Harper & Row, 1989). Further advice about how to do this kind of writing is offered in the section on "response statements" in *Reading Texts: Reading, Responding, Writing,* ed. Kathleen McCormack, Gary Waller, and Linda Flower (Lexington: Heath, 1987); this book also describes ways of developing deeper response to literature and discusses how to move beyond response writing to finished writing, such as an essay.

Reading

Theories of Reader Response. The basic ideas of reader-response criticism, such as the concept of "the implied reader" introduced in Chapter 2 and the concepts of "gaps" and "consistency-building" that form the basis of the approach to reading outlined in Chapter 6, are discussed more fully in two books by Wolfgang Iser: *The Implied Reader* (Baltimore: Johns Hopkins UP, 1974) and *The Act of Reading* (Baltimore: Johns Hopkins UP, 1978). Two useful collections of essays about reader response are *The Reader in the Text: Essays on Audience and Participation,* ed. Susan Suleiman and Inge Crosman (Princeton: Princeton UP, 1980) and *Reader-Response Criticism: From Formalism to Post-structuralism,* ed. Jane P. Tompkins (Baltimore: Johns Hopkins UP, 1980).

Children as Readers. Theoretical considerations of the nature of children's reading are found in Arthur N. Applebee's *Child's Concept of Story: Age Two to Seventeen* (Chicago: U of Chicago P, 1978), Jeff Adams's *The Conspiracy of the Text: The Place of Narrative in the Development of Thought* (London: Routledge and Kegan Paul, 1986) and Marilyn Cochran-Smith's *The Making of a Reader* (Norwood: Ablex, 1984). Cochran-Smith is also the editor of a series of columns about empirical research into children's responses to literature that appears in various issues of the *ChLAQ:* 7.1 (Spring 1982): 42–48; 7.4 (Winter 1982–1983): 23–25; 8.3 (Fall 1983): 37–38; 10.2 (Summer 1985): 83–86; 11.2 (Summer 1986): 100–102; 12.3 (Summer 1987): 94–97.

Children as Implied Readers. Aidan Chambers discusses the implications of a "reader-response" approach for the reading and analysis of children's literature by adults in "The Reader in the Book," *The Signal Approach to Children's Books,* ed. Nancy Chambers (Metuchen: Scarecrow, 1980), 250–275. So do Reinbert Tabbert in "The Impact of Children's Books: Cases and Concepts," *CLE* 10 (1979), 92–102 and 144–149; Peter Hunt in "Childist Criticism: The Subculture of the Child, the Book and the Critic," *Signal* 43 (January 1984): 42–59; Hunt in "Questions of Method and Methods of Questioning: Childist Criticism in Action," *Signal* 45 (September 1984): 180–200; and Margaret Meek in "Symbolic Outlining: The Academic Study of Children's Literature," *Signal* 53 (May 1987): 97–115. There is a special section of articles on reader response called "Literature and Child Readers" in *ChLAQ* 4.4 (Winter 1980). Other important discussions of the child readers implied by texts include three articles in *CLE* 15.1 (1984): Adrienne Kertzer's "Inventing the Child Reader: How We Read Children's Books," 12–21; Roderick McGillis's "Calling a Voice Out of Silence: Hearing What We Read," 22–29; and Carol Billman's "Child Reader as Sleuth," 30–41 (about the way children learn the basic significance of mystery in story).

Responding, Understanding, Judging. Other stimulating discussions of aspects of children's behavior as readers include David Jackson's "First Encounters: The Importance of Initial Responses to Literature," *CLE* 11 (1980): 149–160; Robert Protherough's "How Children Judge Stories," *CLE* 14.1 (1983): 3–13; Nina Mikkelsen's "Literature and the Storymaking Powers of Children," *ChLAQ* 9.1 (Spring 1984): 9–14; Hugh Crago's "The Roots of Response," *ChLAQ* 10.3 (Fall 1985): 100–104 and " 'Easy Connections': Emotional Truth and Fictional Gratification," *Signal* 52 (January 1987): 38–61; Charles Sarland's "Secret Seven Versus the Twits: Cultural Clash or Cosy Combination," *Signal* 42 (September 1983) and "Piaget, Blyton and Story: Children's Play and the Reading Process," *CLE* 16.3 (1985): 102–109; and Barbara A. Lehman's "Child Reader and Literary Work: Children's Literature Merges Two Perspectives," *ChLAQ* 14.3 (1989): 123–128. The repertoire implied by children's texts is discussed in Peter Hunt's "What Do We Lose When We Lose Allusion? Experience and Understanding Stories," *Signal* 57 (September 1988): 212–222; and in John Stephens's "Intertextuality and *The Wedding Ghost*," *CLE* 21.1 (1990): 23–36.

Case Studies: Real Children Reading A number of books discuss the histories of individual children's responses to literature: Dorothy Neal White's *Books Before Five* (New York: Oxford UP, 1954); Dorothy Butler's *Cushla and Her Books* (London: Hodder and Stoughton, 1975), and Maureen and Hugh Crago's *Prelude to Literacy: A Preschool Child's Encounter with Picture and Story* (Carbondale: Southern Illinois UP, 1983). The articles in the Fall 1988 *ChLAQ* (13.3) are about childhood reading experiences, including those of some real and some fictional children. In " 'Plain' and 'Fancy' Laura: A Mennonite Reader of Girls' Books," CL 16 (1988): 185–192, Laura Weaver discusses the inevitable bias her religious background brought to her own childhood reading; Madelon S. Gohlke describes one of her childhood reading experiences in "Re-reading *The Secret Garden*," *College English* 41.8 (April 1980): 894–902, and Roni Natov remembers one of hers in "The Stories We Need to Hear: The Reader and the Tale," *LU* 9 (1985): 11–18.

PART TWO: HISTORICAL AND CULTURAL CONTEXTS

History of Childhood

The pioneering book about the history of childhood is Philippe Ariès's *Centuries of Childhood: A Social History of Family Life* (New York: Vintage–Random House, 1962). The most radical criticism of theories like those of Ariès is Linda Pollack's *Forgotten Children: Parent-Child Relations from 1500 to 1900* (Cambridge: Cambridge UP, 1983).

History of Children's Literature

The classical survey of the history of British children's literature is F. J. Harvey Darton's *Children's Books in England: Five Centuries of Social Life,* first published in 1932; a revised version with additional material by Brian Alderson appeared in 1982 (Cambridge: Cambridge UP). The Spring 1985 and Summer 1989 *ChLAQ* are devoted to historical children's literature, as are a number of the articles in *CL* 14 (1986) and 17 (1989).

Many works about the children's literature of specific places and periods contain "presentist" assumptions, and you should be wary of these. Nevertheless, useful information can be obtained from the following.

Beginnings. For discussions of the earliest times through the Middle Ages, there are Gillian Adams's "First Children's Literature: The Case for Sumer" *CL* 14 (1986): 1-30; Meradith Tilbury McMunn and William Robert McMunn's "Children's Literature in the Middle Ages" *CL* 1 (1972): 21–30; Bennett A. Brockman's "Robin Hood and the Invention of Children's Literature" *CL* 10 (1982): 1–17; and "The Juvenile Audiences of Sir Orfeo" *ChLAQ* 10.1 (Spring 1985): 18–20; a group of articles on children and literature in the Middle Ages in *CL* 4 (1975): 36-63; C. H. Talbot's "Children in the Middle Ages" *CL* 6 (1977): 17–33; D. Thomas Hanks's "Not for Adults Only: The English Corpus Christi Plays" *ChLAQ* 10.1 (Spring 1985): 21–22. For the Renaissance and seventeenth century, consult Warren W. Wooden's *Children's Literature of the English Renaissance,* ed. Jeanie Watson (Lexington: UP of Kentucky, 1986).

The First Literature Exclusively for Children. For the seventeenth and eighteenth century, see Ruth MacDonald's *Literature for Children in England and America from 1646 to 1774* (Troy: Whitston, 1982) and Samuel Pickering's *John Locke and Children's Books in Eighteenth Century England* (Knoxville: U of Tennessee P, 1981).

Some of the most interesting discussions of children's books of the early eighteenth century are by Mitzi Myers. These include "The Dilemmas of Gender as Double-voiced Narrative: or Maria Edgeworth Mothers the Bildungsroman," *The Idea of the Novel in the Eighteenth Century,* ed. Robert W. Uphaus (Colleagues, 1988, 67–96); "Psychology as Self-Expression in Mary Wollstonecraft: Exorcising the Past, Finding a Voice," *The Private Self: Theory and Practice of Women's*

Autobiographical Writings, ed. Shari Benstock (Chapel Hill: U of North Carolina P, 1988); "Impeccable Governesses, Rational Dames, and Moral Mothers: Mary Wollstonecraft and the Female Tradition in Georgian Children's Books," *CL* 14 (1986): 31–60; "A Taste for Truth and Realities: Early Advice for Mothers on Books for Girls," *ChLAQ* 12.3 (Fall 1987): 118–124, "Socializing Rosamund: Educational Ideology and Fictional Form," *ChLAQ* 14.2 (Summer 1989): 52–58; and "Quixotes, Orphans, and Subjectivity: Maria Edgeworth's Georgian Heroinism and the (En)gendering of Young Adult Fiction," *LU* 13.1 (June 1989): 21–40.

The Victorian Period. For the nineteenth century, useful works include: Anne Scott McLeod's *A Moral Tale: Children's Fiction and American Culture 1820–1860* (Hamden: Archon, 1975); Gillian Avery's *Childhood's Pattern: A Study of the Heroes and Heroines of Children's Fiction 1770–1950* (London: Hodder and Stoughton, 1975); Angela and Norman Williamson's "Mamie Pickering's Childhood Reading," *ChLAQ* 9.1 (Spring 1984): 3–6, and 9.2 (Summer 1984): 54–59; Anthony Kearney's "Savage and Barbaric Themes in Victorian Children's Writing," *CLE* 17.4 (1986): 233–240; Peter Merchant's " 'Fresh Instruction o'er the Mind': Exploit and Example in Victorian Fiction," *CLE* 20.1 (Spring 1989): 9–24; and U. C. Knoepflmacher's "Little Girls without Their Curls: Female Aggression in Victorian Children's Literature," *CL* 11 (1983): 14–31, "Resisting Growth through Fairy Tale in Ruskin's *The King of the Golden River,*" *CL* 13 (1985): 3–30, and "The Balancing of Child and Adult: An Approach to Victorian Fantasies for Children," *Nineteenth Century Fiction* 37.4 (1983): 497–530. There are many other books and articles about specific texts by well-known children's writers of the nineteenth century, such as Howard Pyle, Louisa May Alcott, Lewis Carroll, and George Macdonald.

Texts of Early Children's Literature

Patricia Demers includes significant short texts and excerpts from longer ones in *From Instruction to Delight: An Anthology of Children's Literature to 1850* (with Gordon Moyles, Toronto: Oxford UP, 1982) and *A Garland from the Golden Age* (Toronto: Oxford UP, 1983). A wider selection of more complete works can be found in the first seven volumes of *Masterworks of Children's Literature,* under the general editorship of Jonathan Cott (New York: Stonehill–Chelsea House, 1985). A still more extensive selection is the seventy-three volumes of *Classics of Children's Literature,* ed. Alison Lurie and Justin G. Schiller (New York: Garland, 1976–1979).

Selections of Victorian fantasies can be found in Jonathan Cott's *Beyond the Looking Glass: Extraordinary Works of Fairy Tale and Fantasy* (New York: Stonehill–Bowker, 1973), Uli Knoepflmacher's *A Christmas Carol and Other Victorian Fairy Tales* (New York: Bantam, 1983), and Jack Zipes's *Victorian Fairy Tales: The Revolt of the Fairies and Elves* (New York: Methuen, 1987). There are also editions of many individual books available; for instance, many nineteenth-century children's novels are available as Penguin Puffin Classics.

Piaget and Other Developmental Theorists

Piaget. Piaget outlined his ideas about childhood in an extensive series of books; the ones most relevant to children's reception of literature are *The Language and Thought of the Child* (English translation, 1926), *The Moral Judgement of Children* (1932), *Play, Dreams, and Imitation in Childhood* (1962), and with B. Inhelder, *The Psychology of the Child* (1969).

Piaget and Children's Literature. Almost any discussion of children and the reception of literature published in the last fifty years reveals Piaget's influence; two works that do so in a rigorous way are Arthur N. Applebee's *Child's Concept of Story: Age Two to Seventeen* (Chicago: U of Chicago P, 1978) and Nicholas Tucker's *Child and the Book: A Psychological and Literary Exploration* (Cambridge: Cambridge UP, 1981). Neil Philip reviews this book, and Tucker responds to the review, in *CLE* 12 (1981): 160–167.

Piaget's Critics. Books critical of various aspects of Piaget's theories are *Alternatives to Piaget: Critical Essays on the Theory,* ed. Linda S. Siegel and Charles J. Brainerd (New York: Academic, 1978); *Recent Advances in Cognitive Developmental Research,* ed. Charles J. Brainerd (New York: Springer-Verlag, 1983); Jean-Claude Brief's *Beyond Piaget: A Philosophical Psychology* (New York: Teachers College P, 1983); and Susan Sugarman's *Piaget's Construction of the Child's Reality* (Cambridge: Cambridge UP, 1987). Carol Gilligan offers a powerful feminist critique of developmental theories in her work *In a Different Voice: Psychological Theories and Women's Development* (Cambridge: Harvard UP, 1982).

Other Developmental Theories. While Piaget's ideas have had the most influence on our ideas about children and literature, other psychological theories of development have had a strong effect. Among these are Lawrence Kohlberg's stage theory of moral development, described in a number of essays collected in *The Philosophy of Moral Development* (San Francisco: Harper & Row, 1981) and L. S. Vygotsky's *Thought and Language* (Cambridge: MIT P and Wiley, 1962), which adds to Piaget's interest in internal cognitive structures a focus on a child's development through social interactions. Erik Erikson's theories of stages of identity development, explained in his *Childhood and Society* (New York: Norton, 1950) have had an impact on the study of literature and adolescence.

The Context of Contemporary Childhood

There is a vast body of material about the lives of children in the contemporary world, produced by psychologists, sociologists, librarians, educators, and children's literature specialists. I list here only a few books that I have found particularly stimulating.

Assumptions about Childhood. In *For Your Own Good: Hidden Cruelty in Child-Rearing and the Roots of Violence* (trans. Hildegarde and Hunter Hannum, New

York: Farrar Straus Giroux, 1980), Alice Miller reveals the cruelty inherent in still common ideas of child rearing. Two books deal with recent changes in our attitudes toward childhood: David Elkind's *The Hurried Child: Growing Up Too Fast Too Soon* (Reading: Addison-Wesley, 1981) and Neil Postman's *The Disappearance of Childhood* (New York: Dell Laurel, 1984). In *On Learning to Read: The Child's Fascination with Meaning* (New York: Vintage–Random House, 1982), Bruno Bettelheim and Karen Zelan describe how assumptions about the limitations of children control the content of reading series.

Descriptions of Children. Two acute observers of children are Robert Coles in *The Moral Life of Children* (Boston: Houghton Mifflin, 1986) and *The Political Life of Children* (Boston: Houghton Mifflin, 1986) and Vivian Gussin Paley in *White Teacher* (Cambridge: Harvard UP, 1979), *Wally's Stories: Conversation in the Kindergarten* (Cambridge: Harvard UP, 1981), *Boys and Girls: Superheroes in the Doll Corner* (Chicago: U of Chicago P, 1984), *Mollie Is Three: Growing Up in School* (Chicago: U of Chicago P, 1986), and *Bad Guys Don't Have Birthdays: Fantasy Play at Four* (Chicago: U of Chicago P, 1988). In *Philosophy and the Young Child* (Cambridge: Harvard UP, 1980) and *Dialogues with Children* (Cambridge: Harvard UP, 1984), Gareth B. Matthews describes philosophical conversations he has had with young children.

Censorship

One of the subjects mentioned in the chapter on assumptions about childhood, the censorship of children's books, has evoked heated discussion. Attempts to censor children's books in schools or libraries are reported almost daily in newspapers. An overview of the issues surrounding censorship can be found in a series of articles published in *ChLAQ*, edited by Amy McClure: 7.1 (Spring, 1982): 39–42; 8.1 (Spring 1983): 21–25; 8.3 (Fall 1983): 41–43; 8.4 (Winter 1983): 35 (by Taimi Ranta); 9.1 (Spring 1984): 36–37 (by Louise S. Musser); 9.2 (Summer 1984): 77–78, 80 (by Diane Chapman); 10.3 (Fall 1985): 137–139 (by Mark I. West); 12.1 (Spring 1987): 40–43 (by James Gellert); 12.2 (Summer 1987): 103–105 (by Patrick Shannon). Another stimulating article is "Tricks of the Text and Acts of Reading by Censors and Adolescents," *CLE* 18.2 (1987): 89–96, in which Hamida Bosmajian discusses the repressive values hidden in supposedly inflammatory and often censored texts.

Mark West surveys censorship cases in *Children, Culture and Controversy* (Hamden: Archon, 1988). In *Children's Literature in Hitler's Germany: The Cultural Policy of National Socialism* (Athens: Ohio State UP, 1984), Christa Kamenetsky offers a detailed discussion of censorship in a particular place and time. A provocative article about an important American case is Joan DelFattore's "Religious Implications of Children's Literature as Viewed by Religious Fundamentalists: the Mozert Case," *ChLAQ* 14.1 (Spring 1989): 9–13. In his gripping book *Storm in the Mountains: A Case Study of Censorship, Conflict and Consciousness* (Carbondale: Southern Illinois UP, 1988), James Moffett provides a detailed description of a case he was himself involved in. I discuss an interesting example of hidden censorship that I discovered myself in "The Case of the Disappearing Jew," *CLE* 10 (1979): 44–48. In "Censorship in Children's Paperbacks," CLE 11 (1980): 180–191, Jessica Yates presents evidence of a number of similar acts of unacknowledged censorship in paperback editions.

The Contexts of Culture and Ideology

Theory. In *Marxism and Literature* (Oxford: Oxford UP, 1977), Raymond Williams offers a provocative discussion of ideology and culture. Fascinating interpretations of the meanings of specific cultural objects such as soap powder and cruises can be found in Roland Barthes's *Mythologies* (London: Cape, 1972); the last essay in this book, "Myth Today," offers a valuable overview.

Those interested in the application of political approaches to children's literature should consult Robert D. Sutherland's "Hidden Persuaders: Ideologies in Literature for Children," *CLE* 16.3 (1985): 143–157; Peter Hollindale's "Ideology and the Children's Book," *Signal* 55 (January 1988): 3–32; and the selection of essays in *How Much Truth Do We Tell the Children? The Politics of Children's Literature,* ed. Betty Bacon (Minneapolis: MEP Publications, 1988). It includes Ruth B. Moynihan's "Ideologies in Children's Literature: Some Preliminary Notes" and a number of essays on class and race.

Jack Zipes approaches fairy tales from the context of politically oriented theories in *Breaking the Magic Spell* (Austin: U of Texas P, 1979) and *Fairy Tales and the Art of Subversion* (London: Heinemann,1982). *LU* 3.2 (Winter 1979–1980) is devoted to essays about social issues in children's literature; *ChLAQ* 11.2 (Summer 1986) contains essays about children's literature and society. Also about cultural issues are my "Cultural Arrogance and Realism in Judy Blume's *Superfudge,*" *CLE* 19.4 (1989): 230–241; and Derek Eales's "Enid Blyton, Judy Blume, and Cultural Impossibilities," *CLE* 20.2 (1989): 81–89.

Minorities. *Cross-Culturalism in Children's Literature,* eds. Susan R. Gannon and Ruth Anne Thompson, (West Lafayette: ChLA Publications, 1989) contains selected papers from the 1987 Children's Literature Association conference. *LU* 11.1 (1987) includes essays devoted to the literature of American minorities, and has pieces on children's texts about Jews, Chinese-Americans, old people, and people with disabilities.

Donnarae MacCann and Opal Moore offer thought-provoking opinions in a series of articles in *ChLAQ* under the heading of *Cultural Pluralism;* these include "Cultural Pluralism," 10.4 (Winter 1986): 201–203; "The Uncle Remus Travesty," 11.2 (Summer 1986): 96–99 and 11.4 (Winter 86–87): 205–209; "Paternalism and Assimilation in Books About Chicanos," 12.2 (Summer 1987): 99–102, and 12.3 (Fall 1987): 154–157; "The Ignoble Savage: Amerind Images in the Mainstream Mind," 13.1 (Spring 1988): 26–30; and "On Reading Institutions," 13.4 (Winter 1988): 198–200. MacCann is also editor of *The Black American in Books for Children,* 2d. ed. (Metuchen: Scarecrow, 1985). Another revealing examination is Rudine

Sims's *Shadow and Substance: Afro-American Experience in Contemporary Children's Fiction* (Urbana: NCTE, 1982).

Discussion of similar issues in regard to portrayals of native North Americans can be found in a special issue of *Canadian Children's Literature* 31–32 (1983). I also recommend Norman J. Williamson's " 'Indian Tales': Are They Fish or Fowl?" *ChLAQ* 12.2 (Summer 1987): 70–73.

Media and Popular Culture as Contexts for Children's Literature

Discussions of various aspects of popular culture can be found in *Studies in Entertainment: Critical Approaches to Mass Culture,* ed. Tania Modleski (Bloomington: Indiana UP, 1986). Television is the particular focus in Raymond Williams's *Television: Technology and Cultural Form* (New York: Schocken, 1974), John Fiske and John Hartley's *Reading Television* (London: Methuen, 1978), *High Theory/Low Culture: Analysing Popular Television and Film,* ed. Colin MacCabe (New York: St. Martin's, 1986), and Roger Silverstone's *Message of Television: Myth and Narrative in Contemporary Culture* (London: Heinemann, 1981).

Ariel Dorfman discusses popular culture for children in *The Empire's New Clothes: What the Lone Ranger, Babar, and Other Innocent Heroes Do to Our Minds* (New York: Pantheon, 1983); Jack Zipes discusses fantasy in the mass media in *Breaking the Magic Spell: Radical Theories of Folk and Fairy Tales* (Austin: U of Texas P, 1979).

The relationships between children's literature and popular culture are the subject of special sections in the spring 1982 *ChLAQ,* in the Summer 1987 *ChLAQ,* and of the articles in *LU* 11.2 (1987). The *LU* material includes Leo Zanderer's "Popular Culture, Childhood, and the New American Forest of Postmodernism" (7–33). *LU* 12.2 (1988) includes Peggy A. Bulger's "Princess of Power: Socializing Our Daughters Through TV, Toys, and Tradition" (178–192). There are four essays on "Children's Literature and the Media" in *CL* 9 (1981); a special section on the same topic can be found in the Fall 1982 *ChLAQ.*

Film

Theory and Critical Analysis. Some useful introductions to film theory and criticism are Roy Huss and Norman Silverstein's *Film Experience: Elements of Motion Picture Art* (New York: Delta–Dell, 1968); Lincoln F. Johnson's *Film: Space, Time, Light and Sound* (New York: Holt, Rinehart and Winston, 1974); J. Dudley Andrew's *The Master Film Theories: An Introduction* (New York: Oxford UP, 1976); *Film Theory and Criticism,* ed. Gerald Mast and Marshall Cohen (New York: Oxford UP, 1974); and Leo Braudy's *World in a Frame: What We See in Films* (Chicago: U of Chicago P, 1984). More theoretical works are Seymour Chatman's *Story and Discourse: Narrative Structure in Fiction and Film* (Ithaca: Cornell UP, 1978) and Christian Metz's *Language and Cinema* (The Hague: Mouton, 1974) and *The Imaginary Signifier: Psychoanalysis and the Cinema* (Bloomington: Indiana UP, 1986).

Children's Movies. Movie versions of children's novels are the subject of the essays in *Children's Novels and the Movies,* ed. Douglas Street (New York: Ungar, 1983). The movies produced by the Walt Disney studios are the subject of Frances Clarke Sayers's "Walt Disney Accused," *Children and Literature: Views and Reviews,* ed. Virginia Haviland (Glenview: Scott, Foresman, 1973), 116–125; Richard Schickel's *Disney Version* (New York: Simon and Schuster, 1969); Jill May's "Walt Disney's Interpretation of Children's Literature," *Jump Over the Moon: Selected Professional Readings,* eds. Pamela Petrick Barron and Jennifer Q. Burley (New York: Holt, Rinehart and Winston, 1984), 461–472; and Lucy Rollin's "Fear of Faerie: Disney and the Elitist Critics," *ChLAQ* 12.2 (Summer 1987): 90–93.

PART THREE: LITERARY CONTEXTS

Children's Literature as a Genre

The characteristics of children's literature as a genre are Jacqueline Rose's central concern in *The Case of Peter Pan: or The Impossibility of Children's Fiction* (London: Macmillan, 1984). This is a controversial and provocative book; deciphering its dense jargon is well worth the effort. Zohar Shavit's *Poetics of Children's Literature* (Athens: U of Georgia P, 1986) is a less successful attempt to determine the general attributes of children's literature, and it is marred by many historical inaccuracies.

In "Fiction for Children: Some Essential Differences," *Writers, Critics and Children,* ed. Geoff Fox (New York: Agathon, 1976), Myles McDowell makes some useful suggestions. So do Peter Brooks in "Towards Supreme Fictions," *The Child's Part,* ed. Brooks (Boston: Beacon, 1969), 5-14; Natalie Babbitt in "Happy Endings? Of Course, and Also Joy," *Children and Literature,* ed. Haviland (Glenview: Scott, Foresman, 1973), 155–159; and "Something Has to Happen," *LU* 9 (1985): 7–10; Neil Philip in "This Way Confusion?" *Signal* 43 (January 1984): 12–18; and Felicity Hughes in "Children's Literature: Theory and Practice," *ELH* 45 (1978): 542–561. Particularly perceptive are Charles Sarland's "Chorister Quartet" and Aidan Chambers's "Reader in the Book"; both can be found in *The Signal Approach to Children's Books,* ed. Nancy Chambers (Harmondsworth: Kestrel, 1980).

Since stories and storytelling are so central to children's literature, narrative theory may offer clues to the nature of the genre as a whole. That is Peter Hunt's suggestion in "Narrative Theory and Children's Literature," *ChLAQ* 9.4 (Winter 1984–1985): 191–194. Many of the articles in the Fall 1985 issue of *Studies in the Literary Imagination* (18.2), devoted to the subject of children's literature and narrative theory, have provoked stimulating dialogue in commentaries by Phyllis Bixler *CLE* 18.1 (Spring 1987): 54–62; Nancy Huse *ChLAQ* 12.1 (Spring 1987): 51–53; and Margaret Higgonet *CL* 17 (1989): 143–150.

Other books and articles deal less centrally with this subject, but make useful suggestions about it. These include Roger Sale's *Fairy Tales and After: From Snow White to E. B. White* (Cambridge: Harvard UP, 1978); C. S. Lewis's "On Three Ways of Writing for Children," *Children and Literature,* ed. Haviland, 155–159;

and various texts about the pastoral and mythic dimensions of children's literature: Sarah Gilead's "Undoing of Idyll in *The Wind in the Willows,*" *CL* 16 (1988): 145–158; Elliott Gose's *Mere Creatures: A Study of Modern Fantasy Tales for Children* (Toronto: U of Toronto P, 1988); Anita Moss's "Spear and the Piccolo: Heroic and Pastoral Dimensions of William Steig's *Dominic* and *Abel's Island,*" *CL* 10 (1982): 124–140; Pat Pinsent's "Paradise Restored: The Significance of Coincidence in Some Children's Books," *CLE* 20.2 (1989): 103–110; Philippa Pearce's "Writer's View of Childhood," *Horn Book Reflections,* ed. Elinor Whitney Field (Boston: Horn Book, 1969), 49–53; Geraldine Poss's "Epic in Arcadia: The Pastoral World of *The Wind in the Willows,*" *CL* 4 (1975): 80–90; and Sarah M. Smedman's "Springs of Hope: Recovery of Primordial Time in 'Mythic' Novels for Young Readers," *CL* 16 (1988): 91–108.

Critical Theory

Terry Eagleton's *Literary Theory* (Minneapolis: U of Minnesota P, 1983) is an excellent overview of the critical theories outlined in Chapter 8; it's especially valuable because Eagleton takes an aggressively political stance that encourages readers to enter into a dialogue with him. Those interested in getting a flavor of the work of many different theorists might look at anthologies like *The Critical Tradition: Classic Texts and Contemporary Trends,* ed. David H. Richter (New York: Bedford-St. Martin's, 1989) or *Critical Theory Since 1965,* eds. Hazard Adams and Leroy Searle (Talahassee: Florida State UP, 1986). *Critical Terms for Literary Study,* eds. Frank Lentricchia and Thomas McLaughlin (Chicago: U of Chicago P, 1990) offers understandable essays devoted to key terms in literary theory such as "ideology," "interpretation," and "canon."

Feminist Approaches

The best introductions to the many varieties of feminist criticism are selections of essays: *Writing and Sexual Difference,* ed. Elizabeth Abel (Chicago: U of Chicago P, 1982) and *The New Feminist Criticism: Essays on Women, Literature and Theory,* ed. Elaine Showalter (New York: Pantheon, 1985); the latter contains a useful bibliography.

About Children's Literature. Feminist approaches to children's literature are the subject of a special section in the Winter 1982 *ChLAQ;* of Lissa Paul's "Enigma Variations: What Feminist Criticism Knows about Children's Literature," *Signal* 54 (September 1987): 186–202; of Bronwyn Davies's *Frogs and Snails and Feminist Tales: Preschool Children and Gender* (Sydney: Allen and Unwin, 1989); and of my own "Children's Literature as Women's Writing," *ChLAQ* 13.1 (Spring 1988): 31–34. This last piece gave rise to a response: Jean Perrot's "Written from the International Androgynous!! A Plea for Our Common Hide (and Seek!)," *ChLAQ* 14.3 (Fall 1989): 139–141. Among the articles in *Gender and Reading: Essays on Readers, Texts and Contexts,* eds. Elizabeth A. Flynn and Patrocinio P. Schweikart (Baltimore: Johns Hopkins UP, 1986) is Elizabeth Segel's " 'As the Twig is Bent . . . ': Gender and Childhood Reading."

Feminist Readings. The essays in *CL* 17 (1989) offer feminist approaches to specific texts. Other readings of particular texts include Anita Moss's "Frontiers of Gender in Children's Literature: Virginia Hamilton's *Arilla Sun Down*," *ChLAQ* 8.4 (Winter 1983): 25–27; Elizabeth Lennox Keyser's "Contemporary Gothic for Girls: Julia Cunningham's *Tupenny*," *CLE* 17.1 (1986): 88–101 (with a response from Cunningham); Marianne Hirsch's "Ideology, Form, and 'Allerleirauh': Reflections on Reading for the Plot," *CL* 14 (1986): 163–168 (a response to a male-oriented psychoanalytical reading of this Grimm fairy tale); Nancy Veglahn's "Images of Evil: Male and Female Monsters in Heroic Fantasy," *CL* 15 (1987): 106–119; Susan S. Kissel's " 'But When at Last She Really Came, I Shot Her': *Peter Pan* and the Drama of Gender," *CLE* 19.1 (1988): 32–41; Lissa Paul's "Dumb Bunnies: A Revisionist Re-reading of *Watership Down*," *Signal* 56 (May 1988): 113–122; and my own "Teaching Girls About Men: Attitudes to Maleness in Teen Magazines," *Studies in Popular Culture* 9.1 (1986): 103–118. Claudia Nelson's "Beast Within: *Winnie-the-Pooh* Reassessed," *CLE* 21.1 (1990): 17–22 may or may not be a parody of an extreme feminist approach; Carol A. Stanger's "Winnie the Pooh Through a Feminist Lens" *LU* 11.2 (1987): 34–50 is more clearly serious in its intentions.

Psychoanalytical Approaches

Psychoanalytical Texts. *The Freud Reader,* ed. Peter Gay (New York: Norton, 1989) is an excellent introduction to Freud's ideas. For Jung, a good introduction is *The Portable Jung,* ed. Joseph Campbell (New York: Viking, 1971). For Lacan, a standard text is *Ecrits: A Selection,* trans. Alan Sheridan (New York: Norton, 1977). Jane Gallop offers some much-needed help with Lacan's complex ideas in *Reading Lacan* (Ithaca: Cornell UP, 1985).

About Children's Literature. *Opening Texts: Psychoanalysis and the Culture of the Child,* eds. Joseph H. Smith and William Kerrigan (Baltimore: Johns Hopkins UP, 1985) includes a number of essays on children's literature. In *Narratives of Love and Loss: Studies in Modern Children's Fiction* (London: Verso, 1987), Margaret and Michael Rustin present readings of texts that make use of an eclectic blend of psychoanalytical and sociological approaches. *CL* 18 (1990) contains a number of essays using psychological approaches and a response section that offers discussions of the validity of this sort of reading.

Freudian Readings. Freudian discussions of children's literature include Michael Egan's "Neverland of Id: Barrie, *Peter Pan,* and Freud," *CL* 10 (1982): 37–55; Jean-Marie Apostolides's "Tintin and Family Romance," *CL* 13 (1985): 94–108; Wolfgang Mieder's *Kiss of the Snow Queen: Hans Christian Andersen and Man's Redemption by Woman* (Berkeley: U of California P, 1986); Michael Reed's "Female Oedipal Complex in Maurice Sendak's *Outside Over There,*" *ChLAQ* 11.4 (Winter 1986–1987): 176–180; and Hamida Bosmajian's "*Charlie and the Chocolate Factory* and Other Excremental Visions," *LU* 9 (1985): 36–49.

Jungian Readings. Among many Jungian readings are Nancy-Lou Patterson's "Angel and Psychopomp in Madeleine L'Engle's " 'Wind' Trilogy," *CLE* 14 (1983): 195–203; Sally Rigsbee's "Fantasy Places and Imaginative Belief: *The Lion, the Witch, and the Wardrobe* and *The Princess and the Goblin,*" *ChLAQ* 8.1 (Spring 1983): 10–12; Elliott Gose's *Mere Creatures: A Study of Modern Fantasy Tales for Children* (Toronto: U of Toronto P, 1988); Phyllis Stowell's "We're All Mad Here" (about *Alice in Wonderland*), *ChLAQ* 8.2 (Summer 1983): 5–8; Sue Misheff's "Redemptive Journey: The Storytelling Motif in Andersen's 'The Snow Queen,' " *CLE* 21.1 (1990): 1–7; Hamida Bosmajian's "The Cracked Crucible of *Johnny Tremain,*" *LU* 13.1 (June 1989): 53–66; and David L. Russell's "Pinocchio and the Child-Hero's Quest," *CLE* 20.4 (1989): 203–213.

Bibliotherapeutic Approaches. Discussions of children's literature which recommend bibliotherapy—the use of fictional texts in helping children understand and deal with their problems—have a psychological focus, but tend to make shallow assumptions both about psychology and about the ways in which we read and respond to texts. Among texts with such an approach are Masha Kabakow Rudman's *Children's Literature: An Issues Approach* (Lexington: Heath, 1976).

Archetypal Approaches

Northrop Frye's magnum opus is *Anatomy of Criticism: Four Essays* (Princeton: Princeton UP, 1957). Articles about children's literature that take a Fryean approach include Stephen D. Roxburgh's " 'Our First World': Form and Meaning in *The Secret Garden,*" *CLE* 10 (1979): 113–119; and Raymond Wilson's "*Slake's Limbo:* A Myth-Critical Approach," *CLE* 18.4 (1987): 219–226. Virginia Wolf presents archetypal analyses in "Paradise Lost? The Displacement of Myth in Children's Novels," *Studies in the Literary Imagination* 18.2 (Fall 1985): 47–64; "The Cycle of the Seasons: Without and Within Time," *ChLAQ* 10.4 (Winter 1986): 192–196; "The Linear Image: The Road and the River in the Juvenile Novel," *Proceedings of the Thirteenth Annual Conference of the Children's Literature Association,* eds. Susan Gannon and Ruth Anne Thompson (West Lafayette: ChLA Publications, 1988); and "From the Myth to the Wake of Home: Literary Houses," *CL* 18 (1990): 53–67.

Structuralist Approaches

Claude Lévi-Strauss's structural approach as applied to anthropology and mythology is described in *The Savage Mind* (Chicago: U of Chicago P, 1966) and *The Raw and the Cooked* (New York: Harper & Row, 1969). A particularly useful piece is "The Structural Study of Myth," *Structural Anthropology,* (Garden City: Doubleday Anchor, 1967), 202–228.

The application of structuralist ideas to literature is outlined in Jonathan Culler's *Structuralist Poetics* (Ithaca: Cornell UP, 1975) and Robert Scholes's *Structuralism in Literature: An Introduction* (New Haven: Yale UP, 1974). Culler and Scholes offer descriptions of the work of a number of European structuralists. Among the most interesting are Vladimir Propp, *Morphology of the Folktale* (Austin: U of Texas, 1970) and Roland Barthes, especially his *S/Z* (New York: Hill and Wang, 1974) and *The Pleasure of the Text* (New York: Hill and Wang, 1975).

Structural approaches to children's literature are the subject of a special section of the Fall 1982 *ChLAQ*. Peter Neumeyer offers "A Structural Approach to the Study of Literature for Children," based on Propp (*Elementary English* 44.8 [December 1977]: 883–87). In "Maurice Sendak's Ritual Cooking of the Child in Three Tableaux: The Moon, Mother, and Music," *CL* 18 (1990): 68–86, Jean Perrot offers a reading of Sendak modeled on Lèvi-Strauss's *Raw and the Cooked.*

Narrative Theory

All kinds of approaches to narrative are outlined in Wallace Martin's *Recent Theories of Narrative* (Ithaca: Cornell UP, 1986). Another guide is Shlomith Rimmon-Kenan's *Narrative Fiction: Contemporary Poetics* (London: Methuen, 1983). Uses of narrative theory in the analysis of children's literature are the subject of Peter Hunt's "Narrative Theory and Children's Literature" and of the Fall 1985 issue of *Studies in the Literary Imagination,* listed above under "Children's Literature as a Genre."

Post-Structuralist Approaches

Post-structural theories center on the work of Jacques Derrida. Those who wish to undergo an unusual experience should read his complex prose in *Of Grammatology* (Baltimore: Johns Hopkins UP, 1976), *Writing and Difference* (Chicago: U of Chicago P, 1978), or *Dissemination* (Chicago: U of Chicago P, 1981). For an organized overview that communicates all of Derrida's ideas but none of his tone or spirit, there is Jonathan Culler's *On Deconstruction* (Ithaca: Cornell UP, 1982). Apart from my own "Hidden Meaning and the Inner Tale: Deconstruction and the Interpretation of Fairy Tales," *ChLAQ* 14.3 (Fall 1989): 143–148, there has been little discussion of deconstruction and children's literature.

As I write, the latest trend in literary study is a focus on what is called "the new historicism"—a blend of literary practices that emerge from Lacanian psychoanalytic theory, deconstruction, and political and cultural analysis. A good introduction is offered by the essays in *The New Historicism,* ed. H. Aram Veeser (New York: Routledge, 1989). With its focus on the way societies create and distribute power by means of marginalizing various groups within it (such as children), the new historicism is a promising source for insights into children's literature.

The Canon

There has been a great deal of controversy about the literary canon—the group of texts considered to be particularly worthy of study—especially in the light of feminist attacks on it. Some provocative essays on this subject are collected in *Canons,* ed. Robert von Hallberg (Chicago: U of Chicago P, 1984). Frank Kermode has interesting insights into canonical works, in both *The Classic: Literary Images of Permanence and Change* (Cambridge: Harvard UP, 1983) and *Forms of Attention* (Chicago: U of Chicago P, 1985).

For a discussion of the idea of a canon in relation to children's literature, see "Matthew Arnold, a Teddy Bear, and a List of Touchstones," my introduction to *Touchstones: Reflections on the Best in Children's Literature,* ed. Perry Nodelman, vol. 1, (West Lafayette: ChLA Publications, 1985). The essays in this and the two other volumes of the series discuss the picture books, novels, and collections of tales named as touchstones for children's literature by a committee of the Children's Literature Association.

PART FOUR: TYPES OF CHILDREN'S LITERATURE

Poetry

Discussion of some important children's poets, and a variety of opinions about children and poetry, can be found in *Touchstones: Reflections on the Best in Children's Literature,* ed. Perry Nodelman, vol. 2 (West Lafayette: ChLA Publications, 1987). *LU* 4.2 (Winter 1980–1981) is a special issue devoted to children's poetry. A discussion of books considered for the Signal Poetry award (given for volumes of poetry published in Britain) has appeared annually in the May issue of *Signal* for a number of years; it often includes penetrating comments on a variety of books. *ChLAQ* frequently publishes a column devoted to children and poetry; some that offer either useful models of analysis or commentary on controversial issues are Robert Bator's "Punching Marginal Holes in Poetry," 7.1 (Spring 1982): 48–49; Malcolm Usrey's "Child Persona in *Taxis and Toadstools,*" 7.2 (Summer 1982): 39–40; Robert diYanni's "Kenneth Koch Revisited," 9.1 (Spring 1984): 38–39; Anthony L. Manna's "In Pursuit of the Crystal Image: Lee Bennett Hopkins' Poetry Anthologies," 10.2 (Summer 1985): 80–82; Paul B. Janeczko's "Confessions of a Collector" (on the making of anthologies), 12.2 (Summer 1987): 98, 110; and Richard Lewis's "The Blossom Shaping: An Exploration of Chinese Poetry with Children," 12.4 (Winter 1987): 191–193.

The Bat Poet. Considerable attention has been focused on one book about poetry for children: Randall Jarrell's *Bat Poet* (New York: Macmillan, 1963). It is discussed in my own "The Craft or Sullen Art of a Mouse and a Bat," *Language Arts* 55 (April 1978): 467–472, 497; in Peter Neumeyer's "Bat Poet: An Introduction to the Craft," *ChLAQ* 9.3 (Summer 1984): 51–53, 59; in Jerry Griswold's *Children's Books of Randall Jarrell* (Athens: U of Georgia P, 1988); and in Richard Flynn's "Happy Families Are All Invented: Randall Jarrell's Fiction for Children" *CL* 16 (1988): 109–126.

As these critics note, *The Bat Poet* is both a good story and an excellent introduction to the writing and reading of poetry. Another fine introduction is a carefully constructed anthology edited by X. J. and Dorothy Kennedy, *Knock at a Star: A Child's Introduction to Poetry* (Boston: Little, Brown, 1982).

Nursery Rhymes. Nursery rhymes have a special history and raise special questions. Iona and Peter Opie's fascinating *Oxford Dictionary of Nursery Rhymes* (Oxford: Oxford UP, 1951) offers complete histories of many rhymes.

Children and Poetry. There are two important books about the subject of introducing children to the reading and writing of poetry: Kenneth Koch's *Rose, Where Did You Get That Red? Teaching Great Poetry to Children* (New York: Random House, 1973) and Myra Cohn Livingston's *Child as Poet: Myth or Reality* (Boston: Horn Book, 1984). Livingston is highly critical of Koch.

Other useful discussions of children's experiences of poetry are Andrew Sebbs, Geoff Fox, and Brian Merrick's "Teaching Poetry," *CLE* 13.1 (1982): 39–55; John Gough's "Poems in Context: Breaking the Anthology Trap," *CLE* 15.4 (1984): 204–210; Vernon Scannell's "Poetry for Children," *CLE* 18.4 (1987): 202–209; Edward J. Reilly's "Reading and Writing Haiku in the Classroom," *ChLAQ* 13.3 (Fall 1988): 111–114; and Francis E. Kazemek's " 'When Shuttled by the / Playful Hand': The Poetry of William Carlos Williams and the Elementary Literature Curriculum," *CLE* 20.2 (Summer 1989): 111–119.

Picture Books

Theories of Art and Perception. There is a more extensive discussion of the approach to picture books I have outlined in Chapter 10 of this book in another work of mine: *Words About Pictures: The Narrative Art of Children's Picture Books* (Athens: U of Georgia P, 1988). In writing this book, I drew on a large body of art theory, especially E. H. Gombrich's *Art and Illusion: A Study in the Psychology of Pictorial Representation* (New York: Pantheon, 1961); "Visual Image" *Scientific American* 227 (September 1972): 82–94; John Berger's *Ways of Seeing* (London: British Broadcasting Corporation; Harmondsworth: Penguin, 1972); and Norman Bryson's *Vision and Painting: The Logic of the Gaze* (New Haven: Yale UP, 1983). Useful books specifically about the theory of illustration include David Bland's *The Illustration of Books,* 3d ed. (London: Faber and Faber, 1962); William M. Ivins's *Prints and Visual Communication* (1953; New York: De Capo, 1969); and Edward Hodnett's *Image and Text: Studies in the Illustration of English Literature* (London: Scolar Press, 1982). The journal *Word and Image* is devoted to studies of the relationships between text and illustration. No. 2.2 (April–June 1986) specifically examines children and illustration. In *Research into Illustration: An Approach and a Review* (Cambridge: Cambridge UP, 1984), Evelyn Goldsmith concisely summarizes much of the psychological research into the perception of visual images as it might apply to children's response to pictures.

Children and Picture Books. In addition to *Words About Pictures,* studies devoted to children's picture books are Donnarae MacCann and Olga Richard's *The Child's First Books: A Critical Study of Pictures and Texts* (New York: Wilson, 1973); Joseph H. Schwarcz's *Ways of the Illustrator: Visual Communication in Children's Literature*

(Chicago: American Library Association, 1982); and Lyn Ellen Lacy's *Art and Design in Children's Picture Books* (Chicago: American Library Association, 1986).

A number of children's literature journals have devoted special issues to the topic of picture books. These include *LU* 7–8 (1983–1984); *CL* 19 (1991); *ChLAQ* 6.4 (Winter 1981–1982); *ChLAQ* 9.1 (Spring 1984); and *ChLAQ* 15.1 (Spring 1990) (on visual literacy). *Image and Maker,* ed., Peter Neumeyer and Harold Darling (La Jolla: Green Tiger, 1984), a collection of essays about children's illustration, includes Stephen Canham's "What Manner of Beast? Illustrations of 'Beauty and the Beast.'" Another exploration of the topic is Betsy Hearne's "Beauty and the Beast: Visions and Revisions of an Old Tale: 1950–1985," *LU* 12.2 (1988): 74–111.

Other essays that provide a variety of theoretical approaches to children's picture books are Olga Richard's "Visual Language of the Picture Book," *Jump Over the Moon,* eds. Barron and Burley (New York: Holt, Rinehart and Winston), 157–166; Kenneth Marantz's "Picture Book as Art Object: A Call for Balanced Reviewing," *Signposts to Criticism of Children's Literature,* ed. Robert Bator (Chicago: American Library Association, 1983); Stephen Roxburgh's "Anno's Counting Book: A Semiological Analysis," *ChLAQ* 7.3 (Fall 1982): 45–52; and "A Picture Equals How Many Words? Narrative Theory and Picture Books for Children," *LU* 7–8 (1983–1984): 48–52; Hugh Crago's "Who Does Snow White Look At?" *Signal* 45 (September 1984): 129–145; Sonia Landes's "Picture Books as Literature," *ChLAQ* 10.2 (Summer 1985): 51–54; William Moebius's "Introduction to Picturebook Codes," *Word and Image* 2.2 (April–June 1986): 63–66; John Stephens's "Language, Discourse, and Picture Books," *ChLAQ* 14.3 (Fall 1989): 106–110 (on picture books as conveyors of verbal language); and David Lewis's "Constructedness of Texts: Picture Books and the Metafictive," *Signal* 62 (May 1990): 131–146.

Specific Illustrators. Volume 3 of *Touchstones: Reflections on the Best of Children's Literature,* ed. Perry Nodelman (West Lafayette: ChLA Publications, 1989) contains a number of essays devoted to specific celebrated picture books and illustrators. Discussions of individual books that might act as models for analyses of other books include several fine articles by Jane Doonan: "The Object Lesson: Picturebooks of Anthony Browne," *Word and Image* 2.2 (April–June 1986): 159–172; "Talking Pictures: A New Look at Hansel and Gretel," *Signal* 42 (September 1983): 123–131; "Two Artists Telling Tales: Chihiro Iwasaki and Lisbeth Zwerger," *Signal* 44 (May 1984): 93–192; "Tony Ross: Art to Enchant," *Signal* 46 (January 1985): 34–53; "*Outside Over There:* A Journey in Style," *Signal* 50 (May 1986): 92–103 and 51 (September 1986): 172–187; and "The Idle Bear," *Signal* 55 (January 1988): 33–47. Other interesting pieces are Jack Zipes's "A Second Gaze at Little Red Riding Hood's Trials and Tribulations," *LU* 7–8 (1983–1984): 78–109; and Jill P. May's "Illustration as Interpretation: Trina Hyman's Folk Tales," *ChLAQ* 10.3 (Fall 1985): 127–131; Geraldine DeLuca's "Exploring the Levels of Childhood: The Allegorical Sensibility of Maurice Sendak," *CL* 12 (1984): 3–24; and Michael Steig's "Reading *Outside Over There,*" *CL* 13 (1985): 139–153.

Fairy Tales

Versions. The many versions of fairy tales available in libraries and bookstores vary both in authenticity and in quality. For accurate renderings of the tales as originally presented, I recommend Angela Carter's versions of Perrault (New York: Bard Avon, 1977) and Ralph Manheim's versions of the Grimm tales (Garden City: Doubleday, 1977). Both capture aspects of the tone of the original texts that are missing in most other translations. For reliable versions of Norwegian tales, Italian tales, or tales of a number of other countries and cultures, the best sources are the many volumes of the Pantheon Fairy Tale and Folklore Library, a series of collections each of which includes tales from one specific country or ethnic group. In *Favorite Folktales from Around the World* (New York: Pantheon, 1986), Jane Yolen presents an entertaining selection of tales from Pantheon volumes.

Critical Analyses. Appreciations of the central fairy tale collections can be found in volume 2 of *Touchstones: Reflections on the Best in Children's Literature,* listed above under "Poetry." A special section devoted to fairy tales appears in *ChLAQ* (Summer 1982); it includes an extensive bibliographic guide to fairy tale criticism by Roderick McGillis. *LU* 12.2 (1988) is devoted to articles about fairy tales.

Tales as Folklore. Folklorists' approaches to the tales are introduced in *World Folktales: A Scribner Resource Collection,* ed. Atelia Clarkson and Gilbert B. Cross (New York: Scribner, 1980). Variant versions of one central tale from around the world and essays about them can be found in *Cinderella: A Casebook,* ed. Alan Dundes (Madison: U of Wisconsin P, 1982). A romanticized view of the tales based on folkloristic approaches but integrating other analyses is Max Lüthi's often persuasive *Once Upon a Time: On the Nature of Fairy Tales* (Bloomington: Indiana UP, 1976). *ChLAQ* 11.3 (Fall 1986) is devoted to the connections between children's literature and folklore. CLE 17.1 (1986) contains Catherine Storr's "Folk and Fairy Tale," 63–69, and Gillian Klein's "Is Going Two Days Now the Pot Turned Down," 53–61.

Psychoanalytical Approaches. In *The Uses of Enchantment: The Meaning and Importance of Fairy Tales* (New York: Knopf, 1976), Bruno Bettelheim presents psychoanalytic interpretations of a number of tales. Among many responses to this controversial book are James Helsig's "Bruno Bettelheim and the Fairy Tales," *CL* 6 (1977): 93–114; Jack Zipes's "On the Use and Abuse of Folk and Fairy Tales with Children: Bruno Bettelheim's Moralistic Magic Wand," a chapter of Zipes's *Breaking the Magic Spell* (Austin: U of Texas P, 1979); and Nicholas Tucker's "Dr. Bettelheim and Enchantment," Signal 43 (January 1984): 32–41. A number of books by Marie Louise von Franz take a Jungian approach: *Interpretation of Fairy Tales* (New York: Spring, 1970); *The Feminine in Fairytales* (New York: Spring, 1972); and *Shadow and Evil in Fairy Tales* (New York: Spring, 1974).

Historical and Cultural Approaches. There are many revealing discussions of the Grimm tales and others in the context of history and culture, including John Ellis's *One Fairy Story Too Many: The Brothers Grimm and Their Tales* (Chicago: U of Chicago P, 1983); *Fairy Tales and Society: Illusion, Allusion, and Paradigm,* ed. Ruth Bottigheimer (Philadelphia: Pennsylvania UP, 1986); Bottigheimer's *Grimms' Bad Girls and Bold Boys: The Moral and Social Vision of the Tales* (New Haven: Yale UP, 1987); and a number of books by Jack Zipes, including *Breaking the Magic Spell,* mentioned earlier in this section; *Fairy Tales and the Art of Subversion: The Classical Genre for Children and the Process of Civilization* (London: Heinemann, 1982); and *The Brothers Grimm: From Enchanted Forests to the Modern World* (New York: Routledge, 1988). Zipes's *Don't Bet on the Prince: Contemporary Feminist Fairy Tales in North America and England* (New York: Methuen, 1986), is both a collection of tales and a number of articles related to them. Anne Wilson offers a critical response to Zipes in "The Civilizing Process in Fairy Tales," *Signal* 44 (May 1984): 81–87; I do the same in "And the Prince Turned into a Peasant and Lived Happily Ever After," *CL* 11 (1983): 171–174, and in a review in *ChLAQ* 9.2 (Summer 1984): 81–82; Zipes responds to the latter in *ChLAQ* 9.3 (Summer 1984): 131–132.

I particularly recommend Maria Tatar's *Hard Facts of the Grimms' Fairy Tales* (Princeton: Princeton UP, 1987). Tatar combines a consideration of both historical and psychoanalytical contexts with a rich interpretive appreciation of the tales.

Nonfiction

The Art of Nonfiction. Discussion of nonfiction can be found in Margery Fisher's *Matters of Fact: Aspects of Non-Fiction for Children* (New York: Crowell, 1972) and Jo Carr's *Beyond Fact: Nonfiction for Children and Young People* (Chicago: American Library Association, 1982). *LU* 6 (1982) is devoted to essays about "Informational Books for Children." *ChLAQ* 10.4 (1987) has a special section devoted to analyses of the artistry of nonfiction texts.

Other discussions of the art of nonfiction are Irving Adler's "Prose Imagination," *Children and Literature,* ed. Haviland, 323–325; Betty Bacon's "Art of Nonfiction," *Jump Over the Moon,* eds. Barron and Burley, 195–204; Joyce Thomas's "Nonfiction Illustration: Some Considerations." *Children and Their Literature: A Readings Book,* ed. Jill P. May (West Lafayette: ChLA Publications, 1983): 122–127; and my own "Non-fiction for Children: Does It Really Exist?," *ChLAQ* 12.4 (Winter 1987): 160–161 and "Facts as Art," *ChLAQ* 10.4 (Winter 1985–1986): 162–163. This last piece includes a list of noteworthy nonfiction selected by Milton Meltzer. Meltzer presents an interesting case of his own in "The Possibilities of Nonfiction: A Writer's View," *CLE* 11 (1980): 110 and 116, and "Where Do All the Prizes Go? The Case for Nonfiction," *Children and Their Literature,* ed. May, 92–97.

History. In *America Revised: History Schoolbooks in the Twentieth Century* (New York: Vintage–Random House, 1979), Frances Fitzgerald shows how American history is rewritten periodically in relation to social and political shifts. Helpful essays on nonfiction about history include Joshua Brown's ''Telling the History of *All* Americans: Milton Meltzer, Minorities, and the Restoration of the Past,'' *LU* 11.1 (1987): 7–25; Barbara Harrison's ''Howl Like the Wolves,'' *CL* 15 (1987): 67–90; and Miriam Youngerman Miller's ''In Days of Old: The Middle Ages in Children's Non-fiction,'' *ChLAQ* 12.4 (Winter 1987): 167–172.

Biography. Biography is the subject of nine essays in *LU* 4.1 (1980). Other stimulating essays about it include Carol Billman's ''Once Upon a Time . . . . Telling Children Biographical History,'' *Proceedings of the Seventh Annual Conference of the Children's Literature Association,* ed. Priscilla Ord (New Rochelle: ChLA Publications, 1982); Geraldine DeLuca's ''Lives and Half-Lives: Biographies of Women for Young Adults,'' *CLE* 17.4 (1986): 241–252; William H. Epstein's ''Inducing Biography,'' *ChLAQ* 12.4 (Winter 1987): 177–179; Marilyn Jurich's ''What's Left Out of Biography for Children,'' *CL* 1 (1972): 143–151; Milton Meltzer's ''Notes on Biography,'' *ChLAQ* 10.4 (Winter 1986): 172–175; and Linda Walvoord Girard's ''Series Thinking and the Art of Biography for Children,'' *ChLAQ* 14.3 (Winter 1989): 187–192.

Science. For discussion of nonfiction about science, see Geraldine DeLuca and Roni Natov's ''Who's Afraid of Science Books? An Interview with Seymour Simon,'' *LU* 6 (1982): 10–27; Patricia Lauber's ''What Makes an Appealing and Readable Science Book?,'' *LU* 6 (1982): 5–9; Billie Nodelman's ''Science Books, Science Education, and the Religion of Science,'' *ChLAQ* 12.4 (Winter 1987): 180–183; and on a significant controversial issue, W. Bernard Lukenbill's ''Children's Books and Differing Views of Evolution—Past and Present,'' *CLE* 19.3 (1988): 156–164.

Fiction

Formula in Children's Fiction. Many articles explore the ways in which children's fiction combines formula and distinctive qualities: Phyllis Bixler Koppes's ''Tradition and the Individual Talent of Frances Hodgson Burnett: A Generic Analysis of *Little Lord Fauntleroy, A Little Princess,* and *The Secret Garden,*'' *CL* 7 (1978): 191–207; Bixler and Lucien Agosta's ''Formula Fiction and Children's Literature: Thornton Waldo Burgess and Frances Hodgson Burnett,'' *CLE* 15 (1984): 63–72; Lois Kuznets's ''Family as Formula: Cawelti's Formulaic Theory and Streatfeild's 'Shoe' Books,'' *ChLAQ* 9.4 (Winter 1984–1985): 147–149; Margaret Higgonet's "Narrative Fractures and Fragments," *CL* 15 (1987): 37–54; and my own "Apparent Sameness of Children's Novels," *Studies in the Literary Imagination* 18.2 (Fall 1985): 5–20.

Home. The significance of concepts of home in children's fiction is the subject of Jon Stott's ''Running Away to Home—A Story Pattern in Children's Literature,'' *Language Arts* 55.4 (April 1978): 473–477; Christopher Clausen's ''Home and Away in Children's Fiction,'' *CL* 10 (1982): 141–152; Lucy Waddey's ''Home in Children's

Fiction: Three Patterns,'' *ChLAQ* 8.1 (Spring 1983): 13–15; and Virginia Wolf's ''From the Myth to the Wake of Home: Literary Houses,'' *CL* 18 (1990): 53–67.

•

Bachelard. On a related topic, a number of critics make uses of the philosopher Gaston Bachelard's concept of ''felicitous space'' as central to children's fiction: Lois Kuznets in ''Toad Hall Revisited,'' *CL* 7 (1978): 115–128; Hamida Bosmajian in ''Vastness and Contraction of Space in *Little House on the Prairie*,'' *CL* 11 (1983): 49–63; and Ann Moseley in ''The Journey Through the 'Space in the Text' to *Where the Wild Things Are*,'' *CLE* 19.2 (1988): 86–93. Joyce Thomas discusses Bachelard in relation to fairy tales in ''Woods and Castles, Towers and Huts: Aspects of Setting in the Fairy Tale,'' *CLE* 17.2 (1986): 126–134.

Kinds of Children's Fiction

Fantasy. Theoretical books about fantasy include Tsvetan Todorov's *Fantastic: A Structural Approach to a Literary Genre* (Cleveland: Case Western Reserve UP, 1973); Eric Rabkin's *Fantastic in Literature* (Princeton: Princeton UP, 1976); Brian Attebury's *Fantasy Tradition in American Literature* (Bloomington: Indiana UP, 1980); Kathryn Hume's *Fantasy and Mimesis* (New York: Methuen, 1984); Rosemary Jackson's *Fantasy: The Literature of Subversion* (London: Methuen, 1981); Ursula Le Guin's *Language of the Night*, ed. Susan Wood (New York: Putnam, 1979); and Ann Wilson's *Magical Thought in Creative Writing: the Distinctive Roles of Fantasy and Imagination in Fiction* (Stroud: Thimble, 1983). A particularly useful discussion is Lois R. Kuznets's '' 'High Fantasy' in America: a Study of Lloyd Alexander, Ursula Le Guin and Susan Cooper,'' *LU* 9 (1985): 19–35.

Children's science fiction is the subject of two *ChLAQ* special sections; in 5.4 (Winter 1981) and 10.2 (Summer 1985). I present my own theoretical views in ''Out There in Children's Science Fiction: Forward into the Past,'' *Science Fiction Studies* 37 (November 1985): 285–296.

Adventure. Provocative theoretical books about the nature of adventure stories are Paul Zweig's *Adventurer: The Fate of Adventure in the Western World* (Princeton: Princeton UP, 1974); and John G. Cawelti's *Adventure, Mystery and Romance: Formula Stories as Art and Popular Culture* (Chicago: U of Chicago P, 1976). Margery Fisher's *Bright Face of Danger: An Exploration of the Adventure Story* (Boston: Horn Book, 1986) focuses on texts for children. *ChLAQ* 8.3 (Fall 1983) contains a number of essays about adventure stories, including William Blackburn's interesting ''Mirror in the Sea: *Treasure Island* and the Internalization of Juvenile Romance,'' 7–12. In *CLE* 13 (1982): 115–121, Judith Armstrong writes ''In Defence of Adventure Stories.''

Series. The most widely read American series books, including those about Nancy Drew and the Hardy Boys, were produced by the Stratemeyer syndicate. These texts are discussed in Ken Donelson's ''Nancy, Tom and Assorted Friends in the

Stratemeyer Syndicate Then and Now,'' *CL* 7 (1978): 17–44, and Carol Billman's *Secret of the Stratemeyer Syndicate: Nancy Drew, the Hardy Boys, and the Million Dollar Fiction Factory* (New York: Ungar, 1986). Two provocative general studies are Ann Scott McLeod's ''Secret in the Trash Bin: On the Perennial Popularity of Juvenile Series Books,'' *CLE* 15.3 (1984): 127–140, and Gary D. Schmidt's ''See How They Grow: Character Development in Children's Series Books,'' *CLE* 18.2 (1987): 34–43. *ChLAQ* 14.4 (Winter 1989) contains a number of essays on series books, in a section edited by Schmidt.

Young Adult Fiction. In *Literature for Today's Young Adults* (Glenview: Scott, Foresman, 1980), Kenneth L. Donelson and Alleen Pace Nilsen offer a comprehensive overview. *LU* 2.2 (Fall 1978) contains a number of essays about the adolescent novel. Several texts discuss the novelist Robert Cormier, including Patricia J. Campbell's *Presenting Robert Cormier* (New York: Dell Laurel Leaf, 1985, 1989); Ann Scott McLeod's ''Robert Cormier and the Adolescent Novel,'' *CLE* 12 (1981): 74–81; Sylvia Patterson Iskander's ''Readers, Realism, and Robert Cormier,'' 15 (1987), 7–18; Millicent Lenz's ''Romantic Ironist's Vision of Evil: Robert Cormier's *After the First Death,*'' *Proceedings of the Eighth Annual Conference of the Children's Literature Association* (Boston: Northeastern U, 1981); Frank Myszor's ''See-Saw and the Bridge in Robert Cormier's *After the First Death,*'' *CL* 16 (1988): 77–90; and my own ''Robert Cormier Does a Number,'' *CLE* 14.2 (1983): 94–103.

Some Other Subgenres. In *Animal Land: the Creatures of Children's Fiction* (New York: Morrow, 1975), Margaret Blount discusses animal stories. John Goldthwaite's ''Black Rabbit,'' *Signal* 47 (May 1985): 86–111 and 48 (September 1985): 148–167 discusses the influence of Uncle Remus stories in the development of animal fantasy. Ann Royal Newman surveys the topic ''Images of the Bear in Children's Literature,'' *CLE* 18.3 (1987): 131–138.

Mary Cadogan and Patricia Craig's *You're a Brick, Angela* (London: Gollancz, 1976) is ''a new look at girls' fiction from 1839–1975.'' Jeffery Richard's *Happiest Days: The Public Schools in English Fiction* (Manchester: Manchester UP, 1988) is about school stories. In *On Longing: Narratives of the Miniature, the Gigantic, the Souvenir, the Collection* (Baltimore: Johns Hopkins UP, 1984), Susan Stewart offers a complex theory of fiction about miniatures. Also useful are Leonard R. Mendelsohn's ''Toys and Literature,'' *Sharing Literature with Children,* ed. Francelia Butler (New York: Longman, 1977), 80–84, and Geraldine DeLuca's '' 'A Condition of Complete Simplicity': The Toy as Child in *The Mouse and His Child,*'' *CLE* 19.4 (1988): 211-221.

Critiques of Individual Writers of Fiction. Volume 1 of *Touchstones: Reflections on the Best in Children's Literature,* ed. Perry Nodelman (West Lafayette: ChLA Publications, 1985) contains critical essays on each of the twenty-eight novels or series of novels named by the Children's Literature Association as touchstones for children's literature. For those interested in rich critical dialogue, the nine essays about specific works of children's fiction in *ChLAQ* 11.1 (Spring 1986) include three on *Anne of Green Gables.* There are five articles about *Wind in the Willows* in *CL* 16 (1988). A brief search of children's literature journals will turn up numerous other articles about these two widely discussed books; the only other texts that are as popular as subjects of critical attention are *Little Women* and *Charlotte's Web.*

Other insightful articles on specific fictional texts are: Lynne Rosenthal's "Development of Consciousness in Lucy Boston's *The Children of Green Knowe,*" *CL* 8 (1980): 53–67; Elizabeth Lennox Keyser's " 'Quite Contrary': Frances Hodgson Burnett's *The Secret Garden,*" *CL* 11 (1983): 1–13; and Mavis Reimer's "Family as Mythic Reservoir in Alan Garner's Stone Book Quartet," *ChLAQ* 14.3 (Fall 1989): 132–135.

As yet there are only a few books devoted to the critical analysis of specific authors. One is Neil Philip's *Fine Anger: A Critical Introduction to the Work of Alan Garner* (New York: Philomel, 1981). Two useful books in the Twayne series of critical biographies are Phyllis Bixler's *Frances Hodgson Burnett* (Boston: Twayne, 1984) and Lois Kuznets's *Kenneth Grahame* (Boston: Twayne, 1987). This series continues to publish volumes devoted to a variety of children's writers.

TEACHING LITERATURE TO CHILDREN

The most stimulating books about the teaching of literary skills to children are the ones that express the widest knowledge of both developmental psychology and literary theory: Robert Protherough's *Developing Response to Fiction* (Milton Keynes: Open UP, 1983); *Readers, Texts, Teachers,* eds. Bill Corcoran and Emrys Evans (Upper Montclair: Boynton/Cook, 1987); and Ian Reid's *Making of Literature: Texts, Contexts and Classroom Practices* (Australian Association for the Teaching of English, 1984).

Other useful books are *English Teachers at Work: Ideas and Strategies from Five Countries,* eds. Stephen N. Tchudi and others (Upper Montclair: Boynton/Cook, 1986); Alan C. Purves and Dianne L. Monson's *Experiencing Children's Literature* (Glenview: Scott, Foresman, 1984); and *Using Literature in the Elementary Classroom,* rev ed., eds. John Warren Stewig and Sam Leaton Sebesta (Urbana: NCTE, 1989). Robert E. Probst's *Response and Analysis: Teaching Literature in Junior and Senior High School* (Portsmouth: Boynton/Cook–Heinemann, 1988) discusses work with older children and young adults.

Aidan Chambers's *Introducing Books to Children* (London: Heinemann, 1973) is more about creating enthusiasm for literature than about teaching literary strategies, but it contains much of value. In *The Educated Imagination* (Bloomington: Indiana UP, 1964), Northrop Frye offers a view of what children should learn about literature. Glenna Davis Sloan presents an approach to children's literary education based on Frye's ideas in *The Child as Critic: Teaching Literature in the Elementary School* (New York: Teachers College P, 1978).

Of the various children's literature journals, *CLE* devotes most attention to questions of teaching. "Teaching Literary Criticism in the Elementary Grades: A

Symposium,'' ed. Jon C. Stott, originally appeared in *CLE* 12.4 (1981); 192–206; it is reprinted in *Children and their Literature,* ed. May, 160–172. Other representative *CLE* articles include Terry D. Johnson's ''Presenting Literature to Children,'' *CLE* 10.1 (Spring 1979): 35–43; John Stott's '' 'It's Not What You Expect': Teaching Irony to Third Graders,'' *CLE* 13.4 (Winter 1982): 153–161; Stott's ''Spiralled Sequence Story Curriculum: A Structuralist Approach to Teaching Fiction in the Elementary Grades,'' *CLE* 18.3 (Fall 1987): 148–163; and Shelley L. Knudsen Lindauer's ''Wordless Books: An Approach to Visual Literacy,'' *CLE* 19.3 (1988): 136–142.

Articles about teaching also appear fairly often in *ChLAQ. ChLAQ* 12.3 (Fall, 1987) is a special issue devoted to the topic. Among other useful articles are Linnea Hendrickson's ''Literary Criticism as a Source of Teaching Ideas,'' *ChLAQ* 9.4 (Winter 1984–1985): 202; Sonia Landes's ''Picture Books as Literature,'' *ChLAQ* 10.2 (Summer 1985): 51–54 (about teaching meaning-making strategies for picture books); Barbara Z. Kiefer's ''The Child and the Picture Book: Creating Live Circuits,'' *ChLAQ* 11.2 (Summer 1986): 63–68; Richard Van Dongen's ''Nonfiction, History, and Literary Criticism in the Fifth Grade,'' *ChLAQ* 12.4 (Winter 1987): 189–190 (a description of one teacher's work with a class); Kay E. Vandergrift's ''Meaning-Making and the Dragons of Pern,'' *ChLAQ* 15.1 (Spring 1990): 27–32 (a group's experience of discussing a text).

FURTHER READING

If you are interested in reading about specific texts or the work of specific authors, Linnea Hendrickson's *Children's Literature: A Guide to the Criticism* (Boston: Hall, 1986) is a comprehensive bibliography. Unfortunately, it doesn't cover the work of recent years. But *ChLAQ* 14.2 (Summer 1989) contains ''The Year's Work in Children's Literature Studies 1987,'' and a promise of future annual bibliographies. Meanwhile, many critical journals devoted to children's literature studies are indexed in the annual *MLA [Modern Language Association] International Bibliography,* and some others appear in *The Education Index;* these can be found in most research reference rooms.

The literary dialogue never ends. Since I first wrote this chapter, my readings of texts for children have been deeply affected by the analyses of how adult texts depict and engender ideas of masculinity in *Speaking of Gender,* ed. Elaine Showalter (New York: Routledge, 1989), in Eve Kosofsky Sedgwick's *Between Men: English Literature and Male Homosocial Desire* (New York: Columbia UP, 1985), and in *Epistemology of the Closet* (Berkeley: U of California P, 1990). I've also found three good books about reading: Michael Steig's *Stories of Reading: Subjectivity and Literary Understanding* (Baltimore: Johns Hopkins UP, 1989), Victor Nell's *Lost in a Book: The Psychology of Reading for Pleasure* (New Haven: Yale UP, 1988), and J. A. Appleyard's *Becoming a Reader: The Experience of Fiction from Childhood to Adulthood* (Cambridge: Cambridge UP, 1990). And I'm currently reading Peter Hunt's ambitious *Criticism, Theory and Children's Literature* (Oxford: Basil Blackwell, 1991).

Index